Austria played a prominent role in the worldwide events of 1931 after the largest bank in Central and Eastern Europe, the Viennese Credit-Anstalt, collapsed and led Europe into a financial panic that spread to other parts of the world. The events in Austria were pivotal to the economic developments of the 1930s, yet the literature about them is sparse.

This book tries to fill this gap. Schubert analyzes the crisis using the leading theories of financial crises, identifies the causes of the crises, examines the market's efficiency in predicting events, analyzes how the crisis was transmitted to the real sector, and studies the behavior of the Austrian as well as international authorities as lenders of last resort.

His main conclusion is that, even sixty years after the crisis, many of its lessons are still valid. Managerial and regulatory deficiencies led to the collapse of the bank; the subsequent currency crisis was not an irrational and unexplainable panic by a confused public, but rather a rational response to inconsistencies in policy; and the reactions of the largely unprepared authorities – in Austria as well as abroad – did not help in resolving the crisis quickly.

The Credit-Anstalt Crisis
of 1931

The Credit-Anstalt Crisis of 1931

Aurel Schubert

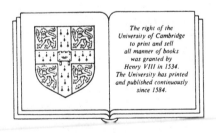

The right of the
University of Cambridge
to print and sell
all manner of books
was granted by
Henry VIII in 1534.
The University has printed
and published continuously
since 1584.

Cambridge University Press
Cambridge
New York   Port Chester   Melbourne   Sydney

CAMBRIDGE UNIVERSITY PRESS
Cambridge, New York, Melbourne, Madrid, Cape Town, Singapore, São Paulo

Cambridge University Press
The Edinburgh Building, Cambridge CB2 2RU, UK

Published in the United States of America by Cambridge University Press, New York

www.cambridge.org
Information on this title: www.cambridge.org/9780521365376

First published 1991
This digitally printed first paperback version 2006

A catalogue record for this publication is available from the British Library

Library of Congress Cataloguing in Publication data
Schubert, Aurel.
    The Credit-Anstalt crisis of 1931 / Aurel Schubert.
        p.   cm.–(Studies in monetary and financial history)
    Based on author's thesis (doctoral–University of South Carolina).
    Includes bibliographical references and index.
    ISBN 0-521-36537-6
    1. Österreichische Credit-Anstalt für Handel und Gewerbe–
History–20th century.   2. Bank failures–Austria–History–20th
century.   3. Business cycles–Austria–History–20th century.
4. Fiscal policy–Austria–History–20th century.
5. Depressions–1929.   I. Title.   II. Series.
HG3020.V540477   1991
332.1′09436–dc20   91-16258
                                                                            CIP

ISBN-13 978-0-521-36537-6 hardback
ISBN-10 0-521-36537-6 hardback

ISBN-13 978-0-521-03029-8 paperback
ISBN-10 0-521-03029-3 paperback

Contents

Tables

Preface

This book is based on my dissertation at the University of South Carolina. In 1983, when I started this research project, the topic seemed primarily of historical and academic interest, as one episode in financial history that has often been cited but never really investigated. At that time, banking crises, supervisory failures, and similar financial problems were not making the headlines of the press – not yet. As my work progressed, the shape of the financial world changed quite dramatically, especially so – but not exclusively – in the United States. Many of the problems that were central to the crisis of the Credit-Anstalt in 1931 suddenly reappeared in the world of present-day finance, haunting banks and their supervisors and endangering the stability of the financial system. Although some of the underlying reasons for the present banking troubles might be quite different from those of the 1930s, others are rather similar. Since some of the mistakes committed in the 1980s are the same as those of sixty years ago, a look back to the financial crisis as it unfolded in 1931 seems warranted and instructive. This is what the present book tries to do by focusing on the causes and consequences of history's biggest bank collapse.

This book could have never been finished without the help and assistance of several people and institutions. I owe a special debt to Michael D. Bordo for his encouragement and his many useful suggestions. Among those who provided helpful comments I wish to thank the following: Michael B. Connolly, John McDermott, Hans Kernbauer, John Mulhern, Larry Neal, and Michael Wagner. The usual disclaimer holds. Seminars on various aspects of the book have been given at the University of South Carolina, the City University Business School in London, the European Economic Association, and the Economic History Association. They all provided valuable suggestions.

For financial assistance I am especially indebted to the Oesterreichische Forschungsgemeinschaft in Vienna. My greatest debt, however, is to my wife Gudrun, who patiently tolerated my restless weekends and sleepless nights and to whom I had to make a promise: never to write a book again.

The Credit-Anstalt Crisis
of 1931

1. Introduction

Those who cannot remember the past are condemned to repeat it.

—George Santayana, 1905

Recent economic developments have led to an increased interest in the interwar period and especially in the banking crises and panics of the 1930s. The threat of defaults of very large debtors or the possible consequences of a stock market crash, plus many other factors, have raised concerns about the stability of the financial systems of individual countries as well as the world. Despite the remarkable resilience the international financial system has shown on several occasions, worst-case scenarios have received considerable attention, some of them even predicting the recurrence of the Great Depression (Batra 1987) and reaping what has been most appropriately termed "the profit of doom" (*Financial Times,* December 4, 1988, V).

Over sixty years have passed since the Credit-Anstalt (CA) crisis, and banks still collapse. The late 1980s actually witnessed the largest numbers of bank failures since the days of the Great Depression, especially so in the United States.[1] With more than 200 collapsed banks a new postdepression peak was reached in that country in 1988, following six consecutive years of record failures.[2] It also marked the first year of a decline in the reserve fund of the Federal Deposit Insurance Corporation, which had been created as a consequence of the epidemic failures of the 1930s. The situation of the American banks worsened further in 1989 and 1990. This has added to the renewed interest in the banking troubles of the 1930s.

[1] From the inception of the Federal Deposit Insurance System in 1933 through 1981, a total of 586 insured banks failed in the United States, while between 1982 and 1988 more than 850 went under; see Barry (1988).

[2] Between 1933 and 1981, the largest number of U.S. banks to have failed in any one year was 17 in 1976.

1

During the 1980s, bank problems were by no means limited to the United States, although – due to its peculiar banking system – the number of failed institutions was by far the largest there. Well publicized failures occurred also in Great Britain (Johnson Matthey Bankers, 1984), in France (Al Saudi Banque, 1988), in Italy (Banco Ambrosiano, 1982), and in many other industrialized as well as developing countries.[3] Reacting to financial distress, more than twenty-five developing countries had undertaken extensive reorganizations of their financial institutions during the decade of the 1980s. But the problems were by no means limited to banks; they also affected other types of financial institutions, especially the savings and loan industry in the United States. At the beginning of 1989, between 500 and 600 of the 3,000 savings and loan associations in the United States were insolvent but owing to the lack of funds in their deposit insurance system, many of the loss-making institutions were allowed to remain in operation.[4]

Despite the large number of bank failures during the 1980s and despite the instabilities in other financial markets, financial crises have been avoided and no loss of confidence occurred in the financial systems of the industrialized world. But today's financial world looks very different from that of the early 1930s. The same applies to the political and economic environment, too. Tremendous technological developments, especially in the field of communications, have blurred the frontiers between financial markets within countries and internationally. The financial markets follow the sun around the globe, and shocks can be transmitted instantaneously. At the same time financial engineering has produced a plethora of new financial instruments with inherent risks, which are much harder to evaluate than for traditional financial assets. The resultant surge in financial flows within individual countries as well as among countries has led to trading volumes unimaginable sixty years ago. Parallel to these developments, bank regulators, central banks, and economic policy makers had sixty additional years to understand

[3] For a list of examples of financial distress during the 1980s, see World Bank (1989).

[4] In August 1989, the bankrupt Federal Savings and Loan Insurance Corporation (FSLIC) was dissolved. On its last day of operations it reported a capital deficit of $87 billion (American billion).

financial markets and to gain experience in containing incipient financial crises.

Despite all these differences, there are many parallels, and some lessons of the 1930s are still valid in today's more sophisticated financial world – lessons with respect to banking and banking regulation, lessons with respect to central banking, and more general lessons concerning the polito-economic environment in which financial institutions operate.

The fear that defaults on the part of large debtor countries, companies, or municipalities could lead to bank failures that could cause chain reactions of considerable damage to the financial system and could even result in a general run on many other banks, leads to the widespread view that "major debtors therefore must be rescued from the threat of bankruptcy to avert the projected dire consequences for banks and for the stability of the financial system" (Schwartz 1986, 11). One of those who do not share this conclusion is Schwartz, who claims that bank failures will not result in financial crises "so long as the security of the private sector's deposits is assured."

The increased academic and nonacademic concern about financial crises has not only created a plethora of interesting articles and papers, but it has also resulted in a growing interest in past banking crises, and among them especially in the catastrophes of the 1930s.

There is a widespread feeling that valuable lessons can be learned from the events of the past: Galbraith (1987, 66) points out, "little is ever really new" in the world of finance. In his view, the public has a "euphoric desire to forget." But studying and analyzing those historic events might make it harder to forget, and thus the "shortness of public memory" might be overcome.

A very special place among the accounts of the 1930s is assigned to the collapse of the Credit-Anstalt,[5] the largest bank of interwar Austria and at that time also the largest bank east of Germany. Many analysts of the 1930s assign great importance to the collapse of this bank. Beyen (1949, 45) concludes, like many other later an-

---

[5] Its official name was "Oesterreichische Credit-Anstalt für Handel and Gewerbe," but its name appears also in different spellings such as "Creditanstalt" or "Kreditanstalt." In this book "Credit-Anstalt" and the abbreviation "CA" will be used, except in original quotes with a different spelling.

alysts that "the crisis of the Austrian Credit-Anstalt started the ball rolling,"[6] and "the ball" stands in this case for the "crisis that was to sweep most countries off the Gold Standard within a few months" (Chandler 1971, 164). Kindleberger (1973, 152) points out that "at the end of May 1931, Austrian financial difficulties ramified widely and led to runs on the banks of Hungary, Czechoslovakia, Romania, Poland, and Germany," while *The Economist* (July 25, 1931, 159) reaches a very similar conclusion when speaking of a "widening circle of distrust and financial difficulty that commenced to spread through Europe with the failure of the Credit Anstalt." According to Chandler (1971, 167) "the crisis was spreading to one of the two great international monetary and financial centers – London" while "the British suspension brought an immediate surge of withdrawals from the United States." The same chain of causality is seen by Vaubel (1984, 259), as he claims that "the accidental collapse of the Austrian Kreditanstalt in May 1931 finally set a chain reaction in motion: the run on the German banks (June–July), the withdrawals from London and the devaluation of sterling (September), the large-scale withdrawals from New York (September–October), and another series of bank failures in the United States (October–January 1932)." In short, the announcement of the crisis at the Credit-Anstalt, "the key banking house of Central Europe . . . rocked the whole economic structure of the Continent" (Hurst 1932, 267), and sent shock waves through the rest of the world.

Considering the pivotal role the Credit-Anstalt crisis played for the economic developments of the 1930s, it is amazing how little attention has been given in the economic literature to these events in Austria. The developments in Germany, Great Britain, or the United States received much more attention and have been analyzed more thoroughly than those in Austria. However, in recent years Austrians have started to review the archives and to study this time period more closely, mainly from a historic descriptive or

---

[6] By the time of the CA crisis the unraveling of the European financial position already had been going on, as Italian banks had to be saved secretly in the spring of 1930, and a bank in Manchester, England, even earlier. We can add as another symptom the fall of the Boden-Credit-Anstalt in Austria in October 1929. However, all these cases of financial distress were solved before they produced any direct large scale consequences, something that did not occur in the case of the CA. In Latin America, Bolivia had already stopped servicing its debt in January 1931 and Peru in March 1931.

sociopolitical approach,[7] adding to the remarkably complete accounts of Federn (1932) and especially Rutkowski (1934). No attempt has been made yet, however, to analyze this bank failure and its repercussions in the context of present-day economic theory of financial crises, or to analyze the links between this bank failure and the currency crisis, or to investigate the effects of these events on the Austrian monetary sector, or to analyze the behavior of the authorities in the light of the lender-of-last-resort theory. This study tries to fill some of these gaps, and to add to the understanding of the effects of financial crises (especially on small open economies) by investigating the experience of a country that was right in the eye of the storm. The goal is to gain from this case study some valuable insight into the mistakes of yesterday, valuable not only for historical reasons but for the fact that the mistakes of yesterday can be repeated as mistakes of tomorrow (or even today) unless they are carefully understood.

The organization of the study will be to first present a diary of the most relevant events of the crisis (chapter 2), before we attempt to shed some light on those events in the context of present-day theories of financial crises. Since considerable confusion exists concerning the characteristics of financial crises, we will try to establish whether the Austrian experience qualified as such a crisis (chapter 3). In chapter 4 we present the causes of the different segments of the crisis in Austria, the causes of the bank failure, the causes of the run on the banks, as well as the causes of the run on the Austrian currency. The efficiency of the stock and foreign exchange markets will also be analyzed (in chapter 5), especially the markets' abilities to predict the crisis. The following chapter (chapter 6) will focus on the channels of transmission of the crisis to the Austrian macroeconomy. The money market as the prime transmitter will be subject to our scrutiny. Since there is widespread agreement among economists that such crises can be stopped by timely and wise intervention, chapter 7 will deal with the role of potential lenders of last resort: Who were they? What did they do? Why did they fail? Alternative policies that could have been pursued and might have led to other outcomes will be touched upon in chapter 8, and some of

---

[7] See, e.g., Ausch (1968), Kernbauer (1981a, 1981b, 1982), Stiefel (1983a, 1983b, 1989), März and Weber (1983b).

the policy implications of this traumatic crisis, which are still relevant in the 1990s, are discussed. Finally, in chapter 9, we will restate the main results. References and comparisons to other countries will be made in most of the chapters.

2. Diary of the crisis

Telling the story of a crisis such as this seems worth while ...
because it offers sheer morbid fascination.

—L. B. Yeager, 1976

On May 8, 1931, the Austrian Credit-Anstalt (Oesterreichische
Credit-Anstalt für Handel and Gewerbe) informed the Austrian government and the Austrian National Bank (ANB) that its 1930 balance sheet had revealed a loss of 140 million schillings, amounting
to roughly 7.5 percent of its total balance sheet or to about 85 percent
of its equity – a shocking announcement even for the Austrian
authorities, who were used to crises. A weekend of continuous secret
top-level meetings followed. In order to avoid any publicity or panic,
even the locations of the meetings were frequently changed.[1]

Bank failures were nothing unusual and new for the Austrian
authorities. The 1920s had already witnessed a series of such events
going back to the collapse of the stock exchange boom and the bear
speculation against the French franc in 1924. This started a wave
of bank collapses, eliminating most of the financial institutions that
had been established during the stock exchange boom following the
end of the hyperinflation and the stabilization of the Austrian currency.[2]

In May 1924 the Allgemeine Depositenbank, a midsized institution that had participated very heavily in the speculation against
the French currency, had to close its doors. Rumors about that
institution's solvency problems had been published in Prague, ig-

---

[1] On Sunday, May 10, 1931, in order to avoid any possible speculation by the press,
the federal chancellor and the minister of finance, the two most important public
officials in the negotiations, even attended the main annual Viennese horse-racing
event, the so-called *Traber Derby* (*Neue Freie Presse*, May 11, 1931, 7).

[2] During 1924 the number of joint stock banks in Vienna dropped from 66 to 36
(Pressburger 1966, 401). Many of the banks that were not eliminated suffered
heavy losses and emerged weakened from this crisis.

niting large withdrawals. A rescue attempt by the five largest Viennese banks failed as the losses turned out to be much larger than initially estimated. The reasons for the collapse ranged from bad management (bad loan portfolio, large expenditures, maturity mismatch, financing of risky speculation) to fraud.[3] In 1926, two important banks, the Centralbank der deutschen Sparkassen, known for holding mainly deposits of savings banks, and the Postal Savings Bank suffered heavy losses. In both cases the government felt compelled to guarantee the deposits in order to avoid panic. The following year two more midsized banks, the Union Bank and the Verkehrsbank, the latter with an extensive network of branch offices, got into trouble and were taken over by the second largest Viennese bank, the Allgemeine Oesterreichische Boden-Credit-Anstalt (BCA).[4] Two years later the collapse of this large bank marked the potentially largest crisis of the 1920s.

In October 1929, after having absorbed a multitude of failing small- and medium-sized banks, the BCA, whose shares were about 50 percent in foreign investors' hands, encountered serious liquidity problems. A range of business errors and an unstable political situation had resulted in large withdrawals. For an extended period the bank was able to meet the demands by taking (excessive) recourse to the discount window of the Austrian National Bank. Once the managing director of the ANB decided to close the discount opportunities, the bank turned to the government for help.

The BCA had very extensive industrial holdings, and a considerable part of Austrian industry depended on this bank for day-to-day financing. Therefore, liquidation of the BCA was never considered a viable solution – a strong partner had to be found. Since it was the second largest bank in Austria, only one domestic bank was considered to be strong enough for such a merger – its main competitor, the Credit-Anstalt. Within only two days the deal was arranged, creating a "superbank" larger than all other Austrian joint stock banks together.

In May 1931 this superbank, "an integral and important part of the financial structure of the world" (Toynbee 1932, 63), was in serious trouble and had to ask the Austrian government and the

---

[3] For a more detailed account of the collapse see Ausch (1968).
[4] The name of this bank is sometimes spelled "Bodenkreditanstalt" or "Boden-Kreditanstalt." When citing quotes, we will use the original spelling.

Table 2.1. *The first reconstruction plan, May 11, 1931 (in million schillings)*

Announced Losses: 139.6		
Cover of Losses:		
State	41.4	
Open reserves	39.6	
Devaluation of shares	29.4	
Rothschild	16.8	
Austrian National Bank	12.4	
	139.6	
New Capital:		Capital Share (in %)
State	58.6	33
Rothschild	13.2	7.4
Austrian National Bank	17.6	10
	89.4	50.4
Remaining Share Capital	88.1	49.6
New Share Capital	177.5	100.0

Sources: Stiefel 1983a, 419, and Pressburger 1966, 461.

National Bank for assistance: An event that, even forty-five years later, was still considered as "the biggest ever bank failure" (*Euromoney,* October 1976, 140) had just started "a new chapter in the melancholy history of postwar banking in Austria" (*Wall Street Journal,* June 23, 1931, 6).

Since the Credit-Anstalt was not a "normal" bank[5] – and the "openly declared bankruptcy of Austria's foremost bank was sure to be followed by numerous business failures"[6] – the laissez-faire oriented Austrian government decided to depart temporarily from its usual economic strategy and accepted a socialization of the losses. Within only three days a reconstruction plan was put together, arranging for covering of the losses by the Austrian state, the reserves, the shareholders, the Rothschilds, and the Austrian National Bank. Moreover, it was decided that the state, the Austrian National Bank, and the Rothschilds should provide new capital, putting the bank on a stronger capital basis than before (see Table 2.1).

The most outstanding feature of this plan was that the share-

[5] März (1982, 191) calls it "by far more equal than other Austrian banking houses."
[6] Ibid., 192.

holders were treated very generously and that the state was to pay for the largest share of the losses, or using White's (1984, 270) words, "nothing more than roundabout transfers from . . . domestic citizens to the shareholders of the threatened bank[s]" took place.[7] The share capital was to be devalued by only 25 percent, instead of more than 80 percent, as would have been justified by the volume of losses, and the state was to contribute 100 million schillings to rescue and reconstruction.

Why did the government depart from its economic principles by involving itself that deeply into the rescue of this bank and by agreeing to become a large shareholder?[8]

First of all, it was the largest bank in Austria with a 1930 total balance sheet the size of the state's expenditures, accounting for about 53 percent of the balance sheet totals of all 25 joint stock banks. About 69 percent of all Austrian limited companies did their business through the Credit-Anstalt, and about 14 percent were very deeply in debt to this bank. Moreover, it had an excellent international reputation, – especially since a member of the Rothschild family, Louis Rothschild, was its president – enjoying better conditions in the financial centers than any of the large German banks.[9]

---

[7] Since more than half of the shares had been in foreign portfolios, a transfer from Austrian taxpayers to foreign and Austrian shareholders occurred. The Austrian authorities were what Guttentag and Herring (1987, 173) called "overly sensitive to the social costs imposed on foreigners from an abrupt failure of the bank."

[8] Actually, with the first reconstruction plan, a slight majority of the shares (89 million schillings or 50.2 percent) came into the hands of the public sector. The Austrian state and the National Bank together held almost 43 percent, the state-owned Kreditinstitut für öffentliche Arbeiten und Unternehmungen another 6.3 percent, and the Postal Savings Bank about 0.9 percent. The state, however, did not "intend to remain so [involved] permanently," but planned to "dispose of its holdings at a suitable moment" (*Financial News*, May 13, 1931, 1), or, as *The Banker* (June 1931, 213) put it, "these shares are not to be held permanently by the government, but will be disposed of as circumstances permit." Sixty years later the Austrian state still, or to be more precise, again holds the majority of the shares of the successor of this bank, and privatization is still, or again, an issue.

[9] The Credit-Anstalt was established in 1855 by a financial group under the leadership of the Viennese Rothschild bank (S. M. von Rothschild) with the participation of several Austrian aristocratic families, such as the Fürstenbergs, the Schwarzenbergs, or the Auerspergs. Its original name was "Kaiserlich-Königlich privilegierte österreichische Credit Anstalt für Handel und Gewerbe." Its initial share capital was by far the largest of any bank in Vienna and the public issue was more than forty times oversubscribed. The promotion of industry and long-

Its stocks were quoted on twelve foreign stock exchanges including New York's, where in 1927 it was the first continental European bank to be introduced, and more than 50 percent of its stocks were in foreign hands. A number of prominent foreign bankers and businessmen sat on its board of directors *(Verwaltungsrat)*.[10] Its business interests extended into eleven banks and forty industrial enterprises in the so called Successor States,[11] and among its creditors were 130 of the most important foreign – especially British and American – banks; "it had probably no rival in the world in respect of the number and importance of its foreign relationships" (*Wall Street Journal*, June 23, 1931, 6). "From the moment of its birth the Credit-Anstalt of Vienna stood in the forefront of international finance," stated *The Economist* (June 27, 1931, 1368). The *Financial News* of London (May 13, 1931, 6) summarized the international standing of the CA in the following way:

The bank has . . . always been considered good for any engagements for, apart from its own first-class standing, it has been backed by the Viennese house of Rothschild, and it was known that, if the worst come to the worst, the Austrian government would continue to support it to the utmost to save Austria from disaster.

That it was not just a "normal" bank can be judged from all these characteristics, as well as from the very poignant statement by a British official in Vienna: "If even the Credit-Anstalt cannot be relied on, everything in Austria must be rotten."[12]

On May 11, 1931, the problems of the bank were announced to the public, together with the reconstruction plan. It was thought that this strategy would preserve confidence in the troubled institution by preventing any interruption of its ordinary business and securing the future of the bank on a new capital basis.

The news of the grave problems of the largest and most prestigious Austrian bank surprised and shocked Vienna. The reactions abroad

term credit was its main goal, and it was modeled after the Crédit Mobilier of the Péreire brothers in France.

[10] Among them were Sir Otto Niemeyer (Bank of England) and Sir Henry Strakosch (Union Corporation, London) both members of the financial committee of the League of Nations, Peter Bark (Anglo-International Bank), Max Warburg from Germany, and the French banker Eugène Schneider-Creuzot.

[11] The states that had been part of the former Austro-Hungarian Empire.

[12] Sir Eric Phipps, minister plenipotentiary of Great Britain in Austria, as quoted in Stiefel, 1983a, 415.

were equally strong. The announcement of the collapse "came as a bombshell to the City [of London]" (*Financial News*, May 13, 1931, 6). *Barron's* (May 18, 1931, 14) reported that "the news of the difficulties [of the Credit-Anstalt] came as a considerable shock to London bankers where it was quite unexpected, as it had been thought the position had been cleared up when the Boden-Kreditanstalt was taken over some time ago."[13]

The foreign reactions to the handling of the situation and the reconstruction plan were very favorable. The announcements by the press were rather optimistic: "Fortunately, it is already clear that the difficulties of the Credit-Anstalt are already being taken successfully in hand, and the very frank and reassuring statement issued this week should go a long way to dispel doubts" (*The Economist*, May 16, 1931, 1044) and "financial opinion is mainly disposed to congratulate all concerned for the masterly way in which they have handled a very delicate situation" (*The Banker*, June 1931, 213). However, these were premature.

Just as unexpected as the problems of the bank was the inability of the reconstruction plan to dispel the doubts of the public. For four days not only did the CA witness a run on its reserves, but so did most of the other Viennese banks. The CA even extended its business hours (until 8:30 P.M.), in order to handle all the required withdrawals.[14]

In only two days the CA lost about 16 percent of its volume of deposits, and within two weeks about 30 percent,[15] as domestic creditors became concerned for the safety and the value of their deposits and withdrew their money from the ailing bank.[16] These large-scale

---

[13] But this merger, with the failing Boden-Credit-Anstalt in October 1929, accounted for 60 million schillings or 43 percent of the reported losses. The other 80 million schillings were said to be equally due to bad debts that had to be written down and to the depreciation of the bank's securities after a year and a half of business depression. In contrast to the problems of the BCA in 1929, no prior withdrawals had occurred, so that the emergence of this crisis originated from the asset side of the balance sheet and not from the liability side.

[14] Despite often-stated claims, the Credit-Anstalt never had to close its doors or suspend business.

[15] Kernbauer (1982, 16) estimates foreign withdrawals between May 11 and May 23 at about 120 million schillings, and domestic withdrawals at about 300 million schillings.

[16] Contrary to a widespread view (e.g., Chandler 1971), mainly domestic creditors, and only to a limited extent foreign creditors, withdrew their money. That was

withdrawals would have rendered this bank illiquid, had not the Austrian National Bank followed parts of Bagehot's rule, and rediscounted freely all the bills presented by the liquidity-strapped institution. Due to the lack of rediscountable trade bills, the CA had to present financial bills – that is, promissory notes – and the Austrian National Bank violated its own charter by accepting those bills.[17] Although the liberal discounting policy managed to stop the panicky fears that means of payment would not be obtainable, creeping distrust of the Credit-Anstalt remained, especially as it became more and more obvious that the true losses would turn out to be much larger than the reported ones. Withdrawals at this institution did not stop.

In order to be able to finance its share in the reconstruction plan, the Austrian government – without any funds at its disposal – had planned to place two- and three-year treasury bonds on the international capital markets. In the meantime it had approached the Bank of England (BofE), and after being rejected,[18] the Bank for International Settlements in Basel (BIS), for a credit amounting to 150 million schillings (approximately 21 million dollars). The BIS reacted favorably to the request, but it took more than two weeks to arrange such a loan, and then only for 100 million schillings.[19] Despite the delay it was considered as a "spectacularly salutory action of international finance" (Glasgow 1931, 112) and bankers in Paris looked "upon the Austrian situation as one more sore spot in the general world picture which has been satisfactorily cleaned up" (*Wall Street Journal*, June 5, 1931, 6).

While the government tried to arrange bridge financing, Austrians, as well as some foreigners, started to convert their schilling holdings into foreign exchange, leading to large-scale reductions in the reserve holdings of the ANB. A group of people emerged who

recognized already by the Austrian parliament when it passed the first governmental guarantee on May 28, 1931 (see *Neue Freie Presse*, May 29, 1931, 15).

[17] "With the permission of the government" (Stiefel, 1983a, 421).

[18] The BofE rejected the Austrian request for help since it considered the BIS in Basel to be in charge of international rescue operations (see Kernbauer, 1982, 13 and chapter 7).

[19] The Austrian National Bank received a rediscount credit amounting to 100 million schillings; eleven central banks extended rediscount quotas amounting to 60 million schillings and the BIS supplied the remaining 40 million schillings. The credit was for a maturity of three months, and the interest rate charged was 5.25 percent.

expected that the Austrian authorities would be unable to adhere to the gold-exchange standard and to defend the Austrian currency in view of the large increases in domestic credit.

When the BIS loan finally arrived, it was not only too late and much too small, but its release was tied to a state guarantee for the credits to the Credit-Anstalt. The Austrian parliament unanimously passed such a guarantee, "after some initial hesitation" (März 1982, 192). The intention was that the minister of finance would be empowered to guarantee for two years all the credits that would be given for the reconstruction and for the current business of the bank. However, the formulation of the guarantee was unclear and did not produce the desired effect. Moreover, "the niggardliness of the sum [of the BIS-credit] and the delay together proved disastrous" (Kindleberger 1973, 131). In less than a week, the money was withdrawn by the public, which distrusted the Austrian currency, and the "sore spot in the general world picture" reemerged. A further BIS credit was promised in case of a prior Austrian issuing of treasury bonds in the international capital markets, but, what with French resistance to plans for an Austro-German customs union could never be realized.[20] In order to avoid foreign repercussions of a possible Aus-

---

[20] In March 1931, Austria and Germany had announced their intention to form a customs union. From then on, France had been the most vocal opponent of such a union. According to the *Wall Street Journal* (May 16, 1931, 1), only five days after the announcement of the CA-crisis "it was reported that under the leadership of French bankers, the Rothschild financial group had offered to the government to arrange the placement [of 150 million schillings of obligations abroad] if Austria abandoned the Austro-German customs union proposal . . ."
In June 1931, France made its support for placing Austrian treasury bonds subject to a formal renunciation by Austria of any project of either economic or political union with Germany. Moreover, it demanded that the Austrian government agree to a thorough examination of its economic and financial position by financial experts of the League of Nations and promise in advance to take any measures that would be recommended by them. These demands were generally judged as political blackmail. *The Contemporary Review* (August 1931, 141), for instance, concluded that "these conditions were unacceptable to Austria, the French offer of help being apparently designed less to help Austria financially than to serve France politically," while *The Banker* (July 1931, 13) criticized "the inability of the French authorities to think in separate terms of financial and political affairs, and their endeavour to use the one as a stick with which to enforce their requirements of the other."
On September 3, 1931, the Austrian foreign minister, Dr. Schober, withdrew the proposal for a customs union with Germany "in view of Austria's urgent need for money" (Toynbee 1932, 113–14). Two days later at The Hague, the

trian moratorium, on June 16 the Bank of England decided to give an emergency short-term credit (for seven days, but renewable on a week-to-week basis) amounting to 150 million schillings to the Austrian National Bank.

Negotiations with the 130 foreign creditor banks, which had formed the so-called Austrian Credit-Anstalt International Committee (representing about 500 million schillings or 37 percent of the liabilities of the CA) led to a standstill agreement that provided for the prolongation of the foreign credits for two years in exchange for an extension of the governmental guarantee to all foreign liabilities of the ailing bank (June 16). The Austrian government had no viable alternative since the representatives of the creditors, led by Sir Robert Kindersley of the Bank of England (who was also president of Lazard Bros. & Co.), had declared "that the consequence of non-acceptance would be the withdrawal of all foreign credits from the bank" (*Daily Telegraph*, June 16, 1931, 13).[21] Four hours after the signing of the agreement, the minister of interior resigned. In his view "a prolongation of the agony of the Credit-Anstalt for two years, at the price of losing her financial freedom" had occurred (*Daily Telegraph*, June 17, 1931, 13). Moreover, the true extent of the liabilities of the bank was still unknown. The Austrian government announced its resignation, and it took four days to form a new one, led by a new federal chancellor. After one week in office, on June 27, 1931, the new government decided to extend its guarantee to virtually all liabilities of the CA. From then on, the Austrian state, with a federal budget of roughly 1,800 million schillings, stood guarantor for 1,200 million schillings of bank liabilities.

The belief of the Austrian government officials that this generous guarantee would induce foreigners to place additional funds at the disposal of the CA proved to be overly optimistic, if not outright mistaken. Withdrawals continued, and the CA had to keep on presenting financial bills to the ANB for rediscounting, and the ANB

Permanent Court of International Justice, by eight votes to seven, "rendered the opinion that the plan was not compatible with the First Geneva Protocol of 4 October 1922, which Austria had accepted as part of the League of Nations scheme of Austrian financial reconstruction" (Toynbee 1932, 114).

[21] The only concession granted to Austria was the possibility of an eventual prolongation of the standstill beyond two years.

accepted those in order to keep the bank afloat.[22] Large increases in the discount rate in June and July (in three steps from 5 percent to 10 percent) did not show any significant effects on either the amount of rediscounting by the CA (since it needed the liquidity regardless of the cost involved) or on the position of the Austrian currency. Even a rate of 10 percent could not stop the capital flight, although such a rate was thought to be able to "draw gold from the moon" (Kindleberger 1973, 159). Money was not seeking the highest ex ante yield, but the highest expected return, that is, the nominal yield adjusted for the probability of default and for the exchange rate risk.

As the government was unable to raise any long-term foreign loans, the foreign reserves kept on declining. The Austrian currency became increasingly backed by financial bills of the – illiquid – Credit-Anstalt, instead of gold and foreign exchange reserves. Finally, on October 9, 1931, five months after the announcement of the bank's problems and after the Austrian National Bank had lost about 700 million schillings in foreign reserves, the government decided to introduce exchange controls.[23] Foreign exchange payments were centralized at the ANB, and Austrians had to register all their foreign exchange holdings. The ANB had the right to buy any or all of them. After two further amendments, any claims on foreigners payable in foreign currency had to be declared. The amounts registered added up to more than 420 million schillings, and the ANB bought about half of them (Kamitz 1949, 183).[24]

In July 1932 the countries that had participated in the original Geneva Accords of 1922 agreed to supply Austria with a new internationally guaranteed loan to the amount of 300 million schillings (Lausanne Protocols).[25] But the money was not raised until August

---

[22] There were, however, constant disputes within the central bank concerning this liberal discounting policy. This point is taken up again in chapter 7.

[23] Only one week later, because of serious inadequacies, the decree had to be amended for the first time and for a second time after four more weeks. Two further supplementary decrees followed in December 1931 and January 1932. On June 23, 1932, the transfer of external debt service was suspended.

[24] On April 6, 1933, the ANB relieved private individuals from the obligation to deliver foreign exchange to the bank. From that date on, the private clearing exchange rate was the only rate of practical significance.

[25] In August 1931 the Austrian government had approached the League of Nations

1933.[26] It yielded 237 million schillings and was mainly used to repay the short-term loans of 1931 and to reduce the short-term state debt with the National Bank (Nötel 1984, 170).

It was not until January 1933, about twenty months after the start of the crisis, that a permanent settlement was reached with the foreign creditors of the bank, and the reconstruction of the CA could finally be started. The main points of this reconstruction were that the bank's old capital was reduced from 177.5 million to 1 million schillings and subsequently increased to 142 million with the Austrian state becoming the principal shareholder of the bank (with about 51 percent) in exchange for assuming responsibility for the majority of its liabilities at the ANB (571 million schillings) and other liabilities. The foreign creditors, on the other hand, received 70 million schillings worth of preferred ordinary stock (49 percent), shares and bonds of a newly created holding company in Monaco, Société Continentale de Gestion, which took over half of the foreign assets of the CA (140 million schillings), and finally a governmental promise to pay annuities in exchange for the remaining 210 million schillings in so-called live claims.[27] This arrangement was, of course, "the implementing of the government guarantee" (*The Bankers' Magazine*, September 1933, 365).

The losses, initially reported as 140 million schillings, turned out to sum up to about 1,070 million schillings, or more than 7 times the announced amount, with the Austrian state and the ANB bearing 700 million schillings or about 70 percent of the losses (Stiefel 1989, 231).[28] The largest fraction of the losses was due to bad debts,

(LofN) for help in selling 150 million schillings of treasury bonds and three members of the LofN secretariat had visited Vienna the same month for a preliminary examination. One month later, the financial committee had recommended the provision of a loan to Austria.

[26] Ausch (1968, 419) claims that the foreign creditors' committee, led by Lionel Rothschild, head of the London branch of the Rothschild family, had influenced the French government not to let the loan be raised until the agreement with the foreign creditors had been finalized.

[27] The creditors received 4.5 percent twenty-year foreign currency bonds with the option of redeeming the bonds in seven years at a 33.3 percent discount. In January 1936, Austria reached a final agreement with the international committee, an agreement that was much more favorable to Austria than the one in 1933.

[28] A sum equivalent to about 40 percent of the volume of state expenditures in 1930.

amounting to about 700 million schillings instead of the 40 million reported in May 1931, an outcome considerably worse than the most pessimistic expectations at the onset of the crisis.[29]

The reorganization of the Austrian banking system was not finished until spring 1934 when the reconstructed Credit-Anstalt took over the active banking businesses of the Wiener Bank-Verein and the Niederösterreichische Escompte-Gesellschaft, the two other remaining large Austrian banks. The capital was increased to 167 million schillings, with the ANB subscribing the additional 25 million schillings.[30] The official devaluation of the schilling by 28 percent was also announced around the time of the banking fusion (with a decree of May 5, 1934). That was the price the market had already established about a year earlier.

[29] However, there have been indications that the CA's assets were devalued more than really justified, putting an excessive burden on the state. Already on June 1, 1931, the *Wiener Börsen-Kurier* had warned that debtors might try to take advantage of the problems of the bank to get their debts unduly reduced, in order to profit as much as possible from the state guarantee (1). This would fit Bernanke's (1981, 155) observation that "if a lender does not develop a reputation for pressing his claims, borrowers have an incentive to become too illiquid in order to force an improvement in terms."

[30] Nötel (1984, 170) estimates the total contributions of the Austrian state, the Austrian National Bank, and the shareholders to the rescue of the three large Austrian banks between 1931 and 1934 at 1,550 million schillings (losses of 1,410 million schillings and new capital of 140 million schillings). According to his estimates about 70 percent of this amount was provided by the state, 25 percent by the shareholders, and 5 percent by the Austrian National Bank. According to Stiefel (1989, 230) the total contribution of the Austrian state and the ANB to the Austrian banks between 1925 and 1936 amounted to 1,137 million schillings.

3. Financial crisis theories and the Austrian experience of 1931

Historic associations, by themselves, never teach lessons. Lessons derive from history interpreted in the light of theories.

—L. B. Yeager, 1976

Definitional problems

Recently, due to the fear of large-scale insolvencies in the international banking sector, considerable attention has been given to financial crises as causes of economic fluctuations, and a respectable volume of literature reflects this renewed interest.[1]

Although their common themes are financial crises, it soon became obvious that this term is used to characterize very diverse facts, and the reader cannot help becoming somewhat confused about the question of what really constitutes a financial crisis. How widespread this confusion is, even within the economic profession itself, is reflected in Schwartz's (1986) study entitled "Real and Pseudo-Financial Crises," where she restates and extends Goldsmith's (1982, 42) view that many of the crises identified in the literature, by Minsky (1982), Kindleberger (1978), and others, were only "at most potential or near crises." The proposition that a financial crisis is like a pretty girl – difficult to define but recognizable when seen (Kindleberger and Laffargue, 1982, 2) – seems to lead to ambiguous results, as some economists see "pretty girls" where others only recognize "pseudo-pretty girls."[2]

The underlying problem is the fact that no clear definition of a financial crisis exists – that is, there is no objective and accepted

---

[1] E.g., Kindleberger and Laffargue (1982), Minsky (1982), James (1984), Schwartz (1986) and Bordo (1986a). For a literature review see Bordo (1986b).

[2] Just as the concept of "prettiness" is relative and a function of the respective culture, so the concept of a financial crisis seems to be a function of the respective school of economic thought.

yardstick by which an economic event can be measured for its qualifications as a financial crisis.

This definitional vacuum leads to apparent inconsistencies in the use of three economic terms, namely "banking crisis," "banking panic," and "financial crisis." Whereas some authors seem to use them indiscriminately (Kindleberger 1978, Minsky 1982, or James 1984), others identify financial crises with banking panics but distinguish them from bank failures (Friedman and Schwartz 1963 or Schwartz 1986), and again others define financial crises in a much broader sense, independently of bank failures or bank panics (e.g., Wright 1977).

The plethora of definitions ranges from very general ones, such as "a situation in which buyers and sellers are unable to find a price at which markets will clear" (ibid., 173), or "a threat to the stability of the system,"[3] or "a sharp, brief, ultracyclical deterioration of all or most of a group of financial indicators – short-term interest rates, asset (stock, real estate, land) prices, commercial insolvencies, and failures of financial institutions" (Goldsmith 1982, 42), or quite similarily, "when changed expectations lead owners of wealth to try to shift quickly out of one type of asset into another, with resulting falls in prices of the first type of asset, and frequently bankruptcy" (Kindleberger and Laffargue 1982, 2), to narrower views, such as expressed by Schwartz (1986, 11), who only identifies a financial crisis when a banking panic occurs "fueled by fears that means of payments will be unobtainable at any price." She is in wide agreement with Gorton (1983, 2), who is most consistent in his terminology, stating explicitly that "a banking panic is not the same as the failure of a single institution." He defines such a banking panic as an abrupt shift in the desired currency deposit ratio, resulting in a decline of the money price of deposits and a banking system that typically suspends convertibility. He avoids entirely the use of the words "crisis" or "financial crisis."

Eichengreen (1987) defines a financial crisis very broadly "as a disturbance of financial markets, marked by falling asset prices and insolvency among debtors and intermediaries, that has ramifications throughout the financial system, destroying the market's capacity to allocate capital." He clearly distinguishes between financial

---

[3] Swoboda, quoted in Kindleberger and Laffargue (1982, 2).

crises and other similar events since his definition "implies a distinction between financial crises on the one hand and panic sales of assets, or bank failures, or debt defaults on the other." In his framework "a financial crisis occurs only when a blockage in one area leads to a systemic seizure."

Instead of attempting to find a common denominator in all these (and many more) definitions, Bordo (1986a) concentrates on extracting the key elements of a typical financial crisis. In his view some or all of the following have to be present in a typical crisis:

1. A widespread change in expectations associated with fear of a change in economic environment.
2. The fear of insolvency of some financial institution(s).
3. An attempt to convert real as well as illiquid financial assets into money.
4. Threats to the solvency of otherwise sound commercial banks and financial institutions.
5. Bank runs that could lead to a general bank panic and to
6. A reduction in the money supply.
7. And finally the whole process could be arrested at the outset by the timely intervention of some authority (the lender of last resort) that lends freely at a penalty rate or engages in open market operations.

In our analysis of the events surrounding the failure of the Credit-Anstalt, we will attempt to distinguish between the failure of this bank (a bank's crisis) and a contagious run on other banks (a bank panic). The term "financial crisis" will be used in a wider sense, in which a bank panic might be a key element (or the precipitating factor). But we allow, more generally, for the possibility that owners of wealth shift quickly from one type of asset into another, including from one money into another.

Timing of the crisis

All the three main branches of the financial crisis literature, namely the Fisher–Minsky–Kindleberger approach, the monetarist approach, and the rational-expectations approach, place heavy emphasis on the timing of a crisis in relationship to the business cycle.[4]

As advocated by Minsky (1977), financial crises are a key element and an essential part of the upper turning point of a business cycle, and consequently coincide with the onset of a business downturn, as the rising interest rates – caused by the previous investment boom

---

[4] These approaches are, however, not mutually exclusive hypotheses.

– will lead to negative present values for investment projects that had been financed in a "speculative" or even Ponzi way.[5] This present value reversal will then result in the inability of businesses and individuals to meet their liabilities (Fisher's [1932] "overindebtedness") or to refinance those debts, forcing them to sell off assets. If the markets for these position-making investments are thin, these transactions will result in large price changes and generate Fisher's "distress selling," potentially leading to a financial crisis.[6] Even if they are initially not "thin," widespread selling off might still lead to the same results.

In contrast to this view of increasing financial instability and collapse at the upper turning point, monetarists consider panics as neither a necessary nor a sufficient condition for a severe contraction (Cagan 1965). In their view, they occur shortly after the business peak and are determined by "special circumstances," with no definite relation to the business cycle. Cagan's conclusions, which are shared by Friedman and Schwartz (1963),[7] are based on his observation that some of the panics occurred at such an early stage of the business cycle downturn that the contractions were not yet deep enough to undermine the financial structure.[8] His argument, that it is extremely doubtful that severe contractions are from the beginning "so special a breed that their full repercussions hit economic activity at large" (Cagan 1965, 266) conforms to Friedman and Schwartz's (1963, 441–2) conclusion that banking panics "have greatly intensified [severe] contractions if indeed they have not been the primary factor converting what would have otherwise been mild contractions into severe ones." Consequently, the timing is independent of the exact business cycle stage, mainly explained by "exogenous" events and "special circumstances" and causality runs from the crisis to the business cycle and not the opposite way, as Minsky's theory would suggest.

[5] For the distinction between hedge, speculative and Ponzi finance, see Minsky (1977).

[6] Whether or not a debt deflation process takes place at this stage depends on "how quickly and aptly the central bank intervenes as a lender of last resort and whether or not government deficits stabilize profits" (Minsky 1982, 33).

[7] They attach great importance to exogenous events, e.g., the failure of a big bank that creates a deterioration of the public's confidence and precipitates runs or panics.

[8] Compare that to Minsky, who argues that not the cycle downturn but the boom undermines the financial structure.

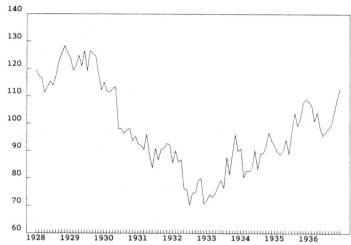

SOURCE: *Wirtschaftsstatistisches Jahrbuch 1937*, p. 7.

Figure 3.1. Production index, 1928–36 (average 1923–31 = 100, seasonally adjusted).

Gorton (1983) challenges this view, as his rational-expectations approach can explain timing, cause, and severity of panics without recourse to "special circumstances." He considers banking panics as rational responses of depositors who wish to smoothe their consumption flows over time. Runs on banks should then coincide with the time when depositors expect a trough to occur, since troughs are the time period when expected low consumption coincides with the likelihood of suspension of convertibility.

How do these approaches to the timing of a financial crisis square with the collapse of the Credit-Anstalt and the events of 1931 in Austria?

The Austrian banking crisis occurred, like the German one, not at the onset but in the middle of a general economic depression (as far as timing as well as the depth of the downturn are concerned).[9] A glance at the path of the production index (Figure 3.1)[10] shows clearly that the summer of 1929 marked the start of the downturn in economic activity. The index reached a peak value of 127 in August 1929 and declined from then on. At the time the Credit-

[9] For a description of the German banking crisis, see James (1984).
[10] Based on production data of ten important commodities, seasonally adjusted, 1923–31=100.

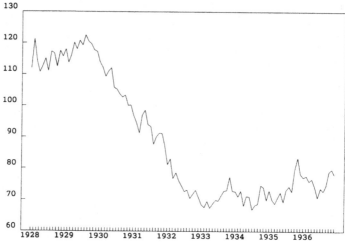

SOURCE: *Wirtschaftsstatistisches Jahrbuch 1937*, p. 7

Figure 3.2. Index of business activity, 1928–36 (seasonally adjusted average, 1923–31 = 100).

Anstalt announced its insolvency, the index had already dropped by about 25 percent to a level of only 96.[11] The index of general business activity reveals a very similar picture for the initial turning point (Figure 3.2).[12]

Consequently, a recession had been going on for about eighteen months by the time the Credit-Anstalt crisis occurred. Obviously this bank crisis did not precipitate the initial economic downturn and was not an integral part of the upper turning point as Minsky would suggest that it should have been. As for the monetarist position, we observe that there was already a depression going on, and not a mild contraction that was subsequently turned into a severe one.

There were signs of recovery, however, but they were definitely destroyed by this crisis, and the (potential) trough was postponed for another year and a half.

According to Gorton's theory, the run should have occurred earlier than it actually did, since the first months of 1931 had already shown weak signs of an impending upturn, so that rational savers

[11] The lowest level of economic activity occurred in December 1932, at a level of only 71.
[12] Computed as the arithmetic average of eight relevant economic indices, seasonally adjusted, 1923–31=100.

would have anticipated the trough earlier and would have acted accordingly.

But some caution is necessary. We have to get back to our initial uneasiness about the lack of precision in the terminology. A distinction has to be made between the failure of the Credit-Anstalt (a bank crisis) and the run on its deposits and those of other banks (a banking panic or banking crisis) and the panicky attempts of the public to exchange Austrian schillings for foreign exchange (a currency crisis).[13]

As for the timing of the failure of the Credit-Anstalt, we will argue that May 1931 had no importance whatsoever, and the crisis took place then solely because the previous year's balance sheet had to be published by the end of May.[14] Since this balance sheet applied to 1930, it appears as if the reported losses had all occurred during that year. Independent investigations, however, revealed a very different picture.[15] They concluded that as far back as the "gold-balance sheet"[16] of January 1, 1925, these yearly statements had been manipulated, in order to present a more favorable picture of the assets and the capital position of the bank, and that the reported profits were not really earned. If these reports are right – and the huge final losses of this institution suggest that they are, since they could not have been accumulated within only one year – we cannot assign any special date to the problems of the Credit-Anstalt. There was no indication that an immediate danger of withdrawals of credits or a suspension of payments had forced the bank's management to disclose the situation.[17]

[13] Friedman and Schwartz, Cagan, as well as Gorton, all talk exclusively about bank panics and their timing, and not about the timing of a bank failure.

[14] If the balance sheet had been due in February or March, the failure and the following runs would have occurred at that point in time. It is, however, more difficult to assess what would have happened if the accounting date had been only in August or September, as the German banking crisis of July 1931 could have had important repercussions on Austria.

[15] Made in the aftermath of the collapse, but never officially published (see Rutkowski 1934, 67–8, and Ausch 1968, 349 and 358).

[16] It was called "gold-balance sheet" because it was based on a revaluation of the assets and liabilities according to their real (gold) value, in order to get rid of the confusion created by the effects of the hyperinflation on those book values.

[17] The timing of the collapse of the second largest bank, the Boden-Credit-Anstalt, which occurred in the fall of 1929, seems to be more consistent with Minsky's hypothesis, and further investigation into that problem could bring valuable results.

But a question remains: Namely, why did the bank disclose its losses in 1931, when it was able to hide them for so many years, without any impact on its international financial standing? Federn (1932), an excellent and knowledgeable expert of the Austrian banking sector of the 1920s and 1930s, assigns credibility to rumors that a newly appointed bank director refused to sign the first draft of the balance sheet and by doing so forced the disclosure of (some of) the losses. Rutkowski (1934) rejects this hypothesis – without specifying the reasons for his doubts – and puts forward his own explanation: that the fear of the worsening economic situation and of increasing political and economic disturbances, because of international opposition to Austria's negotiations with Germany about a customs union, led the bank directors to a disclosure of the situation.

Whichever story one accepts, the disclosure of the losses, and thus the most direct cause of the bank failure, was apparently due to "special circumstances" and some "exogenous events." But these cannot explain the underlying problems of the CA, or the reasons for the run on this and other banks.

Following the disclosure of the problems of the Credit-Anstalt and despite the concurrent announcement of the rescue plan, a scramble for liquidity developed as the public, fearing for the security of its deposits, attached a higher value to cash than to deposits at the Credit-Anstalt. But these developments were not limited to this institution, and the following three days witnessed depositors at many banks seeking to exchange their deposits for currency. As a consequence, the banking system could not have met the public's demands at the initially agreed upon currency price of deposits had it not been for free discounting by the lender of last resort in the person of the Austrian National Bank. The unexpected failure of the largest and most respected financial institution in Europe east of Germany had resulted in a general bank panic, the timing of which was – in a proximate sense – due to an exogenous event ("special circumstances") that changed the public's expectations very dramatically.

After the initial run, the commercial banks, as well as the other financial institutions, had regained the confidence of their depositors and even enjoyed some (considerable) increases in their deposits, as money from the Credit-Anstalt was transferred to other institutions.[18] Checking deposits at the Credit-Anstalt had declined by more than 80 percent between March 1931 and August 1931, and savings deposits had dropped by about 74 percent.[19] This institution's share in Austria of both types of deposits together had declined from 16.3 percent to about 4 percent in less than four months.[20] While the overall volume of checking and savings deposits in Austria had dropped by about 390 million schillings, exactly two thirds of this decline (259 million schillings) had occurred at the Credit-Anstalt and only one third at all other banks and savings banks together.

Do these events qualify as a banking panic and a financial crisis? Using Mundell's definition of a "rush to test the convertibility of an asset into money," we have to conclude affirmatively. Kindleberger and Minsky would also agree. Garber's (1981, 5) requirements for a panic, namely a "run whose timing was not perfectly foreseen," where he defines the run as "a speculative attack on an asset price fixing scheme which causes a discontinuous asset shift in private agents' portfolios" (ibid., 4), are also fulfilled, since in the case of bank runs, the price under attack is the price of deposits fixed in terms of currency. And finally, in Schwartz's (1986, 11) definition, the crucial factor is the public's fear "that means of payments will be unobtainable at any price," which will lead, in a fractional-reserve banking system, to a scramble for high-powered money, resulting in a sudden squeeze on the reserves of the banks. The Austrian experience fits this definition very well. Schwartz states further that a "real financial crisis occurs only when institutions do not exist, and authorities are unschooled in the practices that preclude such a development, and when the private sector has reason to doubt the dependability of preventive arrangements" (ibid. 12).

As far as Austria is concerned, institutions that would have automatically guaranteed the convertibility of deposits did not exist, and most of the scholars would agree with Schwartz that the authorities were "unschooled in the practices" or, at least, behaved as

[18] A still unanswered question is why certain banks gained and others lost deposits, and according to what criteria the public discriminated between these institutions.
[19] At that time they were already guaranteed by the state.
[20] We do not have a breakdown for April, but the combined volume of deposits was about equal to March.

if they were unschooled,[21] and the public had every reason to doubt the dependability of the preventive arrangements. This was especially so, since rumors about much larger losses than those reported were circulating (and they proved to be right, as people found out soon afterward).

We can summarize the previous discussion by stating that the Austrian experience of May 1931, with its big bank collapse and the following short-lived general run, constituted a financial crisis for all the theories reviewed, although convertibility of deposits into currency was never suspended.[22]

Once distrust in the solvency of the other credit institutions had disappeared and the banking panic had been overcome, the financial crisis was not over. Another speculative attack developed as the public started to lose confidence in the ability of the Austrian National Bank to defend the exchange rate of the Austrian schilling, or in Garber's (1981, 4) words, the public believed "that the nature of the price fixing regime [in this case the fixed exchange rate] will change" and started a run for foreign exchange. The development of the foreign reserve holdings of the Austrian National Bank reflects this panic very clearly (see Figure 3.3). After the initial rush to test the convertibility of deposits into high-powered money followed a rush to test the convertibility of one money (the Austrian schilling) into another (mainly American dollars and British pounds).[23] As Hardach (1984, 225) put it, "the crisis of 1931 had been a banking crisis as well as a foreign exchange crisis. Under the gold standard, both crises were fatally interwoven."

Although the National Bank satisfied all demands for foreign exchange[24] the dependability of the preventive arrangements were doubted by the public, as it kept on converting its schilling holdings

[21] This point is taken up again in chapter 7.
[22] Among the more important banks, only the midsized Mercurbank had to close (temporarily) as a side effect of the German crisis in July 1931, since it had close connections with the ailing German Danatbank, which had to be closed on July 13, despite the announcement of a governmental guarantee for its liabilities on the preceding day. Among the smaller financial institutions, Auspitz, Lieben & Co. had to close its doors on May 26 and had to be declared insolvent. Mr. Auspitz was a member of the board of directors of the Credit-Anstalt, but the failure of this bank was not connected to this association but rather due to extensive and unsuccessful speculation by this small bank.
[23] But really into "gold."
[24] Nevertheless, the allocation of foreign banknotes had to be limited at times.

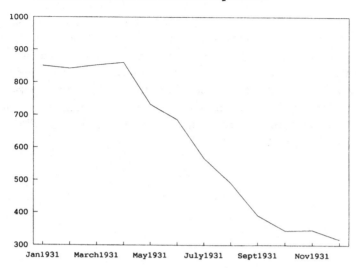

Figure 3.3. Foreign reserves, 1931 (in million schillings).

into foreign monies and continued the depletion of the reserves. As neither international loans nor discount rate changes managed to stop the speculative attack, exchange controls were introduced in October 1931.

In the financial crisis definitions of Kindleberger, Minsky, Mundell, and Flood and Garber, these events qualify as a financial crisis in their own right, while for Schwartz this episode would only constitute a pseudocrisis since she does not accept a run on a currency as a crisis. In her framework, this is only a case of authorities trying to resist the market's evaluation of a currency, while the problem facing the currency is more fundamental, namely the economic policies that are responsible for the currency's plight (Schwartz 1986, 24). The only crisis she would accept here would be the failure of the authorities to adjust their policies when these are the heart of the matter.

Bordo's (1986a, 191) elements of a typical financial crisis would have to be extended. To the "attempt to convert real as well as illiquid financial assets into money," we would have to add "and back into a real asset, such as gold, and safer financial assets, such as guaranteed government bonds."[25]

[25] However, keeping in mind that gold was money at that time.

Since we have established that the 1931 experience in Austria constituted a true financial crisis, and not a mere pseudocrisis, the main question, from a macroeconomic perspective, is whether this episode had effects on the level of economic activity. But before we discuss the importance of these effects for the Austrian experience of the 1930s and the possible channels of transmission, we will turn to the causes of the different stages of the crisis and the efficiency of the asset markets.

4. The causes of the financial crisis

Autopsies are valuable in so far as they are scientifically conducted
to the end that the knowledge gained is made useful in the future.
—Th. F. Woodlock, *Barron's,* February 16, 1931

If we want to identify the main causes of the financial crisis in
Austria in 1931, we have to distinguish among the following: (1) the
causes of the Credit-Anstalt crisis; (2) the causes of the banking
crisis; and (3) the causes of the currency crisis. Obviously, many of
the causes will be shared, since the three different crisis were interdependent.

The causes of the Credit-Anstalt crisis

The causes of the problems of this bank have been discussed quite
frequently in the literature.[1] Nevertheless, as März points out, "the
definite story of the collapse of the Creditanstalt has not yet been
written" (1982, 191). Much of our knowledge goes back to Rutkowski's excellent treatment, and insight into the microeconomic
data of the bank would be required to tell the "definite story" and
to be able to attach relative weights to the different contributing
factors that have already been identified.

Despite the lack of publicly available microdata, we can make
inferences from a variety of direct and indirect sources. For one,
the losses of the bank will give us insight into the causes of the
problems. A comparison to the developments at other, nonfailed,
Viennese banking institutions allows us to isolate the CA specific
causes. A look at other countries provides hints to specifically Austrian developments, and finally investigations and reports made in
1931 help us to reveal some of the internal problems of the company.

[1] See, e.g., Federn (1932), Rutkowski (1934), Ausch (1968), Kernbauer (1981), Stiefel (1983a, 1983b, 1989).

31

However, before we try to investigate the causes of the crisis, we must reiterate that insolvency, not illiquidity, was the initial problem of the bank. Hindsight teaches us this fact, but it was not known to the policymakers in mid-May 1931, when they had to make their crucial decisions.

No withdrawals had occurred before May 12, 1931, that would have created liquidity problems for this bank. "Bank failures can originate on the asset side of the balance sheet, on the liability side, or in shocks affecting both simultaneously, or in rapid succession" (Kindleberger 1985, 4). The problems of the CA originated from the asset side of the bank's balance sheet. Its net worth was simply negative. As Minsky (1982, 146) points out, solvency and liquidity are interrelated.

A decline in net worth – perhaps the result of revaluation of assets – can lead to a decreased willingness to hold debts of a unit and hence to difficulties when it needs to refinance a position. A lack of liquidity may result from what was initially a solvency problem.

This statement characterizes the situation at the CA very well. As the asset-side problems became publicly known, a run caused an immediate spread to the liability side.

The causes of the insolvency of the bank

In order to gain insight into this question, it is worthwhile to analyze first the losses that had occurred at this institution. By identifying the main contributors and their relative weights in the losses, our task of detecting the underlying problems is considerably simplified. Table 4.1 reports an estimate of the losses of the Credit-Anstalt. Adding the 159.6 million schillings of losses that were already included in the adjusted 1930 balance sheet, we end up with a total of close to 990 million schillings, or more than 50 percent of the 1930 balance sheet total.[2]

We observe that about 70 percent of the losses were caused by bad debts. Forty percent of the Austrian debts were total losses, while among foreign debts, the ratio amounted to as high as 66 percent. This confirms our point that the bank might have become the victim of an adverse selection process in the Successor States.

---

[2] More recent estimates put the total losses at 1,070 million schillings (Stiefel 1989, 231).

Table 4.1. *Losses at the Credit-Anstalt*
(in million schillings)

Losses on securities	122.63
Losses on industrial holdings	77.40
Losses on inventory and real estate	11.65
Losses on debtors	602.31
consisting of:	
Losses on Austrian debtors	341.00
Losses on foreign debtors	261.31
	813.99
Losses on current operations (during 1931, 1932)	14.22
Total Losses	828.21

Source: Rutkowski 1934, 104.

The second largest share of losses was owing to the decline in the value of its securities portfolio, reflecting business conditions prevailing in the early 1930s. The losses on its industrial holdings account for still another 10 percent of the overall asset revaluation.

Although the breakdown of the final losses gives us some clear indications of the proximate causes of the insolvency of the CA, the fundamental reasons require additional analysis regarding the Austrian interwar economy and its banking sector.

The fundamental causes. As we demonstrate below, the Austrian economy of the early 1930s was a "prisoner of the hyperinflation experience." The behavior of the economic agents was largely influenced by this traumatic experience. So was the condition of the banking sector. The hyperinflation had left its marks on the balance sheets of the Austrian banks. This deterioration of the internal and external value of the Austrian currency (to about 1/14,400th of its prewar level) deprived the banks of their capital base. As Haber (1928, 78) shows, by 1925 the major Viennese banks had lost between 77.5 and 84.6 percent of their prewar equity (Table 4.2).

The failure of the banks to restore adequate capital endowments after the hyperinflation resulted in a continual worsening of their debt/equity ratios, so that the increasing balance sheet totals were based on a shrinking relative capital basis, and that ventures of these banks were increasingly debt financed – that is, the depositors'

Table 4.2. *Equity of the Viennese banks, 1925, in percentage of 1913[a]*

Credit-Anstalt	15.7
Wiener Bank-Verein	15.4
Boden-Credit-Anstalt	16.2
Niederösterreichische Escompte-Gesellschaft	22.5

[a] After adjustment for new equity issues.
Source: Haber 1928, 78.

Table 4.3. *Debt equity ratio of the Credit-Anstalt*

Year	Ratio
1913	3.64
–	–
–	–
1924 (Jan. 1, 1925)	5.68
1925	6.86
1926	9.28
1927	7.90
1928	8.98
1929	8.82
1930 (June 30)	10.90
1930 (Dec. 31)[a]	9.44
1931	no balance sheet
1932	2.56

[a] Already based on first reconstruction plan of May 1931.
Debt: Creditors + savings accounts + checking accounts
Equity: Share capital + reserves
Sources: Balance sheets of the Credit-Anstalt.

funds were being put at risk, instead of the shareholders'. The debt/ equity ratio of the Credit-Anstalt reflects this development quite clearly (Table 4.3).

We have to be careful, however, since these numbers might be subject to bias, as the bank repurchased some of its own shares without adjusting the capital base and thus effectively reduced its capital base and the security of the creditors.[3] Especially in these times of rapidly falling share values, these assets were immobile and

[3] This was quite common among the banks in Austria and Germany.

so endangered the liquidity of the bank. Moreover, the valuation procedures used might not always have been consistent and realistic. But the trend is very clearly visible. The bank was almost completely deprived of capital, because it had not accumulated adequate means during the posthyperinflation growth period.

The very same phenomenon, if not to an even more extreme degree, occurred in Germany during the 1920s. Before the war, the German banks had about the same debt/equity ratio as the CA (3:1 to 4:1), but this ratio deteriorated during the 1920s, to 15:1 or even 20:1 at the outbreak of the crisis (Stolper 1967, 113). Therefore a relatively small loss was enough to wipe out a bank's capital, and that happened in both countries. Consequently, the Credit-Anstalt was very fragile and had an inadequate capital base, a fundamental cause for its insolvency in 1931. This confirms Minsky's (1982, 138) view that the precondition for a financial crisis (here a bank's crisis) is a "fragile financial structure" that "resulted from the process by which investments and positions in the stock of capital assets are financed."

The lack of capital can be traced back to the hyperinflation, but the other fundamental reasons for the insolvency of the CA are due to decisions reaching even further into the past.

The most crucial and consequential decision was taken in 1918, when the Peace Treaty of Saint-Germain at the end of World War I left the Austro-Hungarian empire divided into three different countries, with the rest of the former territory being spread among four already existing states. Since Vienna had been the financial center of this empire, a choice had to be made between accepting an economic reorientation based on the new political boundaries, or trying to adhere to the economic structure of the prewar period. The banks opted for adhering to a "business as usual" policy – that is to ignore the political changes and to preserve their sphere of influence in the new Successor States. The alternative would have been to attempt to shrink down to a size appropriate to the new Austrian state with only 6 million inhabitants, as compared to more than 50 million they had served in the empire.

The former appeared (in the short run) the less painful route, since shrinking down would have implied large-scale dismissals of bank employees, as well as giving up the influence gained during decades of dominance of the financial markets in these regions. The annual report of the Credit-Anstalt for 1930 (published after the collapse) states that the attempt of this bank to hold its position in the Successor States and even to extend it (as they actually did), was necessary, since the restriction to the Austrian economy would not have provided an institution like the CA with an appropriate field of business (Credit-Anstalt 1931, 11).[4] As Rutkowski (1934, 58) points out correctly, this statement reveals the almost tragic situation of the Viennese bank managers, who would not accept the restriction of their sphere of influence to the small Austrian territory, and who held on to the dream of Vienna as the financial center of the Danubian states, and "virtually became prisoners of their ill considered policy to do business as if the Monarchy still existed" (März and Weber 1983a, 515). "Helped by the undimmed glamour of the name of Rothschild, the Credit-Anstalt emerged from the immediate post-Armistice crisis with its international standing un-impaired" (*The Economist,* June 27, 1931, 1370).

Apart from these arguments, a point can be made on efficiency grounds for preserving the business ties to the industries in the Successor States. These Viennese banks had – over decades – ac-quired an enormous knowledge of the potential borrowers in these states, and a withdrawal would have increased the cost of credit intermediation considerably, as a lot of information would have been lost, and would have had to be gathered first by the new banks. Or, as Guttentag and Herring (1987, 153) put it:

Once the bank has made an initial investment in information about a specific borrower and has developed the right contract and monitoring ar-rangements for that borrower, additional loans can be made to the borrower at lower marginal cost than would be possible for another creditor who has not made the initial investment.

Therefore, the Viennese banks had a comparative advantage in serv-ing those financial needs. This efficiency gain, however, did not accrue to the Austrian economy, but to those of the Successor States.[5]

---

[4] This can be interpreted in different ways. It can either mean "appropriate" for covering the expenses of the institution or "appropriate" for the status of the bank and its officials.

[5] Rutkowski (1934, 58) goes even further and stresses that the Austrian economy suffered harm because of the international business deals of its banks, since those credits supported the Successor States in their strive for autarky, especially since international financial markets were not open to most of them. Moreover, the

The events of May 1931 (and thereafter), however, raise some doubts whether this comparative advantage was used to the benefit of the Viennese banks. As we recall, more than 260 million schillings had been lost to bad debts in the Successor States. This amounted to two thirds of the overall loan volume to foreigners.[6] This poor performance suggests that an adverse selection process might have taken place in those markets. As the Austrian banks and especially the CA had to compete with local banks, the relatively high interest rates charged by Viennese banks might have driven the low-risk borrowers out of this market, leaving the banks with a pool of borrowers with higher than average risk and therefore with very high default rates.[7] Since "borrowers have better knowledge of their own default risk than the bank has ... the familiar adverse selection mechanism makes the quality of the applicant pool (unobservable by banks) dependent on the loan terms offered" (Bernanke 1981, 157). At the same time the monitoring cost of a lender hundreds and thousands of kilometers away had to be considerably higher than for the local banks.

Contemporary reports confirm our conclusions. The *Wiener Börsen-Kurier* (May 18, 1931, 1) reported that whenever there was a considerable profit to be made in foreign centers, the Austrian banks were only allowed to participate with a very moderate share ("out of pity," as it put it); however, when losses were made, they hit Austria and its financial institutions with full force.

This "lemon" aspect of the Austrian loans to the financial markets of Eastern Europe was stressed by *The Economist* (June 27, 1931, 1370):

In the Succession States and the Balkans the credit which the bank [i.e., the CA] had granted had in most cases become illiquid. There the ownership of the best industrial companies had long since passed into stronger hands. What was left abroad was in many cases dependent upon assistance from the bank.

A very similar point was made by Rothschild (1947, 54–5), since he claimed that

the newly created financial institutions of the Succession states ... took the "cream" off the market. They supplied the credit requirements of the new,

point can also be made that Austria's economy would have needed some of those credits since it had suffered under a notorious undercapitalization.

[6] While only about 40 percent of the domestic loans became uncollectible.

[7] This would then be equivalent to Akerlof's (1970) "lemons."

and highly protected, industries of their countries: and the Vienna banks had to employ their funds in less secure fields.

In Federn's words mainly "the long-term loans to unprofitable Czechoslovakian enterprises" were left to the Viennese banks.[8]

Thus, although the breakup of the monarchy was an exogenous political event for the Austrian banking sector, its decision to stay in the eastern credit markets and to take on the role of an inter-mediator between western creditors and eastern borrowers was a largely endogenous decision, and became, as it turned out in 1931, a fundamental cause of the insolvency of the Credit-Anstalt.

Although the first two fundamental causes have led us back to the hyperinflation and even to the Treaty of Saint-Germain, the third cause can be traced back even further, into the middle of the nineteenth century. It is based on "the peculiar nature of the Aus-trian banking system" (Kaldor 1932, 29). Since their establishment, most of the Viennese banks had been "universal banks" – that is, they combined the functions of a commercial deposit bank with those of an investment trust. "The Credit-Anstalt was as much an industrial holding company as a bank . . ." (Stiefel 1983a, 417). The CA had these enormous industrial holdings, because it had already acquired four large Austrian banks, each with extensive holdings. In this respect it was very similar to the large Berlin banks of which the *Wall Street Journal* (May 5, 1931, 9) reported that "bank heads hold directorships in scores of companies, and the banks themselves retain holdings in shares they have issued." This mixed type of deposit and investment bank, "initially created in order to advance growth in an industrial late starter, turned out to be particularly vulnerable in periods of cyclical downturn, much more than purely commercial banks would have been" (Stolper 1967, 112).

The Austrian banks were "universal" in more than one sense of the word. They were not only universal in terms of the banking services they performed, but also in terms of their clientele and in terms of the geographical location of their sphere of influence. This made them very similar to the German banks, very different, how-ever, from the British and American banks. While the servicing of different industries in different locations made them less vulnerable to the effects of a local or sectoral business downturn, in contrast

---

[8] Federn (1932, 411; translated in *Euromoney*, 1976, 145).

to the United States unit banks, which could not branch out in order to reach the optimal size for risk spreading, the fact that they were very closely linked to the businesses actually increased their vulnerability.[9] This was especially so, since the industries did not provide the banks with money, but the banks provided the industries with credit – or as someone put it: "British banks were created for people who had money, while Austrian banks were created for people who needed money."

Every business downturn, and especially the depression of 1929/1930, made this "inherently unsound type of banking" (Kaldor 1932, 30) subject to a double squeeze, one emanating from the losses due to frozen loans, another due to the deterioration of the value of their very extensive portfolio holdings. Being owners of and lenders to the industries, they were hit twice and were caught in a vicious circle, as they had to support unprofitable undertakings ("throw good money after bad") in order to avoid negative effects on the value of their industrial portfolios. As *Die Aktiengesellschaft* (June 15, 1931, 7) analyzed it, the dependence of the industries on the banks became larger than ever, and the purely microeconomic requirements became macroeconomic requirements, as the financing of industry had to be continued even if it did not produce profits for the banks. Moreover, as the public only supplied but hardly demanded stocks after the 1924 stock exchange crash, the banks had only two options: (1) either to buy up the excess supply, or (2) to let the prices decline, which in turn would have adversely affected the value of their own portfolios.

We recall from the aggregate-loss figure that the deterioration of the value of the industrial holdings had contributed a considerable amount to the overall loss of the Credit-Anstalt.[10] This particular organizational structure of the banking sector emerges as a fundamental cause of the bank's insolvency.

The proximate causes. While these fundamental causes set the general framework that made the collapse possible, the proximate

[9] We have to distinguish branch banking from universal banking. Canada, for instance, allowed nationwide branch banking and did not witness any bank failures.

[10] In addition to that, a considerable amount of the frozen loans were due to firms owned by the CA.

causes for the insolvency have to be found in the period closer to the actual event. They can be summarized in three categories: (1) management errors, (2) the business depression, and (3) the ill-fated merger with the Boden-Credit-Anstalt.

Stiefel's (1983b) investigations revealed that inability on the part of the managers played a large role in the losses that occurred. The *Wiener Börsen-Kurier* (May 18, 1931, 1) correctly points out that if a leading director is surprised and astonished when he is informed about the losses of his bank, then he cannot be fit for this position. The fact that members of the board of directors received the "news" from newspapers is another sad outgrowth of the same deficiency. At the same time we read of a director of the bank claiming that "it was best to buy shares of firms that were not quoted on the stock exchange, as one did not then have to lower the book values according to their quoted values" (*Euromoney*, 1976, 146).[11] Sir Robert Kindersley was not exaggerating when he remarked that "the management had been both extravagant and incapable . . ."[12] The *Wall Street Journal*'s (June 23, 1931, 6) conclusion that it was "not bad management" that had created the collapse was premature and incorrect. It is, however, difficult or even impossible to assign relative importance to these managerial mistakes as a proximate cause of the insolvency (and the same applies to the other causes, too).

It seems unnecessary to reflect here on the question whether the Credit-Anstalt would have mastered its problems without the necessary outside help had it not been for the business downturn of 1929/1930. It is unquestionable, however, that a large share of the losses was due to the unexpectedly deep depression in Austria, as well as in the Successor States.[13] This is reflected not only in the

---

[11] A very interesting parallel can be found in the United States. "Because there was an active market for bonds and continuous quotation of their prices, a bank's capital was more likely to be impaired, in the judgment of bank examiners, when it held bonds that were expected to be and were honored in full when due than when it held bonds for which there was no good market and few quotations. So long as the latter did not come due, they were likely to be carried on the books at face value; only actual defaults or postponements of payments would reduce the examiner's evaluation" (Friedman and Schwartz 1963, 356).

[12] Quoted in Stiefel 1983b, 34.

[13] März and Weber (1983a, 501) extend this point to the economic situation during the whole interwar period, as "the deeper causes of the failure of the policy should not be sought in human frailty, but in the poor performance of the Austrian economy even before the onset of the Great Depression."

Table 4.4. *Reported profits of the Credit-Anstalt (in million schillings)*

Year	Profits
1923	7.59
1924	6.32
1925	6.57
1926	7.86
1927	10.11
1928	10.27
1929	8.80
1930	−139.60

Sources: Profit/loss accounts of the Credit-Anstalt.

breakdown of the final losses of the bank but also in the fact that those industries where the CA suffered its heaviest losses, textiles and metal, were among those hit hardest by the recession. A study by Morgenstern (1931, 254) on the development of the values of industrial stocks between 1913 and 1930 revealed that for all industries the prices of their stocks had declined on average to 41.5 percent over this seventeen year period, for textiles and metal, however, even further, to 35.5 and 17.9 percent.

Another piece of evidence on the impact of the business downturn is the development of the profits of the Credit-Anstalt. As the figures in Table 4.4 show, the reported profits had dropped by about 15 percent in 1929 before turning into a loss in 1930.

Unfortunately, however, investigations after the collapse revealed that these numbers did not reflect the true state of affairs in this institution, painting an overly optimistic picture. According to the investigations, losses were already occurring as far back as the mid-1920s. In any case, the rapid worsening of the business climate affected the banking sector, as even the more cautious institutions, like the Niederösterreichische Escompte-Gesellschaft and the Wiener Bank-Verein suffered considerable losses and had to be reorganized.[14]

[14] However, only a few years after the Credit-Anstalt problems arose, i.e., when the business downturn had already been much more pronounced and had persisted for a much longer time period. The Länderbank, which was in French hands but operated in Vienna, did not suffer any losses at all.

It was not only the direct effect of the depression on the bank's customers that led to large-scale losses at the CA, but, as März and Weber (1983b, 435) point out correctly, the bank was put under "considerable pressure from the government to prop up crumbling businesses so as to relieve a steadily worsening economic situation." They conclude therefore that government, business, and union representatives have to share the guilt, since they had insisted on a "business policy which seemed increasingly at variance with the underlying reality" (436). A short-sighted policy to avoid the short-run loss of jobs resulted, in the long run, in much bigger harm, as the unemployment figures show so dramatically. The depression clearly left its mark on the Credit-Anstalt and contributed to its losses.

As the final factor in the determination of the proximate causes, the merger with the Boden-Credit-Anstalt in October 1929 deserves mentioning. The BCA had been the main competitor of the CA, following a very similar – but even more aggressive – business strategy. Just like the CA, it had tried to ignore the economic consequences of the breakup of the monarchy and had attempted to expand its presence in the Successor States. At the same time, it had incorporated a number of failing Austrian banks. In the fall of 1929, political unrest in Austria had led to large-scale withdrawals and to capital flight by the frightened public, and the BCA became increasingly illiquid. Only a generous lending policy on the part of the Austrian National Bank kept this institution afloat. Suddenly, the ANB decided to stop accepting financial bills from this bank and forced it to find a partner for a merger, in order to avoid liquidation.[15] Under the auspices of the government, the Credit-Anstalt decided to take over the ailing institution, with the BCA's shareholders suffering heavy losses.[16]

---

[15] This bank's rediscounting ceiling had already been overextended long before that day.

[16] It is usually claimed that the bank was forced by the government to do so. In this case, the question of the incentives for the CA to obey the government's wish needs clarification. The only effective threat the government might have used was that – if the need should arise – it would refuse to come to the help of the Credit-Anstalt. This, however, might have sufficed to convince Rothschild, as he might have perceived some of the problems in his bank. Further research is necessary to be able to evaluate the implications of such an – indirect – guarantee and the potential moral hazard problems. It seems very likely that

This business transaction was considered a favorable deal for the Credit-Anstalt by contemporary outside observers. The *Wiener Börsen-Kurier* (October 14, 1929, 3), for instance, reported that it was quite sure that the CA would not lose and not even risk anything by taking over the BCA, since the "BCA was and is solvent."

Nevertheless, the merger had a double impact on the CA crisis. For one, it contributed a considerable part to the losses (we recall that out of the 139.6 million schillings of initially reported losses, 60 million schillings were being blamed on the effects of the merger), and is therefore one of the proximate causes of the insolvency. Apart from that, however, it had a fundamental impact on the way the public reacted to the announcement of the CA problems. The parallels to 1929 were obvious, although the BCA crisis had started with illiquidity while the CA crisis with insolvency. Both bank collapses caught the public, as well as most "experts," by surprise. Both banks had a very similar structure, business policy, and clientele, both had very extensive industrial holdings throughout the Successor States, both had built a large banking enterprise on a small capital basis, and they were the two largest banks in Austria. Consequently, it is not surprising, and it was definitely not irrational on the part of the public, that distrust emerged despite the concurrent announcement of the rescue plan.

The decreased willingness of the public to hold debts of the CA and the resulting difficulty of this bank to refinance its position, resulted, as Minsky would have predicted, in illiquidity, as the public ran to convert its CA deposits into cash, fearing larger problems than those that were revealed. This distrust was basically a result of the fact that "the main principle of banking policy [in Austria] was never to dip into declared reserves. Temporary difficulties had to be met from the invisible reserves. . . ." (Layton and Rist 1925, 134).[17] Therefore, any open declaration of losses had to imply lasting difficulties. The surprising announcement of the insolvency as well

the bank officials knew that the CA could count on the government's support, and that, in turn, might have influenced the level of care they applied to their business dealings. At the same time, it might have affected the bank's creditors' tactics in dealing with the Credit-Anstalt. Since they knew that it was an "unsinkable ship," backed by the government, they had every incentive to refuse concessions and to press their claims to the extreme.

17 By "invisible reserves" they refer to "hidden reserves," the result of undervaluing assets.

Table 4.5. *Total foreign debt of the Credit-Anstalt by country of origin (in dollars[a])*

Great Britain	27,000,000
U.S.A.	24,000,000
France	6,000,000
Netherlands	6,000,000
Switzerland	6,000,000
Germany	5,000,000
other countries	2,000,000
Total	76,000,000

[a] 1 U.S. dollar = 7.11 Austrian schillings.
Source: The Economist, July 4, 1931, 16.

as the way the crisis was handled by the bank, the government, and the National Bank became then the proximate reasons for the illiquidity of the Credit-Anstalt.

The causes of the illiquidity of the bank

The fundamental causes. Fundamental to the liquidity problems of the CA was its biased debt structure. The small capital endowment together with the relatively small volume of domestic deposits, forced the CA (as it did all other Viennese banks) to rely very heavily on foreign credits. For the Credit-Anstalt more than a third of its creditors were of foreign origin. Rutkowski (1934, 55) reports that 36 percent or approximately 500 million schillings of all its credits at the time of the collapse came from abroad.[18] Table 4.5 shows the approximate breakdown of the origin of those funds. England and the United States provided the majority of credits to this bank. Foreign private debt was abundantly available, but only on a short-term basis.

As early as 1925 the commissioner general of the League of Nations complained about the eagerness of foreign creditors to lend to Austria:

I am more and more preoccupied by the growing impatience of American banks to grant loans to Austrian official and semi-official corporations. . . .

---

[18] Clarke (1967, 182) estimates the foreign short-term indebtedness of the CA on May 11, 1931, at $100 million, i.e., 700 million schillings.

I have done what I could to control the current, but their eagerness to get rid of their money is stronger than my efforts to let them keep it.[19]

The same point was stressed by Layton and Rist (1925, 122) in their report on the economic conditions in Austria, as they observed that "the chief Viennese banks can obtain at 6 percent more foreign credits than they are able to employ," and at that time the Austrian discount rate was at 10 percent. So that "continuous and large offers of foreign credits from abroad . . . are attracted by the difference of the rates of interest to be obtained in Vienna over those in Western Europe and the United States of America" (123).[20] This phenomenon did not change until 1929, and the ANB's refusal to lower the discount rate led to continuous inflows of foreign credits, or, as the *Wiener Börsen-Kurier* (August 24, 1931, 2) termed it, to a "credit inflation."

The Austrian economy was largely dependent on these short-term credits since only very restricted amounts of long-term funds were obtainable to cover the large structural current account deficit.[21] That is why Sir Eric Phipps concluded that "the extensive short-term credits given to Vienna banks by lenders in London, Paris, Amsterdam, New York and elsewhere . . . really form the economic

---

[19] Cited in Kernbauer 1982, 8.
[20] With respect to the causes of the high interest rates in Vienna, Layton and Rist (1925, 124) had argued already in 1925 that a high bank rate in Austria "is essential for attracting foreign currency. . . . The opinion was expressed to us that, in order to attract sufficient foreign capital, the Bank rate in Austria should normally be at least 1 per cent higher than that in Germany, whilst the German Bank rate should be from 2 to 3 per cent higher than the rate in London." But they also stressed domestic reasons, since a relatively high rate of interest "is even more necessary in order to stimulate the formation of capital in the country itself" (ibid.). Although the interest rates generally followed the path that was given by the ANB's discount-rate policy, they were considerably higher than the official bank rate. The Austrian Institute for Business Cycle Research explained this large discrepancy by the existence of a considerable risk premium charged by the banks, and by the banks' necessity to cover the cost of their oversized apparatus (OIfK 1933, 12). Rothschild (1947, 37) adds to these that "the cost of credit was also raised by the monopolistic policy of the bank cartel which fixed the rates and left a margin of 7 1/2 to 9 1/2 percent between rates paid and charged." Since most of the potential borrowers had no alternative sources of funds, these differentials were not wiped out by arbitrage.
[21] The yearly trade deficit amounted during the 1920s to about 1,100 million schillings. Taking into account the traditional surplus in services, März and Weber (1983a) estimate the average yearly current account deficits at about 790 million schillings.

life-blood of this country."[22] Growing reliance on this type of funds together with the extreme volatility of international short-term capital created financial instability and "a constant potential source of exchange crises" (*The Economist,* September 26, 1931, 553), and, as Minsky (1977, 139) puts it, "in a fragile financial system continued normal functioning can be disrupted by some not unusual event." And the collapse of the Credit-Anstalt was undoubtedly more than a "not unusual event."

The Austrian banks must have known about the problem, one indication being their boycotts of efforts of the ANB to collect data on the extent of this foreign indebtedness (Kernbauer 1982, 15). Adding to this fundamental instability was the fact that these short-term liabilities were tied up in long-term assets. Although the funds were mainly lent out in the form of credits on current accounts (i.e., short-term), these loans were – de facto – rolled over continuously and constituted long-term money that was mainly used to finance capital investments. The product of this policy was then a biased debt structure, a maturity mismatch of the Austrian banks in general and of the Credit-Anstalt in particular. A structure that was inherently unstable, since any unexpected event that would result in reduced inflows or in larger-than-usual withdrawals could render the banks illiquid, and could consequently lead to runs and panics. And that is what happened in 1931.

The proximate causes. The revelation of the drastic decline of the Credit-Anstalt's net worth reduced the public's willingness to hold debts of this bank, and they started to demand cash for their deposits, endangering the liquidity position of the bank. A bank in need of liquid resources has basically three options to refinance its position without becoming illiquid: to borrow money in the market, to sell some of its assets, or to turn to the lender of last resort.

The first avenue, to borrow from other Austrian or foreign banks, was not open to the Credit-Anstalt in May 1931. The Austrian banks needed cash themselves, since there was a danger of an extended run on all banks. Even after the general run had subsided, the relative size of the threatened bank made such a rescue operation by the Austrian commercial banks impossible. The CA was simply too

[22] Quoted in Stiefel 1983a, 417.

big for a domestic private sector solution. The foreign banks, on the other hand, which had lent extensively to the CA before the announcement of the problems, had no intentions of getting further involved. Quite to the contrary, they feared for their existing claims and hoped to get out as soon as possible. A standstill agreement was all that could be reached with them, and that only after long negotiations and a governmental guarantee.

A sudden increase in a bank's cash needs would not cause an illiquidity loss if the bank's assets were perfectly marketable (Guttentag and Herring 1987, 152). Selling off assets in order to raise cash was an avenue the CA had already tried before 1931. In 1930, in order to relieve its already strained liquidity position, it had launched a holding company, the Continental Trust for Bank and Industrial Shares (at Basel, Switzerland), designed to buy up some of the bank's extensive industrial holdings. Partners in this project were the bankers Warburg, Rothschild, Helbert and Wagg, as well as the Schweizer Bankverein. In October 1930, this holding company managed to raise 40 million Swiss francs by placing bonds with a Swiss consortium. Nevertheless, its rather limited activities were judged a failure (*The Times*, May 18, 1931, 20).

Only a few weeks before the outbreak of the crisis, in April 1931, the CA made another similar attempt. This time with the goal of attracting French capital. The Union Internationale de Placement, located in Luxembourg, was established with some of the partners from the Continental Trust and some French and American capital. But no funds were raised in the capital markets. In May 1931, any attempt to liquidate a considerable part of the assets would have been a failure. After more than a year and a half of business depression, prices were very low and potential buyers were very few. The business outlook was too uncertain, especially after the shocking news about this respected bank. Moreover, the liquidity needs of the CA were too big.[23]

Since all these "normal" avenues to strengthen liquidity were not open to the CA, it threatened to close its doors. As too much depended on it – for example, a large part of the payroll of Austrian industry – such a crisis had to be averted. The lender of last resort

[23] The CA did, however, sell some of its assets, e.g., shares in the Laibacher Kredit-Anstalt to local (i.e., Yugoslavian) investors (see *Neue Freie Presse*, June 21, 1931, 19).

had to intervene heavily, even more than allowed by its own statutes.

The causes of the banking crisis

> One terra incognita being seen to be faulty, every other terra incognita would be suspected.
>
> —W. Bagehot, 1962

The announcement of the Credit-Anstalt's losses resulted not only in a run on this institution's reserves, but also in a run on most of the other banks in Vienna. This run forced those banks to turn to the discount window of the Austrian National Bank in order to be protected against expected foreign credit withdrawals. But only after a few days (three to four) did the public realize that the liquidity of those banks was not endangered, and therefore, that their deposits were safe, and the panic subsided. These institutions witnessed an increased inflow of deposits, as former Credit-Anstalt deposits were being transferred.[24] Only when the potential currency crisis became generally recognized, did deposits start to fall again. Initially panic spread to other banks because these institutions were perceived to be very similar to the CA (and to the former BCA). The Credit-Anstalt's failure affected the public's perception of the health of the other Viennese banks – a phenomenon that has been termed in the literature as "reputational externalities" (Summers 1989). This similarity provided the link of distrust that was only overcome when the public became convinced that they could convert their deposits without any difficulty into high-powered money. Therefore, the fundamental reason for the banking panic was the similarity of the situation of all Austrian banks.[25]

The proximate causes can be found in the psychological impact that the announcement of the crisis at the largest and most prestigeous financial institution of Central and Eastern Europe had on the public in Austria. The public's initial mood corresponded with Sir Eric Phipps's assessment that if even the Credit-Anstalt could

---

[24] The Viennese savings banks, for instance, gained 27.6 million schillings or about 2.9 percent in savings deposits in May 1931 (*Statistische Nachrichten*, June 27, 1931, 145).

[25] Although some of them were more conservative in their business policies.

not be relied on, everything in Austria must have been rotten. But no sooner had this general distrust in the banks materialized than it was resolved by the prompt payment by the banks (with the help of the ANB) of every demand by depositors for cash, thus rebuilding the public's confidence and reassuring them that "not everything was rotten." Unfortunately, however, this did not include the Austrian currency, as we will show in the following section.

Causes of the currency crisis

It is clear that the state and the national bank have thus involved themselves in obligations from which . . . inflation can be the only way out.

—N. Kaldor, 1932

As we have pointed out before, the collapse of the Credit-Anstalt was followed by a currency crisis. Since the public expected a change in parity, it engaged in short-term capital transfers (out of the schilling), while the Austrian National Bank believed that the market's expectations were wrong and took steps to keep the exchange rate within the gold points. Their respective actions resulted in large-scale losses of foreign reserves for the ANB, and, as foreign exchange allocations became restricted, in the establishment of black markets. Finally, five months after the outbreak of the crisis, exchange controls were introduced. Inflationary fears by a large segment of the public had led to a speculative attack on the Austrian schilling and to a de facto abandoning of the exchange rate regime.[26]

Therefore, in order to understand the currency crisis, we have to understand why these – rational or irrational – inflationary fears developed. The key to understanding the public's sensitivity with respect to inflation lies in the period 1919 to 1922, the period of the Austrian hyperinflation. This traumatic experience overshadowed all the later developments and left its distinctive mark on them.

At the end of 1918 (i.e., after World War I), the price level in Austria had been about twenty-five times as high as before the war; in January of 1921, this figure had already reached ninety-two times; in January 1922, 830 times; and finally, at the peak of the hyperinflation, in September 1922, 14,153 times the prewar level (Yeager

[26] Formally, however, it was maintained.

1981, 45–6). At the same time, the exchange rate on the United States dollar had reached 16,877 times the 1913 level. In August 1922, then, the Austrian crown was abruptly stabilized, and the "Austrian inflation was essentially stopped cold" (Yeager 1981, 51).

The proximate cause for this unprecedented hyperinflation in Austria was the enormous increase in note circulation during and especially after the war. By the end of August 1922, bank-note circulation had reached a level 2,700 times the estimated prewar level (Walré de Bordes 1924, 50), and 288 times the level of March 1919, the date of the onset of the hyperinflation (Sargent 1982, 49). The expansion of central bank notes stemmed mainly from the bank's policy of discounting treasury bills, but also, as Sargent (1982, 49) points out, from the central bank's practice of making loans and discounts to private agents at nominal interest rates between 6 and 9 percent, when the inflation rate averaged up to 10,000 percent per annum (e.g., from January to August 1922).[27]

This enormous monetary expansion was the proximate reason for the uncontrollable increases in the different price indices. The fundamental cause driving these developments was the chaotic budgetary situation. As its expenditures skyrocketed while its receipts could not keep up at all, the Austrian state ran a large budget deficit. During the second half of 1921, for instance, the government's receipts could not cover more than 35.7 percent of the expenditures (Gratz 1949, 278).[28] Since no other ways of financing were open to the government, it had to sell treasury bills to the Austrian administration of the Austro-Hungarian Bank, and the logical result was the above-mentioned rapid increase in the amount of high-powered money.[29] A vicious circle, or a vicious spiral, developed as

in proportion as the State deficit and the note circulation increased, in proportion as confidence in the future of the currency disappeared, the crown continued to depreciate. But the more the crown depreciated, the more the State deficit increased and the more difficult it became for the state to put its finances in order. (Walré de Bordes 1924, 20)

[27] To this point see also Walré de Bordes (1924, 51–2).
[28] One of the chief causes of the deficit was the supply of food by the government at highly subsidized prices.
[29] Since as "every attempt to obtain credits from foreign banks or from foreign Governments had met with failure . . ." (Walré de Bordes 1924, 28), and Viennese banks were not willing to lend to the state, either (Kernbauer et al. 1983, 351).

People tried to rearrange their portfolios and to reduce the amount of wealth held in this depreciating currency. They fled into the currencies of those countries that did not suffer from hyperinflations and into real assets. The government felt obliged to introduce strict exchange controls. In August 1922 the tailspin of the currency was suddenly stopped, and in September prices reached their peak despite the fact that the selling of treasury bills to the central bank was not terminated until mid-November and high-powered money kept on growing consistently through 1923. Since nothing had changed dramatically in 1922 concerning the proximate cause of the hyperinflation, it was the change in the fundamental cause of the problems that stopped the ongoing disaster so abruptly.

The depreciation of the Austrian crown was suddenly stopped by the intervention of the Council of the League of Nations and the resulting binding commitment of the government of Austria to reorder Austrian fiscal and monetary strategies dramatically. (Sargent 1982, 52)

In particular, the Austrian government had to pledge to establish an independent central bank, that would be forbidden to lend to the government, except on the basis of gold or foreign exchange security.[30] It had to pledge to balance its budget within two years' time. In exchange for this change in the fiscal and monetary regime, an internationally guaranteed loan (650 million gold crowns) was promised and raised in the international capital markets.[31]

The government's willingness to abandon the old fiscal and monetary strategies and to follow fiscal and monetary policies compatible with maintaining the convertibility of its liabilities into dollars reinstated public confidence in the currency, and, as Walré de Bordes (1924, 32) pointed out, "Confidence was the magic power which made everything possible which before had been impossible." This change in the government's strategy resulted then in private economic agents changing their expectations as trust in the economic policies returned and, with it, trust in the currency. "The

---

[30] Article 50 of the statutes of the ANB specified that "neither the Federation nor the provinces nor the municipalities shall in any way, either directly or indirectly, have recourse for their own purposes to the resources of the bank unless they shall have paid in the equivalent of the notes received in gold or in foreign credits" (Sokal and Rosenberg 1929, 123).

[31] As one gold crown equaled 14,400 paper crowns, and one schilling replaced 10,000 paper crowns (in 1925), the net revenue of this bond issue (613 million gold crowns) amounted to about 880 million schillings.

crown became one of the most stable currencies in Europe, earning the nickname of the Alpine dollar" (Yeager 1981, 48). Nevertheless, the experience with hyperinflation left the Austrian public with an increased sensitivity for, and even constant fear of, inflation. At the same time it taught them a very painful but instructive lesson about the links between fiscal and monetary expansion, inflation and exchange rates.

The proximate causes. What kind of changes occurred then in 1931 that made the public lose its trust and confidence in the "Alpine dollar"? On the basis of the previous discussion on the hyperinflation, we have to look for signals of a – perceived – return to policies like those of the 1919 to 1922 period.

As we recall, the initial rescue plan identified the Austrian government as the main contributor to the salvage of the failing bank, with a share of 100 million schillings (41.4 million for losses and 58.6 million for new capital) in exchange for 33 percent of the bank's new share capital. For the state to assume this role was a major departure from its general laissez-faire philosophy, but it was considered to be necessary in order to prevent much greater harm to Austrian industry and economy.[32] It was not intended to be a policy change of any kind. Quite to the contrary, the government preferred intervention in this bank's affairs to intervention at the level of the individual industries and companies, since the latter approach would have been perceived as a complete break with its previous economic philosophy and policy. This was also the reason why it tried – initially – to avoid becoming the majority stockholder of the CA. "The state has no intention whatsoever of remaining a partner of the Credit-Anstalt. At the first opportunity the state will get rid of its shares," reported the *Reichspost* on May 13, 1931. The help to the bank should have been an isolated action made necessary by special circumstances. There is no indication that this action – per se – would have created any adverse expectations with respect to the Austrian currency.

However, what might have already influenced some people's expectations at this stage was the fact that the government did not

---

[32] There had been at least one precedent, since the government had guaranteed the deposits of the Centralbank der deutschen Sparkassen in the summer of 1926.

have the 100 million schillings it had pledged to contribute to the reconstruction of the bank. The *Wiener Börsen-Kurier* (March 23, 1931, 1), on the basis of a report of the General Council of the Austrian National Bank, had already warned in March 1931 of the serious situation of public finance, especially since the issue of the prewar debt had still not been settled satisfactorily and was therefore reducing the private sector's willingness to absorb government debt. Now, Viennese banks had to advance that money, since no cash was left at the treasury. At the same time there were promises of long-term international aid, and – initially – the public had no reasons to doubt those reports.[33] No fundamental change in the fiscal regime had yet occurred.

The events of May 12, 1931, and the following days had, however, a very strong impact on the monetary regime. Distrust in the Credit-Anstalt and, for that matter, in the other banks too, had led to large-scale withdrawals by the public, and – since the ANB followed a "lending freely" policy – to a sharp increase in its bills portfolio and in the amount of high-powered money (Table 4.6).

In the course of only four days (May 12 to May 15) the amount of rediscounted bills increased by at least 328 percent, while high-powered money had increased by 19.4 percent.[34] Bank-note circulation had expanded by 14.6 percent. These were rates of expansion unknown during the preceding years and even unmatched at the height of the hyperinflation during the summer of 1922.[35] During the following weeks, this expansion was not reversed but rather reinforced, as Credit-Anstalt bills – financial bills in their majority – were discounted freely at the National Bank. Inflationary fears of the public were reignited by these developments, and the public

[33] It is difficult to assess what impression the ongoing debate about the customs union with Germany and the strong opposition to this plan by France and other countries had made on the Austrian public and its expectations about international aid.

[34] "At least," because we only have the figures for May 7 and May 15, 69.5 million and 297.6 million schillings. During "normal" months, however, due to seasonal effects, the volume of bills at midmonth used to be lower than during the first week. These figures did not include coins in circulation, since we do not have weekly data on this item.

[35] The highest percentage increase we could detect was for the period August 23 to 31, 1922, when bank-note circulation had actually increased by 17.9 percent. This was not only a somewhat longer time period but included also the last day of the month with its regularily increased demand for cash.

Table 4.6. *Notes and deposits, foreign reserves and bills discounted at the outbreak of the crisis, weekly (in million schillings)*

Day	Notes and deposits at ANB	Foreign reserves	Bills discounted
April 30	1,048.5	860.0	89.2
May 7	1,024.6	855.5	69.5
May 15	1,223.8	826.4	297.6
May 23	1,230.4	780.5	350.0
May 31	1,282.9	732.2	451.3[a]
June 7	1,251.9	677.1	475.4
June 15	1,286.4	698.7[b]	488.2
June 23	1,255.4	661.0	490.2
June 30	1,290.9	658.6	528.7
July 7	1,252.6	639.0	511.3
July 15	1,259.7	622.4	533.9
July 23	1,285.2	592.6	588.4
July 31	1,299.7	566.7	632.1

[a] Bills discounted do not include those 100 million schillings worth of discounts that have been rediscounted by the ANB at the BIS and the other Central Banks participating in the BIS credit.
[b] Includes about half the Bank of England loan of 150 million schillings.
Source: Mitteilungen des Direktoriums der Oesterreichischen Nationalbank, various issues.

realized that the fixed exchange-rate system was inconsistent with the rate of domestic credit expansion.[36] Since a reversal of the policies seemed unlikely, the collapse of the fixed rate was anticipated, and a run on the foreign reserves developed. A speculative attack on the schilling occurred – that is, a discontinuous asset shift in agents' portfolios generated by a belief that an asset price-fixing scheme was about to terminate (Garber 1985, 287). As the public realized that capital gains to hoarding foreign exchange were suddenly available, they rationally demanded this increase in their holdings of foreign exchange (Garber 1981, 8). Table 4.6 reports the development of the reserves of the Austrian National Bank and reflects this speculative attack very vividly.

[36] "Since inflation is usually combined with an increase in note circulation, inflationary fears have been created in the public by the rise in currency" (*Wiener Börsen-Kurier*, June 1, 1931, 1; author's translation), and one week later it reported that fears for the schilling had spread into wide circles of the public and had led to capital flight (June 8, 1931, 1).

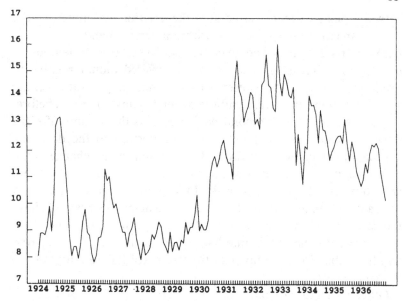

Figure 4.1. High-powered money-production index ratio.

The ANB's liberal lending policy was considered to be a change in the monetary regime, back towards the regime of the immediate postwar period.[37] Since the stabilization of the currency, the ANB had followed a "real bills doctrine." In a speech in 1931 the president of the ANB, Reisch, pointed out that the note circulation was tied to real bills (commercial bills), as the volume of bills could be regarded as a good proxy for the level of capacity utilization of trade and industry, and therefore, for the financial needs of the economy (Reisch 1931, 217). The pursuit of this "needs of trade" approach – of a relatively stable relationship between the note circulation and the nominal level of economic activity – is reflected very clearly in Figure 4.1 in the ratio of high-powered money to the index of industrial production.

Three facts strike the eye of the observer: (1) For most of the time

[37] The Austrian National Bank's functions and duties were very clearly defined in its statutes. Article 1 specified that "the Bank shall use all the means at its disposal to ensure that until the redemption of paper money (bank notes) in specie has been regulated by law, the value of its notes, when expressed in the currency of a country having a gold standard or a stable currency, shall at least not depreciate" (Sokal and Rosenberg 1929, 122).

between the adjustment period after the inflation and mid-1930, the ANB managed to keep the ratio within a narrow band; (2) the two banking crises of 1924 and 1926 are clearly reflected in temporary deviations – that is, increases in high-powered money relative to production, and, for the present analysis most importantly; (3) the 1931 crisis shows the ratio climbing to heights never reached before.

The ratio rose in the second half of 1930 as the volume of high-powered money was not reduced in proportion to the declining volume of production, but this did not yet reflect any change in the policy regime.[38] The business improvement in spring 1931 led to a short downward trend in the ratio. In May 1931, however, this ratio took a quantum leap upward and remained at levels not seen before, indicating to the public that a sudden change in the monetary rule had occurred. The old regime had ended as the real bills doctrine had been abandoned in favor of the rescue (of the liquidity) of the banking sector.

Other indicators of the monetary policy that were used during those years showed a very similar picture and led to the same conclusions. The central bank's weekly statements had never been studied as carefully as in 1931, especially the behavior of the note cover (*Wiener Börsen-Kurier*, June 8, 1931, 1). This interest went well beyond Austria and even Europe, as the *Wall Street Journal* (May 23, 1931, 10) reported that the "National Bank of Austria weekly statement [of May 15] shows circulation of 1,224,000,000 schillings, a new high record. Note cover, at 67%, is still the highest in Europe." Table 4.7 reports the behavior of the note cover after the outbreak of the crisis. Within the first days of the crisis, it declined by about one fifth. Despite the loans of the BIS and the Bank of England and the standstill agreement with the foreign creditors, it continued to decline.[39]

---

[38] There had been critical voices in political as well as journalistic circles because of the perceived inflationary dangers of this increase.

[39] These figures have been computed by dividing the gold and foreign exchange holdings of the ANB by the sum of currency in circulation and deposits at the central bank. The statutory minimum cover was somewhat differently defined. The debt of the government to the National Bank was deducted from money in circulation (without coins), and only the foreign exchange reserves specified in Article 85 of the statutes of the ANB were included. This ratio, which in 1931 had to exceed 24 percent, declined from 37 percent at the end of April to 27.9 percent in May, to reach 24.01 percent in December 1931.

Table 4.7. *Note cover in Austria, May–October 1931 (in percentages)*

Month	Days			
	7	15	23	Last Day
May	83.5	67.5	63.8	57.1
June	54.1	54.3	52.7	51.0
July	51.0	49.4	46.1	43.6
Aug.	48.7	43.1	42.3	40.3
Sept.	39.6	39.3	35.6	33.0
Oct.	29.9	29.1	28.7	28.1

Source: *Mitteilungen des Direktoriums der Oesterreichischen Nationalbank*, various issues.

This perceived change in the monetary strategy then became the proximate reason for the currency crisis, since "any sort of fixed exchange rate is equivalent to a monetary growth rule" and consequently "implies a specific monetary discipline, which, if not followed for one reason or another, will precipitate an exchange rate collapse" (Connolly and Taylor 1984, 205). Movements in domestic credit were then offset by countermovements in the foreign-exchange reserves, as this collapse of the prevailing exchange rate regime was predicted by the public.[40] Figure 4.2 shows very clearly those opposite flows in domestic credit and foreign reserves.

Only very restrictive allocations of foreign exchange – for example, on some days (early June 1931) only 5 percent for dollar notes – prevented foreign reserves from converging towards zero at a faster rate than they actually did (*Wiener Börsen-Kurier*, June 8, 1931, 2). As the authorities did not adjust their policies, the flight out of the schilling continued until exchange controls were introduced on October 9, 1931.[41]

The proximate cause of the currency crisis was the lack of confidence in the authorities' ability to defend the schilling's parity in

[40] An interesting topic for further research would be a comparison to the concurrent developments in Hungary, as that country's authorities decided to introduce a gold value currency (gold pengö) as numeraire (a standard for currency exchange rates), in order to stop withdrawals and capital flight and to induce the return of money (see, e.g., *The Economist*, August 29, 1931, 382, and *Wiener Börsen-Kurier*, August 24, 1931, 2).

[41] It did not stop completely thereafter, but the people had to – and did – become more imaginative about how to circumvent the controls (see Ellis, 1941).

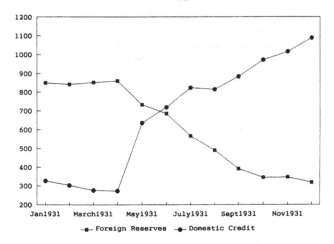

Figure 4.2. Foreign reserves and domestic credit, 1931 (in million schillings).

the light of the liberal lending policy that was followed in order to prevent an immobilization of the Credit-Anstalt. The fixed exchange rate regime was subject to collapse since it conflicted with more important policies. But "the collapse may have ultimately been caused by fundamental events ... drawing down on the central bank's foreign reserves and/or causing it to speed up domestic credit growth by more than anticipated" (Connolly and Taylor 1984, 205).

The fundamental causes. We have identified the change in the monetary regime as the proximate reason for the currency crisis. The fundamental cause, however, was the sad state of the Austrian government's finances. As we recall, the fundamental problem leading to the hyperinflation of the early 1920s had been the complete imbalance between the Austrian government's revenues and expenditures. The League of Nations loan had been granted in order to restore a balanced budget and orderly public finance. The acceptance of this change in the fiscal regime in exchange for the loan had stopped the currency's plunge in August 1922. Thereafter the government had pursued a policy of balanced budgets on current expenditures with moderate deficits when capital investment expenditures are taken into account.

At the onset of the Credit-Anstalt crisis, three adverse events – bad "fiscal news" – affected this policy regime. For one, 1930 had been the first year since stabilization with a budget deficit on current account (17 million schillings), as compared to a projected surplus of 35.4 million schillings.[42] It was mainly due to the increased outlays for unemployment benefits and reduced tax revenues – both effects of the business depression. Including capital investments, the deficit amounted to 261.6 million schillings (11.4 percent of expenditures), as compared to a surplus of 20 million schillings in 1929 (Butschek 1983, 429).[43] The predictions for 1931 that were issued at that time were even less encouraging, as the adverse effects of the business downturn on receipts and expenditures were expected to become even stronger. The first quarter of 1931 alone resulted in a 54.2 million schilling deficit for the current budget and the minister of finance predicted a 150 million schilling deficit for 1931.[44]

The second bad fiscal news was that in May 1931 the treasury had no funds whatsoever at its disposal. Its vaults were simply empty. However, it committed itself to contribute 100 million schillings to the reconstruction of the Credit-Anstalt and had to force Viennese banks to advance the necessary funds.

The most important adverse fiscal news was the acceptance of a (first not clearly defined and then unlimited) state guarantee for the liabilities of the Credit-Anstalt. The potential fiscal implications of this (forced) guarantee constituted a clear departure from the balanced-budget strategy of the mid- and late-1920s. It created contingent liabilities for the Austrian budget of amounts that could not be foreseen, at a time when the continued business downturn was already threatening Austria's fiscal balance, and it increased the present value of expected government debt in a discontinuous way.

---

[42] See *Wiener Börsen-Kurier*, October 19, 1931, 2, and Gruber 1930, 11.

[43] The *Wall Street Journal* (May 18, 1931, 6) reported in this context that "the International Control Committee for the protection of Austrian loans . . . has issued a study indicating that the Austrian government, far from initiating economies, has allowed unnecessary expenditures." The *Daily Telegraph* (May 21, 1931, 11) reported that "the Austrian governments, central and local, spend too much, as their budgets are higher than that of Czechoslovakia, which has 16,000,000 inhabitants, as against 6,000,000 Austrians." Both reports confirm statements made concerning the British situation in 1931, namely that "the first thing at which foreigners look is the budgetary situation" and that "Continental observers looked immediately to the budget when confidence in the sterling was weakened" (quoted in Eichengreen 1981, 10).

[44] Excluding any expenses for the reconstruction of the Credit-Anstalt (*Neue Freie Presse*, June 12, 1931, 2).

Moreover, by this point in time it was already obvious that this crisis would become increasingly intermingled with international politics and that consequently foreign credits could not be counted on to any large extent.[45]

Tax revenues, on the other hand, were declining as the business depression continued and intensified, and the situation in the domestic financial markets was judged to be unfavorable for a bond issue.[46] These were very clear signals for the public to get concerned about a change in the fiscal regime and consequently about inflationary finance, as it had occurred some years earlier. The budget had emerged as the crucial determinant of the state of confidence, because of the popular association of budget deficits with monetary expansion.[47] This regime change led to immediate doubts and fears by experts, by the Bourse, as well as by the general public, as they recognized that the state could be forced under certain circumstances to borrow more than half a billion schillings at the National Bank, and that would be equivalent to inflation (*Wiener Börsen-Kurier*, June 1, 1931, 1),[48] as the new fiscal rule would have repercussions on the monetary rule.[49]

[45] The *Daily Telegraph* had already reported on May 16, 1931, that its correspondent had been informed "by a high official of the French Foreign office that naturally France would not agree to Austria obtaining such a loan [i.e., from the League of Nations] in the face of the Austro-German customs union plan" (11). The news from London was not more encouraging, since the Bank of England "passed the buck" to the BIS in Basel: "We should wish to cooperate in any helpful way, but the position has been essentially changed since March 1926 by the foundation of the BIS. Individual action by Central Banks, for reason of sympathy or even material interest, in such circumstances, has been superseded by corporate action through Basel" (letter by Siepman to Reisch on May 13, 1931; quoted in Kernbauer 1982, 13). (The BIS actually did not start to operate until 1930.) One month later, the BofE did not have these reservations and forwarded a 150 million schilling short-term credit to the ANB.

[46] "Where are the taxpayers to come from?" asked *The Economist* (June 27, 1931, 1379).

[47] Cited from Eichengreen (1981, 5 and 16), who made this point in the context of Britain. The same observation was made by contemporary Austrian observers, like the *Neue Freie Presse* (September 21, 1931, 1), which stressed the fact that the forced abandoning of the gold standard in Britain was strongly influenced by budgetary concerns and the parliament's inability to agree on some budget cutting measures.

[48] Their prediction turned out to be overly optimistic, as the course of the later events showed.

[49] "The Government has committed itself far beyond its strength in according to foreign creditors a guarantee" (*The Economist*, November 28, 1931, 1009).

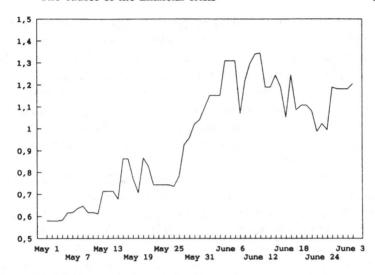

Figure 4.3. Yield spread of bonds in Vienna (in percentage points).

Financing of the government by the central bank was not allowed by law, but the bank had violated its charter before, when it rediscounted financial bills. Moreover, by that time, there had not yet been a test whether the government and the central bank would really obey – in a situation of financial stress – this restriction. Capital flight received an additional and strong impetus as the potential present value of current – but especially of prospective future government deficits – increased enormously. Within only six days (May 31 to June 5), the BIS credit of 100 million schillings was exhausted and the Austrian National Bank requested another but never received it. The BIS, although it had assured the Austrians that it would be ready to help them protect their currency, should the need arise, did not fulfill its promise. With the issue of the state guarantee, the problem of the Credit-Anstalt became a problem of Austrian public finance and of the Austrian currency.

Bond-market data furnishes us with strong empirical evidence on this perceived change in the state of public finance and its repercussions on interest rates. Figure 4.3 represents the yield differential between the 7 percent League of Nations Bond of 1923 (due in 1943) and the 7 percent Austrian International Bond of 1930 (due in 1957) in Vienna. The main difference between these two bonds (in addition to their maturity) was the fact that the first issue was internationally guaranteed and its coupons were paid in American dollars, while the 1930 issue was only backed by the Austrian state and paid in schillings. Since the interest rate risk was very similar, the yield differential can be interpreted as an approximation for the required risk premium for the nonguaranteed schilling issue. Variations in this premium can be regarded as reflecting changes in the perceived credit rating (default risk) of the Austrian state and changes in the purchasing power risk of the schilling relative to the United States dollar.

The curve shows the outbreak of the Credit-Anstalt crisis very clearly, but the announcement of the state guarantee coincided with a much more pronounced jump in the yield differential. Overnight, Austria and its currency became much larger risks, as the state guarantee was expected to have repercussions on the bond and foreign exchange markets. Instead of calming the situation and contributing to a return to normalcy – as intended – the governmental guarantee for the bank's liabilities worsened Austria's credit rating and the prospects for its currency and reduced the likelihood of capital inflows at any given interest rate. The guarantee constituted unfavorable "fiscal news."[50] *The Review of Reviews* (September 1931, 39) summarized very clearly the events of this day when the initial guarantee was announced and its economic implications, stating that "the gravest twenty-four hours in the stormy twelve years of the Austrian Republic pass in doubt over the government's financial future." This doubt left a clear mark on the bond market.

This was especially so since the situation within the CA was not cleared up, even after months of investigations. Nobody knew how much had really been lost and therefore, for how much the state would have to assume responsibility.[51] This fundamental uncertainty was the ideal breeding ground for rumors of all kind.

Sargent's conclusion (1982, 47) about hyperinflation finds strong confirmation as the change in the government's strategy or regime resulted in a change in the public's strategies in choosing portfolios. The inflationary fears – based on the rapid extension of domestic

---

[50] For the role of "fiscal news" in generating inflationary expectations during the German hyperinflation, see Webb 1986.

[51] *The Economist* (October 24, 1931, 758) wrote in this context that with "every day that passes the liability of the Federal State for the Credit-Anstalt is growing, and there is talk of figures running into alarming amounts."

credit and high-powered money – were reinforced. This led the public to dispose of their schilling holdings or schilling denominated assets and to try to acquire as much foreign exchange as possible, forcing the central bank to reduce allocations and to support the exchange rate. Austria had become a prisoner of her inflation experience, since any sizable budget deficit "would at that time immediately have been interpreted by the population as another destruction of the currency."[52]

Bankers, politicians, and journalists alike tried to emphasize that no danger for the stability of the currency existed, pointing out repeatedly that considerable exchange reserves were available at the central bank and that the note cover was still far above the legal requirements.[53] A very strong but unsuccessful – maybe even counterproductive – appeal was made by the president of the Austrian National Bank, Reisch, in an interview on June 15, 1931:

It is unfortunately the fact that during the last few days there has been a certain tendency to exchange the Austrian schilling for foreign currency. It is quite unreasonable, for, as the last bank return shows, the schilling is more than twice as strongly backed as is legally necessary. This tendency can only harm our economic life. There can be no question of our currency being in danger, but the Austrian public, remembering the inflation, is quickly panic-stricken. As it is useless to talk reason in a panic, I have so far avoided the issue of reassuring statements. There is no danger whatever of inflation. (Glasgow 1931, 140)

They all disregarded, however, what Keynes had already emphasized during the 1920s, namely that the size of the government's gold reserves (or, here, foreign exchange reserves) was not the determinant of whether it could successfully maintain convertibility with gold. The determinant was its fiscal policy.[54] The size of the gold reserves and of international borrowing ceilings could only affect the length of time a currency could be defended or the time available to change fiscal policy in order to return to consistency with the fixed exchange rate regime.

The fact that Austria's reserves were largely "borrowed reserves" – originating from short-term capital inflows that more than offset the structural current account deficit – and therefore constituted

---

[52] See Stolper (1967, 116) as he makes this point with regard to Germany.
[53] See various issues of *Wiener Börsen-Kurier;* June 8, 1931, 1; June 15, 1931, 1; or October 12, 1931, 1.
[54] See Keynes (1924, 67, and 1925, 132) as interpreted in Sargent (1982, 45).

outstanding callable debt to foreigners, greatly reduced the probability of a successful defense of the currency until a change in policy should occur. In this sense the adverse balance of trade can be included as one of the factors contributing to the distrust in the parity, since it influenced the probabilities attached to the different possible outcomes.[55]

Austrian fiscal as well as monetary policies were perceived to be inconsistent with the adherence to the gold exchange standard. They constituted and were understood by the public as a reversal of the binding commitment of the government of Austria (in 1922) to reorder its fiscal and monetary strategies. What seemed to be a rational policy move in order to protect the Austrian banking system and the money supply, namely to discount freely and to guarantee all CA deposits, became the cause of a currency crisis and of the loss of most of the foreign exchange reserves. The Austrian public realized that the fixed exchange rate system could not be maintained under the new policy regime, and recognized that there was a potential for capital gains to be made by those who could still buy foreign exchange at the old fixed price. Their attempts to leap "into a disorderly queue to trade at the old price" (Garber 1985, 291) led to reduced allocations by the ANB and to the emergence of black markets in coffeehouses, at street corners, and in apartment-house lobbies, where higher prices were charged (or could be attained). The ANB's attempt to resist this revaluation, in the belief that the market's evaluation was wrong, precipitated the currency crisis. With every week that passed, it became increasingly evident that the real problem was not so much the salvage of the Credit-Anstalt itself as of the entire economy of Austria (*The Economist*, December 5, 1931, 1063). "The cost of salvaging the Credit Anstalt was the gold schilling" (Ellis 1941, 35).

[55] This large trade deficit can be traced back to the breakup of the monarchy and the concurrent destruction of the large economic unit that the monarchy represented. Internal trade had suddenly become foreign trade, and was consequently subject to tariffs and other trade barriers. Austria's sudden dependence on foreign raw materials and foodstuff was at the heart of this trade deficit. Rising protectionism in Europe and especially in the United States (in 1930) added to the already existing problems, and increased the asymmetry between the free flow of capital and the very restricted flow of goods.

5. The financial crisis and market efficiency

In Europe, where the problem is mainly one of nerves, the psychological is nearly always the most important aspect of whatever takes place.

—*The Contemporary Review*, May 1931

We have shown that the Austrian experience of 1931 constituted a true financial crisis and was not just a pseudocrisis. Historic accounts stress very clearly the fact that the markets were surprised by the outbreak of the crisis – or, better, the crises.[1] If this observation happens to be correct – in spite of the fact that crises of this magnitude need time to develop – then we would have to reject market efficiency for this episode. Not all the available information was incorporated into market behavior. Such evidence differs from the results of the vast majority of empirical studies of the behavior of stock markets, foreign exchange markets, bond markets, commodity futures markets, etc.[2]

We recall from above that it was not a single crisis that occurred in Austria in 1931, but a bank failure, a banking crisis, and a currency crisis. Therefore, when we investigate whether the market predicted the crisis, we really have to ask this question separately for the different aspects of the crisis. Two episodes in particular, namely the Credit-Anstalt failure and the currency crisis, should have been reflected in market behavior before the actual events occurred. The stock market and the foreign exchange market are then the main objects of our investigations. First, we will turn to the market for Credit-Anstalt stocks and compare its behavior to that predicted by the efficient market hypothesis.

[1] The usually well informed *Wall Street Journal* remarked on May 14, 1931, that "the news was a distinct shock" (13).

[2] For a review of some of the empirical results see Fama (1970).

The market for Credit-Anstalt stocks

The efficient market hypothesis

The basic idea of the efficient market hypothesis is that security prices at any moment fully reflect all available information.[3] Since the relevant pieces of information are generated (or become available) in a random fashion, those prices are expected to move randomly, if the news is "not delayed or controlled in any systematic manner" (Francis 1980, 645). Thus, "the ideal is a market in which prices provide accurate signals for resource allocation . . ." (Fama 1970, 109). If securities markets are less than perfectly efficient, then some capital will be misallocated since the market prices do not always equal the underlying intrinsic values of the respective companies.

For empirical purposes, varying degrees of market efficiency have been defined, ranging from the weak form to the semi-strong form and, in the extreme case, the strong form, in order to allow us "to pinpoint the level of information at which the hypothesis breaks down" (ibid., 116).

The weakly efficient hypothesis

"Weakly efficient markets are defined to be markets in which past prices provide no information about future prices which would allow a short-term trader to earn a return above what could be attained with a naive buy-and-hold strategy" (Francis 1980, 648). This means, in essence, that there should be no pattern of short-term (daily, weekly, or monthly) price changes that can be used to earn a larger profit than could be earned with a simple buy-and-hold approach to the stock market. Thus, "successive price changes are independent random variables, implying that the past history of the series generates no information that would be useful in predicting future price changes" (Leuthold 1972, 879). If a certain pattern of price changes did exist, this would tend to indicate that stock prices do not adjust to follow their randomly changing intrinsic values.

What is required then is that securities prices basically follow a random walk – that is, successive values must be (1) identically

---

[3] This hypothesis, however, is not restricted to securities but can also be extended to include foreign exchange.

distributed according to some stable distribution and (2) independent of preceding or subsequent observations.

The semi-strongly efficient hypothesis

The semi-strong form of efficiency requires more evidence of efficiency than the weak hypothesis. The question to be investigated is whether current securities prices "fully reflect" all obvious publicly available information, and whether any learning lags exist before the latest news is completely disseminated to the market. If the semi-strong hypothesis is consistent with the behavior of the market, then the market would correctly anticipate earnings changes before they are announced to the public. If the new and relevant pieces of information are not efficiently digested, we will observe an ex-post stock market performance that is not expected. It is the speed of this price adjustment process that gauges how efficient a market is.

The strongly efficient hypothesis

This approach takes the extreme position that all (not just the publicly available) information should be fully reflected in securities prices. Therefore, no individual should have "higher expected trading profits than others because he has monopolistic access to some information" (Fama 1970, 143). In order to be able to reject this hypothesis, all that is needed is to find one insider who has profited from inside information. As Fama (ibid., 150) points out, the strongest form is best viewed as a benchmark against which deviations from market efficiency (interpreted in the strictest sense) can be judged.

The Credit-Anstalt shares

In May 1931, at the time of the announcement of its difficulties, the Credit-Anstalt had a share capital of 125 million schillings. Its shares were quoted not only at the Vienna Stock Exchange but on many other exchanges throughout Europe and the United States, specifically Prague, Trieste, Budapest, Berlin, Breslau (now Wroclaw), Dresden, Frankfurt, Hamburg, Cologne, Leipzig, Munich, and New York. In October 1927, it was the first continental European stock

Table 5.1. *Dividends paid by Viennese banks (in percentages)*

Year	CA	BCA	WBV	NOE[a]
1925	10	14.4	9	12.5
1926	10	14.4	9	12.5
1927	10	15	9	12.5
1928	10	15	7.5	12.5
1929	8.5	—	5	10.5
1930	0	—	5	10.5
1931	0	—	0	0

[a] CA – Credit-Anstalt
  BCA – Boden-Credit-Anstalt
  WBV – Wiener Bank-Verein
  NOE – Niederösterreichische Escompte-Gesellschaft
Sources: Compass, various issues.

company to be introduced into the New York Stock Exchange. This reflects the fact that it occupied a very special place among the European banks. It indicates further, as Rutkowski (1934, 53) points out, that everything had to be done to defend its excellent reputation – that is, to prevent any news from becoming public that could have created doubts about its good standing.[4] The CA's dividend policy seemed to have been geared to this purpose. As "dividend changes may be assumed to convey important information to the market concerning the management's assessment of the firm's long-run earning and dividend paying potential" (Fama et al. 1969, 178–9), the managers of this bank tried to avoid changes in the distributed profits. But, as Table 5.1 points out, this seemed to have been the policy of most of the Viennese banks.[5]

We will pay special attention to the behavior of the shares of the Credit-Anstalt on two of the exchanges, namely Vienna and New York. The CA stocks had been quoted in Vienna since the establishment of this bank in 1855, but they had been introduced to New

[4] Ausch (1968, 356) adopts Rutkowski's point when he generalizes that the Austrian banks kept on paying high dividends, since a reduction in those distributed profits could have led to a drop in share prices and thus would have harmed the image and the creditworthiness of these banks.
[5] The Amstelbank in Amsterdam, which belonged in large part to the Credit-Anstalt, did exactly the same: paying 11 percent every year between 1924 and 1929.

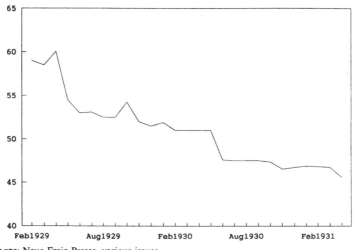

SOURCES: Neue Freie Presse, various issues.

Figure 5.1. Price of CA shares at Viennese Bourse (midmonth values).

York only in 1927.[6] Goldman, Sachs & Co. offered 50,000 American shares, representing 400,000 deposited Austrian shares, since Guaranty Trust Company of New York, as depositary, had issued its certificates for American shares in the proportion of one American for eight deposited (Moody's *Manual of Investments* 1933, 1137). The initial offer was at $80 per American share (about 75 percent above face value). The par value of an Austrian share was 40 schillings.

Figures 5.1 and 5.2 show the development of the prices of the CA shares in Vienna and in New York, respectively (on a monthly basis), while Table 5.2 presents the volumes of trade with CA shares at the New York Stock Exchange (NYSE).

These figures and the table reflect the declining value as well as the declining volume of trade of the CA shares. As for the NYSE, the CA shares were definitely not among the most actively traded stocks, but, nevertheless, there was a reasonable turnover, especially so through 1930.[7]

---

[6] In Vienna, the initial public issue (15 million gulden) was forty three times oversubscribed (see *The Economist*, June 27, 1931, 1369, and Joham 1935, 265).

[7] It is interesting to note that the highest turnover during these three years occurred in the months following the merger of the CA with the Boden-Credit-Anstalt in October 1929.

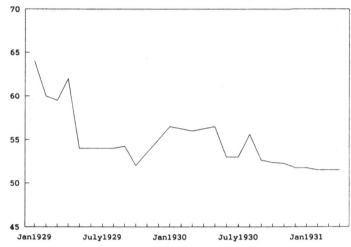

SOURCES: The *Wall Street Journal*, various issues.

Figure 5.2. Price of CA shares at the New York Stock Exchange (end-of-month values).

Table 5.2. *Volumes of sales of CA stocks at NYSE (January 1929–May 1931)*

Month	Years		
	1929	1930	1931
January	1,600	1,300	100
February	1,300	100	400
March	2,200	700	400
April	600	2,300	100
May	200	1,000	900
June	0	2,100	0
July	1,200	400	0
August	1,000	200	0
September	900	300	0
October	4,300	2,200	0
November	3,700	3,200	0
December	6,600	100	0
Monthly Averages	1,967	1,158	380
			(Jan.–May)

Sources: Barron's, various issues.

Analysis of the stock data

The strong form test. The relevant question to be asked is whether any individual investor or group of investors had monopolistic access to information relevant for the price formation of the Credit-Anstalt shares. If we find evidence for the existence of such an informational advantage and for the fact that those concerned profited from this insider information, we have to reject the strong efficiency hypothesis. In this case an interesting follow-up question arises, namely, how far down through the investment community did deviations from the model permeate?

The analysis of the prices and of the sales volumes of the shares of the Credit-Anstalt just prior to the public announcement of the bank's difficulties reveals valuable insight into the question of the efficiency of the market. We have to recall that, although its problems were made public in the evening of May 11, 1931, the management of the bank, the government, and the Austrian National Bank had been informed three days earlier, on May 8. During the three days of negotiations for reconstruction, the troubles were a guarded secret, and no newspaper (or any other type of media) received or published prior information.[8] This course of events made monopolistic gains for insiders possible – insiders being either top managers of the bank, top officials of the government or of the National Bank, or anybody who could have received information from somebody belonging to these groups.[9]

In Table 5.3 we present the development of the price of the Credit-Anstalt stock in Vienna during the trading days just prior to the announcement.

The quotations on the days between information of the government and information of the public reveal an interesting pattern. The last two trading days prior to the public announcement show declines far in excess of the average changes in the value of this

[8] Stiefel (1983b, 32) reports that even some members of the board of directors of the bank only received the news from the newspapers after the official announcement.

[9] It is obvious that top managers of the CA should have had information about the problems far in advance, but, as Ausch (1968, 349) reports, Managing Director Neurath himself was reported to have been completely astonished when confronted with the 1930 balance sheet. Even if this happens to be true, the top officials must have had a few days of advance knowledge compared to the government and the National Bank officials.

Table 5.3. *Price of CA Stock in Vienna, (early May 1931)*

Day	Stock Price	Absolute change	Cumulative change
May 2	45.55	+ .05	+ .05
May 4	45.50	− .05	0
May 5	45.50	0	0
May 6	45.55	+ .05	+ .05
May 7	45.40	− .15	− .10
May 8	45.20	− .20	− .30
May 9	44.75	− .45	− .75
May 11	43.50	−1.25	−2.00

Sources: Neue Freie Presse, various issues.

Table 5.4. *The CA stock at the New York Stock Exchange (early May 1931)*

Day	Volume	Open	Close	Bid	Asked
May 1	0	—	—	51½	53
May 2	0	—	—	51¼	53
May 4	0	—	—	51¼	53
May 5	0	—	—	51¼	53
May 6	100	51¼	51¼	51¼	53
May 7	200	51¼	51¼	51	53
May 9	200	51	51	50⅜	53
May 11	100	48⅝	48⅝	49¼	53

Sources: The Wall Street Journal, various issues, and Barron's, various issues.

stock. The absolute drop in the value of a CA share on May 11 (the trading day just prior to the "news") was larger than any weekly change (drop or rise) since the merger with the BCA in 1929.[10] The data suggest increased selling within the last trading days before public announcement, leading to the suspicion that some insiders might have used their monopolistic access to special information to secure profits.[11] Whether or not this happened to be an isolated incident can be checked by analyzing the New York Stock Exchange data for the same time period and by comparing the results (Table 5.4).

A very similar picture is revealed in New York. May 11 shows a

[10] With the exception of one single week in 1930, when the 1929 dividend was debited.

[11] Unfortunately, we do not have data on the volumes of sales in Vienna. Moreover, only part of the trades was done through the stock exchange.

large negative change (by $2.375), far in excess of the average change during the preceding months. Moreover, it is worth pointing out that during the five trading days prior to the announcement of the losses, more CA stocks were sold at the NYSE than during any of the preceding five months, and more than during the preceding sixty trading days.[12,13]

The very same phenomenon was reported from Budapest, Hungary, where this stock was also listed at the Bourse. According to reports in the *Neue Freie Presse* (May 13, 1931, 14–15), there had been lively discussion in Budapest on the fact that since Saturday, May 9, there had been considerable supply of CA shares, although normally trades in this paper occurred only very infrequently. Moreover, on May 11, according to the same report, the attempt was made to sell a large block of several thousand shares of the CA, but the deal did not materialize.

We can conclude that the events at the NYSE and the Bourse in Budapest confirm the basic observation we made at the Vienna Bourse, namely that a few people seemed to have taken advantage (or attempted to take advantage) of monopolistic information prior to the public announcement. This constitutes evidence against the strong form of the efficient market model, as far as the Credit-Anstalt shares are concerned. The small absolute size of the transactions, however, suggests that those deviations from the model did not permeate very far down through the investment community, but were restricted to a few insiders.

The semistrong form test. The semistrong efficiency hypothesis requires that all the publicly available information should be incorporated in the security's price. Empirical studies usually focus on the price behavior around specific events, examining whether the market had already discounted the expected outcome of the event prior to its occurrence.

In the case of the Credit-Anstalt crisis, we cannot point to any

---

[12] Since the CA stock was not very actively traded in 1931, these volumes were quite small.

[13] Not all the transactions might have gone through the stock exchange, i.e., the bank might have bought those stocks offered by insiders at an agreed price "over the counter." Thus actual volumes traded in New York might have been considerably larger. But we do not have any information concerning this possibility.

specific event that should have had a strong impact on the expected future earnings of the company, apart from the announcement of the collapse. Historical accounts, however, let us believe that there were a number of publicly known facts that influenced unfavorably the business outlook for this bank and should therefore have been incorporated in the public's evaluation of the intrinsic value of the Credit-Anstalt shares.

Walter Federn, one of the most outspoken and knowledgeable economic journalists of that time, points out:

For some years ... it has been a most disturbing matter to be a witness to the Kreditanstalt's repeated losses of millions and millions of schillings through the insolvency of firms, even new firms whose names had barely been known up to their collapse. It is usually claimed that there is sufficient security, but everyone knows how rapidly the value of security dwindles during a crisis.

He states further that he

first became anxious when he asked the leading director of the Kreditanstalt whether corporations should depreciate plant equipment in accord with its cost or its replacement value, and was told that no Austrian company had the resources to do the latter.[14]

At the same time, however, 98 of the 146 Austrian companies listed at the Vienna Stock Exchange paid dividends to their stockholders in 1929 (*Wiener Börsen-Kurier,* July 13, 1931, 1).

According to the *Financial News* (May 13, 1931, 1), in the City of London, there were "quarters which knew of the bank's trouble," but they had "hoped that the losses could be recovered without publicity." To these insiders, "It was known that the Creditanstalt had suffered losses through a number of failures in Central Europe – especially in the textile trade – and that it had been immobilized to a great extent through the absorption of the Bodencreditanstalt."

Since most of this information was publicly available, in an efficient market the public was expected to have adjusted its assumed rates of return to that additional risk and recalculated the intrinsic value of the Credit-Anstalt. The *Neue Freie Presse* (May 17, 1931) pointed out that the problems of the bank had not arisen suddenly, and that everybody could see how the portfolio of this bank had deteriorated.[15] The newspaper analysts were less surprised by the

[14] Federn (1932, 414), as translated in *Euromoney,* October 1976, 146.
[15] One explanation for the apparent inactivity of the public in reacting to these

Table 5.5. *Values of some stocks in CA portfolio (end of year)[a]*

Company	1927	1928	1929	1930	1931
Wienerberger Ziegel	69	45.25	37	23	20
Austro-Daimler	–	12.20	10	4.50	4
Leykam	12.25	9.5	6.5	3	3
Ungarische Allgem.					
Kohle	963	998	750	535	495
Galicia	89.5	62.5	32	19.3	13

[a] For 1931: value of May 9, 1931.
Source: Rutkowski (1934, 47).

crisis per se than by the speed with which it had arrived.[16] The same feelings were shared by some quarters in London, as they expressed surprise that losses amounting to nearly £5 million "could have occurred in the course of one single year" (*Financial News,* May 13, 1931, 1).

This leads us then to other important sources of information on the business conditions, namely the trends in the values of the rather extensive stock portfolio of the Credit-Anstalt, as well as the publicly available data on business failures and bankruptcies. Rutkowski (1934, 47) reports the quotations of some of the stocks of companies that belonged to the CA conglomerate and that were held in considerable amounts in the portfolio of the CA, a sample of which is presented in Table 5.5.

The tremendous depreciation of its assets could not remain without effect on the bank's earnings, and we recall that out of the 140 million schillings of initially reported losses, 40 million were blamed on the depreciated value of the bank's holdings of securities.[17] At the same time, business failures in general increased at a very fast rate from their low in 1929 (Table 5.6).

It seems obvious that these events affected very adversely the bank's earnings power, and must have been reflected in share prices, especially so in the case of the CA, since it controlled more enter-

pieces of information could be an overestimation of the bank's strength because of the widespread belief that the CA had very large hidden reserves.

[16] See *Neue Freie Presse,* May 12, 1931, 2, evening edition.

[17] During 1930 the Viennese stock exchange had lost on average about 17 percent of its value and the volume of shares traded declined by about 50 percent (*Neues Wiener Journal,* April 2, 1931, 2).

Table 5.6. *Number of business
failures (monthly averages)*

Year	Number
1925	256.3
1926	233.5
1927	236.2
1928	188.8
1929	183.2
1930	245.6
1931	316.1
1932	406.3

prises than the two other – remaining – large Viennese banks together.[18]

The informational content of the balance sheets and the profit/
loss accounts of the bank, however, are very limited. In the absence
of effective banking and auditing regulations, the published balance
sheets showed only very highly aggregated figures, hiding more than
they really revealed. With hindsight we know that even those numbers did not conform to the true state of affairs. The same applies
to the dividend payments, considered to be a very important source
of information to the market concerning the management's own
assessment of the firm's long-run earnings potential.

Parallel to these developments, "the American banking difficulties
deprived it [the CA] of an important source of money" (*The Economist*, June 27, 1931, 1370), while its day-to-day business was very
dependent on these short-term funds. This information was also
available to the public.

We can conclude that information on the possible status of the
bank was publicly available, although by no means to a degree comparable to today's standards. Nevertheless, we have to assume that
rational investors would attempt to use any information available
to reduce uncertainty. In trying to assess empirically the implications of the semistrong efficiency hypothesis, we will have to compare the behavior of the CA stock not only to the market in general
but also to the behavior of the nonfailed banks. There might have

---

[18] Reik (1931, 42) lists sixty-five businesses that were dominated by the CA, thirty
by the Niederösterreichische Escompte-Gesellschaft and eighteen by the Wiener Bank-Verein.

been industry-specific effects like a common shock to the entire banking industry at a specific point in time. This is especially relevant since a study by Morgenstern (1931) suggests that over the period 1913 to 1930 the overall value of bank stocks had declined much more than the market average.[19] He compared the 1930 market values of the different industries' capital to the respective 1913 values, adjusted for all new issues of capital. His results suggest that the banking industry's value had declined to 12.63 percent, while a weighted average of all industries had only dropped to 41.54 percent.

One implication of the efficient use of publicly available information is that on the day of the actual event (in our case, the day of the announcement of the collapse) the price of the stock should have already been adjusted. Therefore, we should not observe any violent postannouncement changes in values, but rather a smooth adjustment over the weeks and months prior to the actual event, that is, the asset exchange out of CA stocks should have taken place in an orderly manner, far in advance of the event.

Analyzing the valuation of the CA shares in New York on the trading days right after the official statement, we observe a virtual collapse of the price (Table 5.7).

The behavior of the CLOSE values, as well as the BID and ASKED values confirm Fama's (1970, 126) view that "when important new information comes into the market, it cannot always be immediately evaluated precisely. Thus sometimes the initial price will overadjust to the information, and other times it will underadjust." In any case, the collapse of the bank was "new information," not yet discounted at the time of its public announcement. The postcollapse price behavior shows that very vividly.[20] By May 15, the market

---

[19] A similar but less extreme result had been computed by the Austrian Institute for Business Cycle Research in 1933 (see Oesterreichisches Institut für Konjunkturforschung 1933, 13), indicating that from 1923 to 1932 the overall value of bank stocks had declined by 80.4 percent, while the market as a whole had declined by only 77.1 percent. The two methods used were somewhat different, since Morgenstern's average decline is based on an unweighted average of all industries, while the OIfK's measure is based on a weighted average, using the total market values of the shares of each industry.

[20] The strong volatility in the ASKED price reflects the sharp fluctuations in the evaluation of the situation after the shocking announcement. The *Wall Street Journal* (May 14, 1931, 13) reported, for instance, that on May 13, despite a lack of bids, the ASKED price was moved up to 50 "reflecting the improved sentiment." The following day it dropped back to 32.

Table 5.7. *Price of CA stock at NYSE after the announcement of the bank's difficulties*

Day	Close	Bid	Asked
May 11	48⁵/₈	46³/₄	47¹/₂
May 12	—	12	37
May 13	—	—	50
May 14	—	27	32
May 15	27	—	50
May 16	—	—	50
May 18	—	23	50
May 19	26	—	25
May 20	—	—	25
May 21	25	—	50

Sources: *The Wall Street Journal*, various issues.

had revaluated its price, since the stock suffered only relatively minor losses afterward. The adjustment from $48.625 to $27 per American share (i.e., a decline by 44.5 percent) was far in excess of the official devaluation of the stock's value by 25 percent.[21] Under these conditions the semistrong efficiency hypothesis must be rejected.

The *Wall Street Journal* (May 18, 1931, 6) described the events in Vienna in the following way: "Austrian shares of the Creditanstalt have been suspended from the Vienna Bourse after falling Tuesday [i.e. May 12, 1931] to 30 from 42.5.[22] On May 13, about 6,000 CA-shares were offered for sale in Vienna, but no deals and quotations resulted, because of the large price differences between bids and prices asked (*Neue Freie Presse*, May 14, 1931, 16). Similar situations were also reported from Berlin, Prague, and Budapest. On June 1, the quotation of CA shares in Vienna was down to 15 schillings, for a nominal value of (then) 30 schillings. Four weeks later, on June 27, *The Economist* (1379) reported, in reference to the Viennese Bourse:

The shares of the Credit Anstalt ... represent a very doubtful value. For weeks there has been no official quotation, and unofficially the value of the

---

[21] This was especially so on the first day after the news, when the BID price declined by 74 percent, while the ASKED price only dropped by 22 percent.

[22] According to the *Neue Freie Presse* (May 13, 1931, 14) the CA shares on that day received support (from unidentified sources), in order to keep the price from falling below 30 schillings.

shares is assumed to be eight to ten schillings, which means that, since the announcement of the crisis, they have fallen a further 75 per cent.

This confirms all our conclusions about the postcollapse price behavior in New York. The market acted surprised, and the semistrong efficiency hypothesis cannot be accepted for the behavior of this bank's stock prices.[23]

An alternative and more rigorous way to check for the semistrong form of efficiency is to investigate whether any abnormally large (negative) returns had occurred prior to May 12, so that at least a partial adjustment of the market value to the increased risk can be detected. In order to detect such extraordinary effects on prices (or returns), we have to abstract from the general market conditions – that is, the normal, expected returns. One way is by estimating the relationship between the CA stock and the general market conditions (market model):

$$R(i)(t) = a(i) + b(i) \cdot R(m)(t) + u(i)(t)$$

where $R(i)(t)$ is the return on the CA stock in month t, i.e., $\{[P(t) - P(t-1)]/P(t-1)\}$.

$R(m)(t)$ is the return on the market, using a stock market index.

$u(i)(t)$ is the error term.

$a(i)$, $b(i)$ are the coefficients to be estimated.

This model represents the monthly rates of return of the CA shares as a function of the corresponding return on the market.[24] The period over which we estimated the market model was January 1929 to December 1930,[25] excluding the months just prior to the announcement of the collapse. The estimated coefficients are reported in Table 5.8.

[23] A very similar misjudgment had occurred in autumn of 1929, when the Boden-Credit-Anstalt had to be saved. Its shares were quoted at that time at almost 200 percent of their nominal value, while the shareholders received only a fraction (about 15 percent) of that, when their bank became merged into the Credit-Anstalt. The postcollapse period was characterized by a large price adjustment, as the market had not correctly anticipated the weakness of the bank by October 1929.

[24] As stock market indices we used two different series available for the Vienna Stock Exchange (OIfK and Statistisches Zentralamt), and the Dow Jones Industrial Average for the NYSE.

[25] For Vienna from February 1929 to December 1930.

Table 5.8. *Market model, regression coefficients for CA stocks*[a]

	a(alpha)	b(beta)	R-square	DW[b]
Vienna (1)	−.0031	.0714	.029	2.61
	(−.8398)	(.7723)		
Vienna (2)	−.0034	.0429	.007	2.65
	(−.8130)	(.3635)		
New York	−.0036	.1997[c]	.202	2.01
	(−.4593)	(2.3052)		

[a] t-values in parentheses
[b] Durbin-Watson statistics.
[c] Significant at the 10 percent level.

The results indicate that the market model performs very poorly for the Viennese Bourse, but reasonably well for New York. In Vienna it can only explain a very small portion of the variability, and the so-called beta coefficients are not significantly different from zero. Therefore, the value of the CA stock does not seem to have been driven by developments of the overall market.[26] In New York the model performs considerably better, explaining about 20 percent of the overall risk. The beta coefficient shows that the systematic risk of the CA shares was only about one fifth of that of the market.

In order to find evidence whether the behavior of this stock was more industry specific than CA specific, we constructed stock indices for nonfailed banks for Vienna as well as for New York, and regressed the returns of the CA shares on the returns of these bank indices.[27]

The results (Table 5.9) suggest that in New York the bank index performed considerably worse than the Dow Jones index of thirty industrial shares in explaining the behavior of the price of the CA shares. This indicates that the behavior of the CA stock was very different from that of the American banking industry (as explained

---

[26] Some of the possible explanations for this unusual behavior will be touched upon later.

[27] We used an arithmetic average of the stock values of two banks in New York (Bank of America and First National Bank), and of three Viennese banks (Austrian National Bank, Niederösterreichische Escompte-Gesellschaft, and Wiener Bank-Verein).

Table 5.9. *Regression coefficients for CA stocks regressed on bank industry index*[a]

	a	b	R-square	DW
Vienna	−.0037	.0827	.024	2.70
	(−1.0214)	(.7021)		
New York	−.0077	.0532	.025	2.38
	(−.9204)	(.7275)		

[a] t-values in parentheses.

Table 5.10. *Regression coefficients for nonfailed banks regressed on the market*[a]

	a	b	R-square	DW
Vienna (1)	−.0003	.3879[b]	.243	1.99
	(−.0519)	(2.5314)		
Vienna (2)	.0030	.4853[b]	.239	2.11
	(.4422)	(2.5043)		
New York	.0088	.9139[b]	.486	2.42
	(.4756)	(4.4560)		

[a] t-values in parentheses.
[b] Significant at the 10 percent level.

by those two representative banks). In Vienna, the results for the banking industry index lead to the same conclusions as in New York.

When the market model was estimated for the overall banking industry, in order to assess the degree of covariance between the (nonfailed) banks and the market, a much closer connection was found in New York as well as in Vienna (see Table 5.10).

This reinforces our previous results about the predominance of CA specific effects, as compared to industry specific effects or that the CA stock showed very idiosyncratic behavior.[28]

The ultimate goal is to test whether the CA collapse was antici-

[28] It is conceivable that the CA had financial and managerial or other characteristics that were considered different from the other banks analyzed here. The implicit governmental guarantee for this bank might be one of those factors that played a role. We recall März's (1982) statement that "the CA was more equal than the other banks."

Table 5.11. *Abnormal returns for CA stocks in 1931*[a]

Month	Vienna			New York	
	(1)	(2)	(3)	(4)	(5)
Jan.	.0101	.0072	.0087	−.0000	−.0003
	(.5869)	(.4223)	(.5054)	(−.0005)	(−.0081)
Feb.	−.0045	−.0015	.0009	−.0276	.0017
	(−.2312)	(−.0707)	(.0524)	(−.7029)	(.0424)
March	.0012	.0013	.0012	.0218	.0091
	(.0711)	(.0756)	(.0709)	(.5843)	(.2222)
April	−.0204	−.0201	−.0211	.0281	.0159
	(−1.2108)	(−1.1767)	(−1.2473)	(.7431)	(.3739)
May	−.0346[b]	−.0383[b]	−.0373[b]	−	−
	(−1.8552)	(−2.0701)	(−2.2613)	−	−

[a] t-statistics in parentheses (computed by dividing the prediction error by its variance).
[b] Significant at the 10 percent level.
Column 1 is based on the Stock Index of the Statistisches Zentralamt.
Column 2 is based on the Stock Index of the OIfK.
Column 3 is based on the Index of Nonfailed Banks.
Column 4 is based on the Dow Jones Index.
Column 5 is based on the Index of Nonfailed Banks.

pated by the market and therefore incorporated into the valuation of the stocks. Therefore the possible existence of abnormal (negative) returns prior to the announcement of the news has to be investigated. If the collapse was anticipated, negative abnormal returns for the CA would be observed. Using the market models estimated above as the benchmark cases, the expected (normal) returns for January through April 1931 (mid-May for Vienna) were estimated and compared to the actual returns. The "abnormal" returns being the difference between the "normal" and the "actual" ones. Table 5.11 presents those abnormal returns for the CA stock in Vienna and New York, either on the basis of the general model (columns 1, 2, and 4) or on that of the banking industry returns as the comparison series (columns 3 and 5).

The results suggest that prior to May 1931 no abnormal (negative) returns had occurred. The cumulative abnormal residuals for Vienna are all negative, but very similar in size to those of May; for New York, they even turn out to be positive. There is no indication that the market had adjusted its required rate of return to the increased risk of default. Only the May 1931 residuals show significant negative values, which were caused by the large price drops in the days just prior to May 12.

The two test methods used generated consistent results. The semistrong hypothesis has to be rejected for the behavior of the Credit-Anstalt stocks, just as the strongest form had to be. The lack of any significant negative abnormal returns during the weeks and months prior to the collapse, as well as the postcollapse behavior of this stock price, does not conform to the efficiency postulate. The market did not anticipate the crisis.

The weak form test. Since both the strong and the semistrong hypotheses had to be dismissed, only the weakest form of market efficiency remains to be investigated. This model, a form of the random-walk hypothesis, is based on the hypothesis that the first differences of the price series should be purely random.[29] If this model is correct the series will proceed by a sequence of unconnected steps, starting each time from the previous value of the series. All the series tested, monthly (for Vienna and New York) and weekly (for Vienna), using different lags showed no evidence for any substantial linear dependence between lagged returns on the CA shares (Tables 5.12 and 5.13). Lagged returns could only explain an insignificantly small percentage of the variation in current returns.

On the basis of these results, the random-walk hypothesis seems to be confirmed for the behavior of the prices of the Credit-Anstalt shares. This implies that no trading rules with substantial expected profits were possible. The test for the weak efficiency hypothesis has been passed.

Conclusions on the stock market behavior. The empirical tests showed that the strong as well as the semistrong hypothesis had to be rejected for the behavior of the market for CA shares during 1929 to 1931.[30] Only the weakest form seemed to conform to the market's

---

[29] If $P(t)$ is the price of the stock on a given day, or in a given month, and $u(t)$ has a mean of zero and is uncorrelated with $u(t - k)$, for all k not equal to zero, then

$$P(t) - P(t - 1) = u(t).$$

[30] These results apply only to this particular stock and not to the Viennese or New

Table 5.12. *First order serial correlation coefficients, for one and two months returns on CA stocks*[a]

Stock market		Differencing interval	
		1	2
Vienna[b]		− .1625	− .3026
		(− .7169)	(−1.4030)
	R-square	.021	.079
New York[c]		− .3657	− .3005
		(− .6455)	(− .5181)
	R-square	.016	.011

[a] t-statistics in parentheses.
[b] Time period: Vienna March 1929–May 1931.
[c] Time period: New York February 1929–May 1931.

Table 5.13. *First order serial correlation coefficients for 1, 2, 3, and 4 weeks returns on CA stocks*[ab]

	Differencing interval (weeks)			
	1	2	3	4
	−.0492	−.0561	−.0270	−.0233
	(−.4432)	(−.5084)	(−.2426)	(−.2081)
R-square	.003	.003	.001	.001

[a] t-statistics in parentheses.
[b] Time period: October 11, 1929 to May 7, 1931.

behavior, confirming that past price changes did not provide information on future price changes, which would have allowed traders to earn short-term returns in excess of those attained with a simple buy-and-hold strategy. Neither all the existing information nor the subset of publicly available information was fully incorporated into the prices of these stocks, leading us to the tentative conclusion that this particular market behaved – to a large extent – inefficiently. Since many of the recent studies on stock-market efficiency support the weak as well as the semistrong hypothesis, we are left with a puzzle to be resolved. What were the possible reasons for this apparent deviation from the efficiency postulate?

York stock markets in general. We are dealing with only one specific company, and there might be what Fama et al. (1969, 183) termed "eccentricities of specific cases."

In our view, a considerable part of the observed behavior can be traced to manipulations on the part of the bank itself. Two forms of manipulation can be distinguished: (1) direct manipulation of the stock prices, and (2) indirect manipulation.

By direct manipulation, we understand the fact that the Credit-Anstalt influenced the price of its shares by buying them up, whenever increased selling would have depressed the price.[31] As Hodson (1932, 209) states, "The bank held, in accordance with Central European custom, a large portion of its own shares. . . ." The bank's resources were large enough to affect the price of its shares, and it used this power in order to control the market.[32] Evidence on this point provides a report of an independent commission that looked into the CA problems[33] stating that in 1929 the CA had bought about 17 percent of its own stocks and by the end of that year held about 22 percent. These 470,000 stocks exceeded the amount of CA stocks issued at the New York Stock Exchange in 1927 (400,000). The CA (and for that matter the BCA and perhaps other Viennese banks too) did not, as the law would have required, reduce the share capital accordingly.[34] It held those repurchased shares as part of its own assets, reducing the equity available to cushion any losses of the bank.[35] It interfered with the price determination in this market,

---

[31] März and Weber (1983a, 512) talk in this context of a "ruinous policy of buying up stocks so as to create the impression of stability" that "was pursued with such consistency that the banks did not hesitate to intervene, when their own securities were offered for sale."

[32] "It exerted a great influence upon the Bourses of Vienna and elsewhere" (*The Economist*, June 27, 1931, 1369).

[33] II. Bericht der Besonderen Kommission vom 1. Juli 1932, p.18/19, as cited in Ausch 1968, 357.

[34] The relevant regulation was contained in paragraph 32 of the so-called Aktien-regulativ.

[35] German banks were following the same practice, actively supporting their own as well as other shares. According to Born (1967, 60) most of the big German banks held on to their own shares they had bought back, and did not accordingly reduce the capital outstanding. The most extreme example was the Danatbank, which held about 50 percent of its own stocks at the time of its collapse in July 1931. The Deutsche Bank, however, did use the repurchased shares "to reduce its capital, which was considered too large" (*Wall Street Journal*, May 5, 1931, 9). But this practice was not restricted to bank shares. The *Wall Street Journal* (ibid.) reports that "when the market declines the big [German] joint-stock banks seek to hold up shares in the interest of their customers, besides their own, because they make advances liberally against securities. . . . Shares would have fallen lower without support from the banks, most of which created syn-

reducing the role of the fundamentals. Consequently, the price could not fulfill its economic double function of providing – correct – information and incentive. Misallocation of capital was then the consequence.

In addition to this distortion of the price mechanism, the Credit-Anstalt gave misleading signals to the market concerning its own financial standing and that of its dependent industries. The dividend payments and the balance sheets on which they were based did not reflect the true earnings of the company. Dividends were used as a means of manipulating the market's valuation of the bank's stocks, and as Ausch (1968, 358) puts it, the dividends were not adjusted to the profits, but the (reported) profits to the dividends. A very similar conclusion appears in a report of the Austrian Institute for Business Cycle Research from 1933 (OIfK 1933), pointing to the fact that Austrian bank stocks did not recover from price drops after dividend payments, and concluding that these dividends must therefore have been paid out of the companies' capital stocks and not their earnings. This then is what we consider an indirect manipulation of the stock prices. The only systematic sources of information to the market – the dividends – were highly unreliable or even outright wrong.[36] Attempts to get additional information on the status of the banks, such as the National Bank's project to assess the short-run foreign indebtedness of the Austrian banking sector, were boycotted.

Apart from the bank's own influence on the price of its stock, there is still another – related – factor that might have played a considerable role. The Rothschilds and their friends and business associates were large-scale holders of CA stocks.[37] Since the Credit-Anstalt was always considered to be a "Rothschild bank" and had a member of the Austrian branch of this family as its president, it was in the business interest of these stockholders to prevent any

dicates for the purpose, granting credits to them." März and Weber (1983a, 514) stress the same fact at the CA, since it not only bought its own shares in order to bolster their value but also bought those of its major client firms.

[36] Banks did not have to publish more than a yearly balance sheet. During 1928–30, additional mid-yearly statements were issued, but only with a time lag of several months.

[37] They acquired, for instance, 25 million schillings of new shares, out of the 40 million schillings issued after the merger with the BCA in October 1929 (Ausch 1968, 331).

declines in the value of this stock, since the signaling effect and its repercussions would be potentially much more unfavorable and expensive than supporting the value of this stock. The adverse effect on the efficiency of the market is then the same as the effect of the bank buying back its own shares.[38,39] Moreover, a large part of the shares were in institutional portfolios, like that of the Austrian Postal Savings Bank. These owners did not necessarily react to news in the same way as profit-maximizing investors would have done. Their utility functions were different.[40]

Given these circumstances our empirical results about the very limited efficiency of the market for Credit-Anstalt stocks appear much less surprising. The banks in general and the CA in particular were powerful enough to influence the markets for their shares and to distort the informational contents of the price quotations and render those markets partly inefficient. The market was manipulated and did not transmit the correct information concerning the incipient failure of the largest Central European bank.[41] The evening of May 11, 1931, brought to the majority of the people a truly surprising message. The "news" was "new," indeed.[42]

[38] To be able to test this hypothesis, we would need detailed data on the holders of CA stocks and the changes of ownership over time.

[39] Federn, the contemporary observer, points out that the Rothschilds had a rule never to sell shares they had acquired. They were always buyers in the market (1932, 418). In the case of the Credit-Anstalt, Federn observed that they had bought a considerable amount of the reflowing shares (419).

[40] In this context it is interesting to note that on the occasion of its last capital increase before the collapse – just after the merger with the BCA – the CA did not give the old shareholders a right to purchase new shares but allocated them to a government-owned bank (Kreditinstitut für öffentliche Unternehmungen und Arbeiten), to the members of the board of directors of the former BCA, and to foreign friends of the Credit-Anstalt, led by the Rothschilds (see Rutkowski 1934, 71). These were "strong hands," which could be trusted to hold on to those stocks, even in bad times.

[41] This situation was by no means unprecedented. As already mentioned above, at the time of the collapse of the Boden-Credit-Anstalt its shares were still quoted at almost 200 percent of their nominal value. Also, as Rutkowski (1934, 68–69) points out, only a very small amount of those shares were in the hands of (small) investors; most of them were in fixed hands in France, Belgium, England, and at the Austrian Postal Savings Bank. In addition, about 25 percent were in the bank's own portfolio.

[42] An interesting little notice can be found in the *Neue Freie Presse* on May 12, 1931 (evening edition, 2), where an official of a Berlin bank (Bank für auswärtigen Handel), the shares of which were held to 30 percent by the Credit-Anstalt, is quoted as saying that his bank had recognized the unfavorable developments

The market for foreign exchange

As we have shown above, the Credit-Anstalt crisis led to a crisis of the Austrian currency. The proximate reason for this foreign exchange crisis was the liberal lending policy of the Austrian National Bank following the immobilization of the CA, while the fundamental cause was the sad state of Austrian public finance. If the foreign exchange market had been efficient, it should have predicted this crisis before the problems actually occurred and culminated.

First of all, we have to define what market efficiency means in the context of foreign-exchange markets. The hypothesis of market efficiency is a "joint hypothesis of rational expectations and perfect markets (i.e., competitive markets with low information and transactions costs)" (Frankel 1980, 1086), or, more specifically, that people form their expectations of the spot rate rationally, given the information at their disposal, and that the mean of their expectational distribution is reflected in the market's forward rate.

One way to test this hypothesis is to determine whether the forward exchange rate is an unbiased forecast for the future spot rate, or, in other words, whether "the expected value of the future spot rate, given the current information set, is equal to the current forward rate" (Frankel 1980, 1087).

A crucial methodological point is then the definition of the information set that the market participants are considered to have when they form their expectations.

Empirical evidence for Germany during the 1920s shows that the behavior of the foreign exchange market was consistent with the implications of the efficient market hypothesis during the German hyperinflation as well as during the "normal" period after stabilization of the currency (Frenkel 1980).

As far as Austria during 1931 is concerned, rigorous empirical testing of this hypothesis is precluded, since the necessary data is not at our disposal. We recall that the hyperinflation experience had reduced the value of the Austrian currency to 1/14,400th of its prewar level, and that from August 1922 on stability had returned, and the so-called Alpine dollar emerged. Foreign exchange restrictions pre-

at the Credit-Anstalt about a year before May 1931 and had acted accordingly. The following day, however, this bank rejected those reports as fabricated and incorrect (*Neue Freie Presse*, May 13, 1931, morning edition, 4).

vailed then for several years, and no open market for forward kronen existed. By the use of a forward exchange policy,[43] the ANB managed to attract large foreign credits for Austria and thus "greatly facilitated the economic reconstruction of the country" (Einzig 1961, 420). He reports further that "during the years of stability an open market had developed in Vienna for Forward Exchanges against schillings . . ." (ibid., 426). Unfortunately no data on quotations in this forward market are available to us.[44]

This lack of forward exchange data, however, does not preclude us completely from investigating the question whether the market had predicted the occurrence of the currency crisis and had acted accordingly. We cannot test the efficient market hypothesis per se, but we can still attempt to show that the market's behavior was not obviously inconsistent with the basics of the efficiency postulate.

We recall from our discussion of the causes of the currency crisis that it was really the public's behavior – rational, given its information set – that had led to the collapse of the exchange rate. Asset holders' expectations of future exchange rates are largely influenced by their prediction of future supplies of this money relative to other national monies, adjusted for expected changes in the demand for it. Therefore, the changes in the fiscal and monetary regime that were recognized by the market had signaled to it that the stability of the currency might have been in jeopardy, and this precipitated the run out of the schilling – in order to avoid capital losses or to secure capital gains. As the market participants recognized that the continuation of the fixed exchange rate conflicted with more important policies (namely securing the liquidity of the banking sector) they attacked the currency. Although it seemed unexpected and irrational to the authorities, the speculative attack was rational, as the fundamental inconsistencies in the policies of the authorities

---

[43] Foreign banks bought from the ANB spot kronen (and later schillings) and resold them to the ANB for later delivery at a low discount ("Kostdevisen"). This enabled those banks or alternatively the Austrian borrowers to pass on the exchange-rate risk to the ANB. The ANB provided thus a substitute for the lacking open market in forward kronen and quoted artificial forward margins at which arbitrage was profitable.

[44] Weber (1980, 123–4) showed that for Switzerland a close relationship existed between the monetary base and the exchange-rate expectations of the domestic and foreign wealth holders, which governed the capital flows. Each major shift in the approximate base was accompanied by a change in the forward rate.

were not reversed until the foreign reserves had approached complete depletion. Moreover, it was endogenously timed, on the basis of the perceived regime switch.

Foreign short-term credits by the Bank for International Settlements and the Bank of England, intended to stabilize the currency, could not restore confidence in the Austrian currency. However, they increased the potential capital gains to speculators, releasing more foreign exchange. Therefore less of the public's wealth had to be held in the depreciating schilling.

We cannot share the view put forward in *The Economist* (July 25, 1931, 174) that the timing of the Austrian crisis was a

blessing in disguise for Austria, for it became possible to raise for the protection of the currency, credits from the BIS ... [and] the Bank of England. ... This start in advance of the other debtor countries has proved to be advantageous to Austria in view of the credit requirements of Germany and Hungary.

These credits postponed the end of the authorities' intervention in the foreign exchange market and the introduction of exchange controls, but did not prevent or stop the sudden shift of reserves from the ANB to the public, as the domestic credit expansion, which had triggered the collapse, and the public finance problems, continued.

The public recognized that the continuous expansion in the domestic credit component of the money supply, given a fixed exchange rate, must have resulted in a collapse as the reserves were bound to fall beyond a certain limit. Once that limit was reached, the Austrian authorities did not devalue the currency or let it float, but introduced exchange controls and maintained the old exchange rate. The imposition of controls then resulted in black market exchange rates considerably above the official ones, reflecting the market's evaluation of the intrinsic value of the schilling (based on its information set).

There are then mainly three sets of information that provide us with evidence on the public's expectations concerning the value of the Austrian schilling: (1) evidence from official foreign exchange markets; (2) evidence from the gold and the bond market; and (3) evidence from the black market. Some newspaper reports concerning other markets will add complementary information.

Austria, during the interwar period, adhered to the gold exchange standard. The Austrian National Bank stood ready to supply all the foreign exchange demanded at the given parity (fixed to the United States dollar).[45] Consequently, the official exchange rate of the United States dollar in Vienna, or of the Austrian schilling in New York, does not show a lot of variation and cannot be used to measure the market's expected devaluation of the Austrian currency. In such a fixed exchange-rate system, changes in the confidence of the market in a currency are reflected not so much in the price of the currency as in the changes in the foreign exchange reserves of the respective central bank. As long as enough reserves are at the disposal of this central bank, the adjustment will not occur through price changes but quantity changes. As we recall from above, the reserves of the Austrian National Bank underwent very fast depletion, starting in May 1931. These reserve losses reflect mounting distrust in the schilling and the expected devaluation, but they do not indicate the extent of the market's discount for this asset.

Table 5.14 reports the price of the Austrian schilling at the Zürich (Switzerland) market, between January 1931 and December 1932. With the announcement of the Credit-Anstalt crisis, a discount on the schilling developed that increased consistently until exchange controls were introduced. But the ANB prevented the discount from becoming larger than a few percentage points.

More complete information, however, can be obtained from the markets for gold and for League of Nations bonds. Table 5.15 presents the agio on the schilling price of gold. With the introduction of the requirement of proof of necessity for foreign exchange on September 23, 1931 (following England's abandonment of the gold standard) an agio developed that reached 44 percent by the end of November and stabilized at about 20 percent during the summer of 1932.

Although the gold price did not start to rise from parity until the ANB's introduction of controlled allocations of foreign exchange, the bond market provides us with clear evidence that from the

---

[45] Austria was committed to return to gold convertibility (redemption of bank notes in specie). Article 83 of the statutes of the ANB provided that the bank shall resume specie payments when the federal debt to the bank had been reduced to 30 million gold crowns (43.2 million schillings). In view of the CA crisis, parliament decided to abolish this commitment on May 13, 1931, and it was formally canceled in an extraordinary general meeting of the shareholders of the ANB on June 17, 1931.

Table 5.14. *Price of the Austrian schilling at the Zürich exchange (monthly in percentage of parity)*

1931		1932	
Jan.	99.6	Jan.	na
Feb.	99.8	Feb.	na
March	100.1	March	na
April	100.1	April	na
May	100.0	May	79.7
June	99.3	June	78.1
July	98.9	July	83.2
Aug.	98.8	Aug.	84.0
Sept.	98.5	Sept.	84.9
Oct.	na[a]	Oct.	84.8
Nov.	na	Nov.	84.5
Dec.	na	Dec.	84.0

[a] Not available.
Source: *Monatsberichte des OIfK,* Heft 2, 1935.

Table 5.15. *Agio on the schilling price of gold in 1931–2 (in percentages)*

1931		1932	
September:	November:	January:	April:
23............2	2............28	6............30	6.........14
24............3	3............24	27...........32	
25............8	7............20	30...........35	May:
28..........2.5	9............28		4.........20
29............5	16...........24	February:	9.........25
	20...........32	2............42	18........30
October:	23...........36	11...........36	
1..............8	24...........44	17...........34	June:
2............13			2.........36
6............20	December:	March:	17........30
21...........30	16...........41	3............32	
27...........32	17...........39	17...........28	July:
	22...........36	22...........20	21........25[a]
	24...........32		

[a] From early August until end of December 1932, 20%.
Source: *Wirtschaftsstatistisches Jahrbuch* 1932, 364.

Table 5.16. *League of Nations bond 1943, quotation in Vienna and New York (monthly averages)*

Month	Vienna	New York	Difference absolute /	%
Jan. 1931	108.2	105.4	2.8	2.7
Feb.	106.9	105.5	1.4	1.3
March	106.7	107.2	− .5	− .1
April	107.2	106.6	.6	.1
May	110.2	106.9	3.3	3.1
June	114.0	106.9	7.1	6.6
July	113.0	106.4	6.6	6.2
Aug.	111.0	104.8	6.2	6.0
Sept.	111.0	102.9	8.1	7.9
Oct.	118.6	94.0	24.6	26.2
Nov.	120.5	90.0	30.5	33.9
Dec.	126.8	82.7	44.1	53.3
Jan. 1932	121.7	89.5	32.2	36.0
Feb.	124.8	90.5	34.3	37.9
March	124.3	93.7	30.6	32.7
April	113.8	88.6	25.2	28.4
May	110.7	79.1	31.6	39.9
June	107.3	78.1	29.2	37.4
July	108.0	88.1	19.9	22.6
Aug.	107.0	86.8	20.2	23.3
Sept.	108.0	90.1	17.9	19.9
Oct.	106.9	92.2	13.9	15.1
Nov.	106.1	91.8	14.3	15.6
Dec.	108.4	89.8	18.6	20.7

Source: Wirtschaftsstatistisches Jahrbuch 1932, 365.

moment of the announcement of the CA crisis, the market's evaluation of the Austrian schilling deteriorated. In Table 5.16 the prices of the 1923 to 1943 League of Nations Bond in Vienna and New York are presented.

Although the valuation of this security just prior to the start of the crisis was almost equal in both markets, a widening gap developed from May 1931 on, mainly reflecting the market's different evaluation of the Austrian and the American currency. There is large-scale correspondence between the bond price difference and the agio on the gold price, reflecting consistency in the market's valuation of the Austrian currency.

The message received from an analysis of both markets, for gold and for bonds, is very much the same. Early in the crisis the public came to believe that a change in the official parity was imminent, and they were willing to pay a premium for gold, foreign exchange, and assets denominated in foreign exchange. The value of this premium moved parallel in all these markets, and it anticipated the eventual devaluation of the Austrian currency quite correctly.

While the National Bank was "adhering rigidly to the official rates for foreign exchange" (*The Economist,* October 24, 1931, 758), the market valued the schilling at a large discount, reaching a maximum of 44 percent in late November 1931, or, as *The Economist* put it, "the restricted allotment of notes . . . led, as always in such times, to the growth of clandestine transactions, in which notes, gold and, recently, also silver are negotiated at a premium" (October 3, 1931, 615).[46] "The rapid ebbing away of devisen reserves had created a shortage of foreign exchange immediately after the Credit-Anstalt collapse, so that transactions of any importance proceeded on a premium basis for gold currencies" (Ellis 1941, 40).[47] This chronic scarcity of foreign exchange and the consequent restricted allocations by the ANB led to the emergence of parallel markets.[48] The public desired to alter the composition of its portfolio of financial assets, but the ANB's restricted allocations hindered this adjustment. The potential buyers of foreign exchange were willing to pay a premium in order to be able to make their desired portfolio adjustments.[49]

Following a Viennese tradition, the trading places for those black

[46] The publishing of the prices in those parallel markets was forbidden even before exchange restrictions were introduced (Pressburger 1969, 95).

[47] A similar deterioration in the value of the schilling was observed abroad, starting in June 1931 (Pressburger 1969, 92).

[48] The *Wiener Börsen-Kurier* (June 8, 1931, 2) reports that allocations fell sometimes as low as 5 percent (United States dollar) and 50 percent (Swiss franc). After Great Britain had gone off the gold standard, "the National Bank has drastically curtailed the issue of foreign currency. Of the means of payment demanded at clearing scarcely 10 per cent has been allowed" (*The Economist,* October 3, 1931, 615).

[49] Once exchange controls were introduced, "by means of the severe punishment regulations it [i.e., the National Bank] has suppressed private trading, in which considerably higher prices had figured" (*The Economist,* October 24, 1931, 758). There was another interesting consequence of the increased hoarding of foreign exchange by the public: Insurance contracts against burglary, theft, fire damage, and other kinds of losses of cash in private custody enjoyed a remarkable boom (*Neue Freie Presse,* September 20, 1931, 21).

market transactions were – predominantly – coffeehouses. While the official exchange rate at the Vienna Bourse was administratively determined by the ANB, the black market exchange rate was determined by the interaction of supply and demand for foreign money in that market. Unfortunately, we do not have data on the day-to-day prices in those coffeehouse markets.

Ellis (1941, 40) reports that in September "the informal (but still legal) coffeehouse dealings involved premia of 10–15 percent," while *The Economist* (October 10, 1931, 661) states that "unofficial trade with foreign means of payment" was done in those markets with prices "up to 12 percent above official rates."[50]

While the public fled increasingly into these coffeehouse markets, businesses pursued a different approach, since they recognized the potential depreciation and encountered problems with securing the foreign means of payment for use at a later date. They started to "add a gold clause to their invoices" while the government took "the view that the Austrian schilling [was] perfectly stable and that a gold clause [was] therefore of purely theoretical significance" (*The Economist,* October 31, 1931, 808).

The premiums on foreign exchange as well as on gold are only one piece of evidence that the market had predicted the currency problems and acted accordingly. The public responded also with an unseasonal surge in imports in the summer of 1931, as people attempted to flee into real and especially foreign goods, in order to protect themselves against the anticipated inflation and depreciation.[51] The *Wiener Börsen-Kurier* (November 16, 1931, 3) reported a strong demand for textiles, furniture, shoes, and jewelry – at a time when the number of registered unemployed was rising strongly and already surpassed 300,000. Kamitz (1949, 184) points out that the imports of Swiss watches were unusually high. The businesses, on the other hand, tried to protect themselves by importing large quantities of raw materials.[52] The drive to hedge themselves against

---

[50] When these numbers are compared to the agio of the gold price and the price discrepancy of the League of Nations bonds at that time, they seem to reflect somewhat larger discounts prevailing in the coffeehouses than in the regular markets.

[51] Expected increases in import tariffs have been traditionally used to explain this surge. Unfortunately, we cannot discriminate empirically between these competing hypotheses.

[52] Kamitz (1949, 183) reports for instance that in the fourth quarter of 1931 imports

inflation induced the public to invest in houses, also something rather unusual for a business depression of the depth this one had reached in mid-1931. *The Economist* (October 3, 1931, 615) considered it "worthy of note that a strong demand for real estate has again set in and houses containing small flats are being sought." Those who could not shelter themselves in real estate, rediscovered the stock market as a hedge against inflation, thus producing a stock market boom – again an atypical phenomenon during a severe depression.

The generally accepted explanation of this boom [was] the desire of the public to have their money placed in some substantial way, as the foreign currency control regulations in the different countries make it impossible to convert the money into foreign means of payment or to invest it in foreign business. (*The Economist*, December 12, 1931, 1123)

But the Austrian National Bank "probably regarded the rise in stock prices as an undurable symptom of fear for the schilling" (*The Economist*, December 19, 1931, 1178) and the boom was only very short-lived.

We can summarize that there is ample evidence that, in spite of all efforts by the authorities, the market anticipated inflation and a currency crisis, starting with the early days of the Credit-Anstalt crisis.[53] The public recognized the inconsistencies of the adherence to the gold exchange standard in combination with the massive expansion of domestic credit and the inability of the Austrian government to preserve orderly public finances in the light of the guarantees for the liabilities of the Credit-Anstalt. One price of the salvage of the Credit-Anstalt was the gold parity of the schilling, and that was clearly recognized by the market as early as mid- to late May 1931. The behavior of the authorities who considered the market's evaluation to be wrong cost Austria its entire foreign exchange reserves, without being able to stop the decline of the currency.

---

of rubber were up (relative to one year earlier) by 125 percent, of raw iron by 63 percent, and of chemical fertilizers by 55 percent, all rather unusual during a severe and deepening business depression.

[53] To do justice to the authorities, we have to point out that there was lack of unanimity among officials concerning the liberal lending policy of the ANB and the potential danger for the currency, since the vice president and the managing director of the ANB opposed this policy. As far as the state guarantees are concerned, at least one minister was against them, and the general guarantee for the foreign liabilities on June 16, 1931, led to the fall of the government.

It was not until 1934 that this devaluation was finally officially accepted.[54] The new parity (28 percent below the old one) was consistent with the market's evaluation.[55] The authorities' attempts to resist a rational evaluation of the value of the Austrian schilling without changing the underlying policies had resulted in the currency crisis.

[54] From mid-1932 on, an increasing part of the transactions was done on a "private clearing" basis, i.e. at free market rates and not at the official ones.

[55] The main decline had been stopped by July 1932, when the signing of the Lausanne Protocols made the issuing of an international long-term loan appear secured. The danger of a possible monetization of the government debt seemed to be successfully avoided. The actual loan, however, was only received a year later. There is a striking similarity in these events to the 1922 Geneva Protocols and their effects on exchange rate expectations.

6. The financial crisis and economic activity

> Financial crises, like contagious disease, threaten not only the host organism, namely the financial market, but the entire economic environment in which the host resides.
>
> —Eichengreen and Postes, 1987

The evidence and the channels of transmission

The banking and currency crisis of 1931 clearly coincided with adverse developments in economic activity in Austria. Historic accounts point out that after sharp drops in output and large increases in unemployment during 1930, in the spring of 1931 the trough seemed to have been passed, and a slow recovery seemed to be on its way. The Austrian Chancellor Ender stated in March 1931, during a parliamentary session, that for Austria the trough of the economic depression had already been reached (Kernbauer et al. 1983, 378), and the press frequently announced an easing of the crisis.[1] The highly respectable Austrian Institute for Business Cycle Research ("Oesterreichisches Institut für Konjunkturforschung") pointed out repeatedly that the crisis had started to fade away (OIfK, February 26, 1932, 17), that the first symptoms of recovery had appeared, and that a considerable improvement had occurred in the securities market (OIfK, 1933, 6). In April 1931, the first large domestic bond issue since World War I, the Austrian Housing Loan, turned out to be a great success. It was more than 50 percent oversubscribed, and as *The Times* (April 14, 1931, 21) reported, it was "taken to herald the

---

[1] Very similar observations have been made for the United States as well as for Germany. According to Bernanke (1983, 257), an incipient recovery in the United States degenerated into a new slump during the mid-1931 crisis, while for Friedman and Schwartz (1963, 313) the first four or five months in 1931 had "many of the earmarks of the bottom of a cycle and the beginning of revival." According to James (1984, 69), referring to Germany, "in the spring of 1931 there had been signs that the recovery might begin soon."

success of any forthcoming Austrian issues abroad." These events were interpreted "as a sign of approaching better times"[2] and the general mood was slightly optimistic – at least compared to the year before.[3]

In May 1931, signs of optimism and hope disappeared instantly and were changed into a "mood of catastrophe" (Bachinger and Matis 1974, 121). The evening of May 11, 1931 changed the outlook completely. The announcement of the losses at the Credit-Anstalt destroyed any expectations (or illusions) of recovery and a return to prosperity, since, if the CA had a problem, the Austrian economy had a problem.

Some of the economic time series reflect very clearly both the reasons for the hope of recovery and the impact of the outbreak of the banking and financial crisis. The stock market index (Figure 6.1), considered to be a leading indicator of business activity, had basically stopped its decline in December of 1930 and showed a healthy recovery in February and March 1931, creating hopes for improvement in the economy. The events of May 1931 left a clear mark on the development of stock prices, and they fell rapidly and uninterruptedly until September 1931. The index of business activity (Figure 6.2), a composite index serving as an overall measure for the state of the economy, had reached a trough in March 1931, and showed an upward trend in April and May. The events during the second half of May, however, turned the index to down again. The clearest and strongest effect can be detected in the path of the number of unemployed, a lagging indicator. During March to June 1931, it showed – if adjusted for seasonal factors – declines in the number of unemployed (Figure 6.3), reflecting the somewhat improved business climate. This encouraging trend was then completely reversed in July 1931, and – disregarding seasonal influences – sixteen months of uninterrupted increases in the number of jobless followed until October 1932, with the turnaround not occurring until mid-1933.

[2] See, for example, the statement of the president of the Niederösterreichische Escompte-Gesellschaft, one of the remaining three large banks in Austria, on the occasion of the presentation of the 1930 balance sheet in April 1931 (The Times, April 20, 1931, 24).

[3] That not all the economic news was positive is shown very vividly by a short notice in the Wall Street Journal of May 11, 1931 (8): "Mitterberg, Salzburg, copper mine, most important in Austria, closed. All miners dismissed. Hope to reopen when the copper price improves."

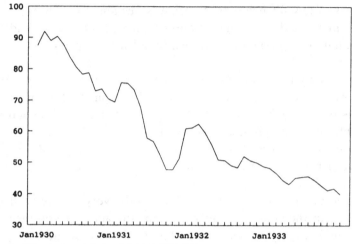

SOURCE: *Wirtschaftsstatistisches Jahrbuch* 1937, 399.

Figure 6.1. Stock index, 1930–3 (mid-monthly values, 1923–1932 = 100).

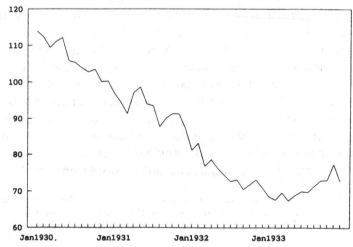

SOURCE: *Wirtschaftsstatistisches Jahrbuch* 1937, 7.

Figure 6.2. Index of business activity, 1930–3 (seasonally adjusted, 1923–31 = 100).

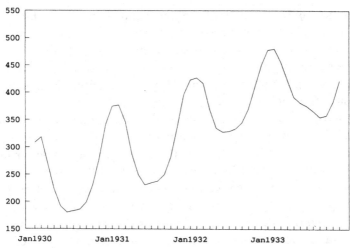

SOURCE: *Statistisches Handbuch der Weltwirtschaft* 1936, 215.

Figure 6.3. Number of unemployed, 1930–3 (in thousands).

Additional evidence of a deteriorating situation can be seen in the behavior of the Gross National Product, the number of business insolvencies, the amount of imports and exports, the volume of check clearing and many other indices.

The evidence from all these graphs and the other time series clearly supports the view that the banking crisis made a difference for aggregate economic activity in Austria. It either worsened an ongoing recession or even aborted an incipient recovery, and postponed the trough of the crisis by almost two years. In short, it turned a strong recession into the Great Depression.

What then were the possible channels of transmission of the disturbances from the banking and currency crisis to economic activity in Austria?[4]

---

[4] Ideally, the relationship among the different series, monetary and nonmonetary, and the impact of the crisis on all of them, the transmission channels and their interaction, could be explained with a structural model of the Austrian interwar economy. The data currently available to us, however, does not allow us to build such a full scale model. Moreover, as Eichengreen (1983) points out correctly, building such a model requires exogenous variables and a priori knowledge to justify the decision to omit potential linkages among variables. Therefore, "when the very purpose of the exercise is to identify the channels through which cyclical impulses were transmitted, rather than to estimate the relative importance of channels already identified, this procedure is tantamount to assuming one's conclusions" (153).

Bordo (1986a, 193) identifies three channels through which (in a simple quantity theory framework) financial crises are able to affect economic activity. The first possible channel works through changes in the money supply, the second through changes in money demand (velocity), and the third is a direct link to real output without transmission through the monetary sector.

Banking panics are expected to affect the money stock through their effects on the money multiplier. The public's loss of confidence in the banking sector and the concurrent scramble for high-powered money result in a downward shift in the desired deposit-currency ratio, and if convertibility is maintained, in a shift in the actual ratio. This increase in the public's preference for cash relative to deposits will, ceteris paribus, result in a decline in the multiplier and consequently in a contraction in the money stock. The banks, under attack, will on their part attempt to strengthen their liquidity position by withdrawing interbank deposits, rediscounting bills, recalling loans or refusing to roll over old loans. Their quest for high-powered money will have similar effects on the money stock, reducing the multiplier through a decline in the deposit/reserve ratio. Unless the monetary authorities manage to offset the reduction in the multiplier by increases in high-powered money, the money stock will contract and exert downward pressure on income.

The public's scramble for liquidity is likely to affect money demand, as people resort to hoarding currency or change the composition of their portfolios. Whether the overall money demand will be changed depends on factors such as the extent of the confidence crisis, the sophistication of the financial markets, and the existence of alternative assets.

The third channel of transmission, the direct (nonmonetary) link between a financial crisis and economic activity, has been identified with increased cost of credit intermediation, due to a reduced effectiveness of the financial sector. The cost of credit intermediation, in Bernanke's (1983) framework, includes screening, monitoring, and accounting costs, as well as the expected losses inflicted by bad borrowers. A banking panic will thus lead to a contraction of the banking system's role in the intermediation of credit. Their accumulated expertise at evaluating potential borrowers, establishing long-term relationships with customers, and offering loan conditions that encourage potential borrowers to self-select in a favorable way (ibid., 263) will be used less efficiently. The increases in the cost of credit intermediation will result in higher borrowing costs and/or in fewer people receiving loans from the banking sector. This interference with the normal flow of credit might have an effect on aggregate economic activity, independent of the effects resulting from the interplay of the changes in money supply and money demand.[5]

The Austrian money stock, 1923 to 1936

Although there exists a range of published data on different monetary series in Austria, no estimates for monetary aggregates have yet been attempted. Therefore, we construct an empirical definition of the Austrian money stock for most of the interwar period, between the stabilization of the currency (establishment of the Austrian National Bank) and 1936. We estimate two money stock series, a narrow one and a broader one. The narrow money stock (M1) is based on currency in the hands of the public plus checking and current account deposits at commercial banks, savings banks, and the Austrian Postal Savings Bank. The broader definition (M2) includes all the components of M1 plus savings deposits at those financial intermediaries.[6] The two series and their components are shown in Table 6.1.

The money stock estimates

The estimation of the M1 series is based on currency in the hands of the public (i.e., currency in circulation minus currency at banks, savings banks, the Austrian Postal Savings Bank, and the Austrian National Bank), plus checking deposits at commercial banks, sav-

[5] Other indirect – nonmonetary – effects on economic activity are also conceivable, such as wealth effects emanating from reduced wealth of stockholders and of holders of other securities that might have declined in value, or effects following a depreciation of the home currency.
[6] While the definitions of money used here may turn out, in the light of further research, to be less than perfect, they seem adequate for present purposes, and for a first attempt to analyze the behavior of money during the interwar years in Austria.

Table 6.1. *M1 and M2 and their components, 1923 to 1936 (in million schillings)*

Year	M1	Currency	Deposits
1923	2079.1	645.9	1433.2
1924	2603.4	782.5	1820.9
1925	2801.2	867.0	1934.2
1926	3454.7	921.3	2533.4
1927	3621.0	960.9	2660.1
1928	3942.1	1011.3	2930.8
1929	3981.7	1058.3	2923.4
1930	3886.4	1081.6	2804.8
1931	2994.6	1183.8	1810.8
1932	2463.7	926.9	1536.8
1933	2371.1	948.5	1422.6
1934	2187.6	932.0	1255.6
1935	2222.9	922.4	1300.5
1936	2137.6	927.8	1209.8

Year	M2	Currency	Deposits
1923	2178.5	645.9	1532.6
1924	2910.0	782.5	2127.5
1925	3430.7	867.0	2563.7
1926	4359.7	921.3	3438.4
1927	4786.3	960.9	3825.4
1928	5402.0	1011.3	4390.7
1929	5636.2	1058.3	4577.9
1930	5819.6	1081.6	4738.0
1931	4695.3	1183.8	3511.5
1932	4298.3	926.9	3371.4
1933	4232.3	948.5	3283.8
1934	4123.6	932.0	3191.6
1935	4278.2	922.4	3355.8
1936	4244.0	927.8	3316.2

ings banks, and the Postal Savings Bank, plus current account deposits at commercial banks and the savings banks.[7]

For the overall period under consideration, 1923 to 1936 (using end of December data), the money stock had only grown by about 2.8 percent. But this overall development does not reflect the very

[7] This total was then adjusted by the difference between all interbank deposits and the deposits and other sight liabilities at the National Bank. Moreover, since the schilling had not been introduced until 1925, the amounts expressed in kronen were converted into schillings at the official conversion rate of 1 schilling = 10,000 kronen.

Table 6.2. *Money growth, M1 and its components (in percentages)*

Year	M1	Currency	Deposits
1924	22.5	19.2	23.9
1925	7.3	10.3	6.0
1926	21.0	6.1	27.0
1927	4.7	4.2	4.9
1928	8.5	5.1	9.7
1929	1.0	4.5	-0.3
1930	-2.4	2.2	-4.1
1931	-26.1	9.0	-43.8
1932	-19.5	-24.5	-16.4
1933	-3.8	2.3	-7.7
1934	-8.1	-1.8	-12.5
1935	1.6	-1.0	3.5
1936	-3.9	0.6	-7.2

different pattern of money growth during distinct subperiods. We can identify at least three different periods:

1. The period of growing money stock from 1923 to 1929.
2. The period of declining money stock from 1930 to 1934.
3. An oscillating period from 1935 to 1936.

From 1923 to 1928, M1 was growing at about 12.8 percent per year (see Table 6.2).[8] These large increases were suddenly interrupted in 1929, when our estimates show a drop in the growth rate to about 1 percent compared to 8.5 percent in 1928. The following five years (1930 to 1934) were characterized by a continuous decline in the money stock at an average rate of 12.0 percent, offsetting most of the increases from the first subperiod. This large average rate of decline is caused mainly by two years, 1931 and 1932, which showed rates of decline of 26.1 and 19.5 percent, respectively. The following slight increase in 1935 (1.6 percent) was more than offset by another decline in 1936 (3.9 percent).

Investigating the changes in the two components, currency and deposits, we find that the main influence on the changes in the money stock came from fluctuations in the amount of deposits, while the amount of currency was not subject to the same absolute variations. Moreover, currency did not start to decline until 1932, while the amount of deposits had already peaked in 1928. Deposits

[8] Based on logarithmic differences.

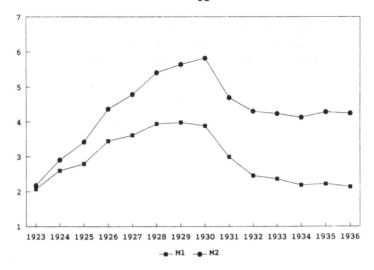

Figure 6.4. Money stock, M1 and M2 (in billion schillings).

in 1936 were about 15.6 percent below their level in December 1923. The growth pattern of deposits is very similar to the one observed for the overall money stock. The most remarkable year is again 1931, with a rate of decline of the sum of current and checking deposits of 43.8 percent.

Apart from our estimates for the narrow money stock (M1), we estimated another, broader series, that includes the full amount of savings deposits in Austria (M2).[9]

Figure 6.4 reveals the increasing discrepancy between the two monetary aggregates, due to the fact that savings accounts behaved very differently over the cycle than did checking and current account deposits. The tremendous growth in savings is quite clearly reflected in the fact that, in 1936, the level of M2 was about 95 percent above its 1923 level, while M1 had only grown over the same period by 2.8 percent. However, just as in the case of the narrower definition, three distinct subperiods can be distinguished. A growth period through 1930, a declining period between 1931 and 1934, and then oscillation during 1935 to 1936 (Table 6.3).

[9] As mentioned above the savings at the credit associations are not included. Since they constituted more than 20 percent of the savings deposits, the money stock will be underestimated. However, we would expect that the changes in savings deposits at those institutions were not very different from the changes at the savings banks. But this issue is left to further research.

Table 6.3. *Money growth, M2 and its components (in percentages)*

Year	M2	Currency	Deposits
1924	29.0	19.2	32.8
1925	16.5	10.3	18.7
1926	24.0	6.1	29.4
1927	9.3	4.2	10.7
1928	12.1	5.1	13.8
1929	4.2	4.5	4.2
1930	3.2	2.2	3.4
1931	−21.5	9.0	−30.0
1932	−8.8	−24.5	−4.1
1933	−1.5	2.3	−2.6
1934	−2.6	−1.8	−2.8
1935	3.7	−1.0	5.0
1936	−0.8	0.6	−1.2

Growth over the 1923 to 1928 period averaged 18.2 percent as compared to about 12.8 percent for M1. During 1929 and 1930 it slowed down considerably (4.2 percent and 3.2 percent), reducing the average yearly growth rate over the whole expansion period from 1923 to 1930 to about 14 percent. The contractionary period, 1931 to 1934, reduced the stock of money in its broad definition by 34.4 percent, even below the level of December 1926.[10] Just as in the case of M1, most of the decline was due to only two years, 1931 and 1932. The contraction of 1932, however, was considerably less severe than for the narrow money stock (8.8 percent vs. 19.5 percent). The oscillating period shows modest growth in 1935 (3.7 percent) and virtual stagnation in 1936 (−0.8).

The behavior of the money supply in 1931

As far as our analysis is concerned, the most important and interesting time period is the year 1931, and especially the period between May 12 (the public announcement of the problems of the Credit-Anstalt) and October 9 (the introduction of exchange controls). We recall that during 1931 the money stock in its narrower definition

[10] This overall decline was strikingly similar to the one witnessed in the United States, where the money stock fell by 33 percent between August 1929 and March 1933.

Table 6.4. *High-powered money in 1931, monthly (in million schillings)*[a]

| End of Month | High-powered money | | Foreign[b] | Domestic component |
	Seasonally unadjusted	Seasonally adjusted		
January	1,176.4	1,208.6	850.1	326.2
February	1,144.9	1,191.0	842.0	302.9
March	1,128.7	1,170.0	852.1	276.6
April	1,133.5	1,164.6	860.0	273.5
May	1,368.0	1,385.9	732.2	635.8
June	1,377.5	1,364.6	685.6	718.9
July	1,389.1	1,348.7	566.6	822.5
August	1,304.4	1,289.9	490.3	814.2
September	1,275.0	1,267.1	391.7	883.4
October	1,315.5	1,303.9	344.3	971.3
November	1,362.0	1,346.1	346.4	1,015.7
December	1,406.9	1,342.8	317.6	1,089.4

[a] Components might not add up exactly due to rounding.
[b] The foreign component does not include the foreign assets included in "other assets."

had declined by 23 percent (at an annual rate of 26.1 percent) and in its broader definition by 19.3 percent (at a rate of 21.5 percent). This strong and (during the time period under analysis) unprecedented monetary shock for the Austrian economy occurred despite an unusually large increase in the monetary base (more than 10 percent).[11] Therefore, we have to pay special attention to the behavior of the multiplier and especially to the changes in its components, the deposit–currency (D/C), and the deposit–reserve (D/R) ratios.

As we pointed out in chapter 4 above, the unprecedented increase in high-powered money occurred mainly during one month, May 1931, and even then almost exclusively during one week. These were the four days following the announcement of the losses of the CA, the most crucial days for the later developments. The unadjusted monetary base expanded during May 1931 at a monthly growth rate of 18.8 percent, while the seasonally adjusted base grew at a rate of 17.4 percent (Table 6.4).

By further analysis we find that growth in domestic assets of the

[11] The word "unusually" is meant in comparison to the rate of growth during the preceding five years.

Austrian National Bank (ANB) was responsible for this upward jump in the base, rising by one and a half times the increase in high-powered money, while the following decline in foreign exchange reserves offset only part of the excess growth. This expansion in domestic assets was the result of an increase in the volume of bills discounted by 405 percent between April 30 and May 31.[12] We know, however, that these figures underestimate the developments, since there is ample evidence that the ANB pursued a "window dressing" policy by including some of the financial bills of the ailing bank under "other assets," in exchange for foreign exchange reserves that were hidden in the same balance sheet item. An alternative method used was to place money in foreign banks under the condition that they lend it back to the Credit-Anstalt.

The weekly series of notes and demand deposits at the central bank[13] shows that the monetary base had declined during the week preceding the crisis, and that the run on the CA and the other banks led to an expansion of the base at a weekly rate of 17.8 percent (Table 6.5). The following weeks witnessed much more moderate changes.

As we argued in chapter 4, it was exactly this unprecedented and unexpected expansion in the amount of high-powered money that precipitated the inflationary fears and the run on the currency by (parts of) the public.

We cannot analyze the behavior of the money multiplier and the ratios on a weekly or monthly basis; nevertheless a lot of information is to be gained from the available data concerning the impact of the banking crisis on the behavior of the public and the banking sector. The narrow multiplier dropped from 3.1 at the end of 1930 to only 2.13 in December of 1931, while the broader one declined from 4.58 to 3.34. These rates of contraction of 36.2 and 31.6 percent, respectively, were due to declines in both ratios, D/C and D/R. For the M2 definition, the public's scramble for liquidity and for safety let the D/C ratio decline at a rate of 39 percent (from 4.4 to 3.0), and for the narrower money stock the respective rate of decline amounted to 52.8 percent, from 2.6 to 1.5. These changes in the ratios – in isolation – would have reduced the money stock by 25.5

[12] Compared to May 7, 1931, even 550 percent.
[13] Used here as a proxy for the monetary base, since the data on coins in circulation are not available on a weekly basis.

Table 6.5. *Notes and deposits, foreign reserves and bills discounted at the outbreak of the crisis, weekly (in million schillings)*

Day	Notes and deposits at ANB	Foreign reserves	Bills discounted
April 30	1,048.5	860.0	89.2
May 7	1,024.6	855.5	69.5
May 15	1,223.8	826.4	297.6
May 23	1,230.4	780.5	350.0
May 31	1,282.9	732.2	451.3
June 7	1,251.9	677.1	475.4
June 15	1,286.4	698.7[a]	488.2
June 23	1,255.4	661.0	490.2
June 30	1,290.9	658.6	528.7
July 7	1,252.6	639.0	511.3
July 15	1,259.7	622.4	533.9
July 23	1,285.2	592.6	588.4
July 31	1,299.7	566.7	632.1
Aug. 7	1,261.9	546.7	614.3
Aug. 15	1,217.0	524.3	591.8
Aug. 23	1,192.2	504.5	586.5
Aug. 31	1,215.7	490.3	624.3
Sept. 7	1,193.7	472.3	620.3
Sept. 15	1,162.8	456.4	604.9
Sept. 23	1,141.9	407.0	630.3
Sept. 30	1,185.5	391.7	688.5
Oct. 7	1,201.7	358.9	736.2

[a] Includes about half the Bank of England loan of 150 million schillings.
Sources: Mitteilungen des Direktoriums der Oesterreichischen Nationalbank, various issues.

and 28.8 percent respectively, thus making the currency ratio the main contributor to the behavior of the money stock in 1931. This result conforms fully with the conclusions of Friedman and Schwartz (1963) and Cagan (1965) for the United States. "There was no more sensitive indicator of the state of public confidence in the banks than the deposit/currency ratio" (Friedman and Schwartz, 1963, 123).[14]

Although we are not able to present any exact figures for the D/C

[14] Boughton and Wicker (1979) show, however, that bank failures were not the only cause of the fall in the D/C ratio in the United States, but that changes in interest rates as well as changes in income also had their respective influences.

Table 6.6. *Savings and checking deposits in 1931, monthly (in million schillings)*

Month	Credit-Anstalt	Banks in Vienna	Total in Austria
January	320.7	592.3	1,941.1
February	322.5	598.4	1,968.2
March	322.7	601.7	1,981.5
April	322.9	596.6	1,970.0
May	na[a]	290.9[b]	1,700.0[b]
June	na	na	na
July	na	na	na
August	63.7	329.4	1,592.3
September	na	235.9[c]	1,453.3[c]
October	na	225.3	1,407.3
November	na	220.2	1,399.5
December	na	221.7	1,383.5

[a] Not available.
[b] From May on (with the exception of August) without Credit-Anstalt.
[c] From September on without foreign exchange deposits (about 98.5 million schillings in August 1931).
Sources: *Mitteilungen des Direktoriums der Oesterreichischen Nationalbank,* various issues.

ratio during the most interesting period, May 1931 to October 1931, we have enough data to be able to trace out its approximate development. As far as deposits are concerned, we know that checking and savings deposits amounted to 1,970 million schillings at the end of April 1931 and had dropped to 1,592 million by August of that year (see Table 6.6). This amounted to a decline by 21 percent. The volume of these deposits kept on declining afterward, however, at a slower pace.[15]

For current account deposits, no monthly data are at our disposal. We know, however, that they declined from about 2,619 million schillings on December 31, 1930, to about 1,556 million at the end of 1931. We assume that the development of this series, although stronger in its decline, was somewhat parallel to that of checking and savings deposits.

At the same time as the volume of deposits was contracting that strongly, first because of an internal drain created by the public's fear for the security of its deposits and then due to the external drain caused by fear for the currency, the amount of currency in circu-

[15] After taking into account that from September on, *Kassenscheine* (bank notes) in foreign currency were no longer included in the reported figures.

lation witnessed a very different development. Note circulation in Austria virtually exploded during May 1931, followed by further ups and some smaller downs during the rest of the year. The amount of currency held by the public increased parallel to the amount in circulation. A disaggregation of the note circulation into the different categories of schilling bills reveals very interesting insights into the whereabouts of the additional currency. The number of bills, as well as the values of the categories, show that 66 percent of the 156 million schillings of expansion occurred in the 1,000 schilling category, the highest denomination, which more than doubled in the course of one month (see Table 6.7). The share of these bills increased from 8.9 percent to 16.7 percent of the number of notes in circulation. Most of the remaining increase reflected an expansion in the volume of the second highest denomination, the 100 schilling category.[16]

In order to understand these changes correctly, we have to put the value of a 1,000 schilling bill into perspective. The average balance on savings accounts at the Postal Savings Bank in 1931 was only 412 schillings and on checking accounts about 1,696 (Wagner and Tomanek 1983, 252–3). An analysis of household expenditures in 1931 reported that the median family in the sample incurred total yearly expenditures amounting to 4,000 to 5,000 schillings.[17] We know from the income tax statistics for 1930 that half of the taxpayers had yearly income tax bases of up to 3,000 schillings (OIfK 1933, 10). And finally, we recall from chapter 5 that 1,000 schillings would have bought about twenty three shares in the Credit-Anstalt on May 11, 1931.

The important point about all these figures is that 1,000 schilling bills represented a very large amount of money. Therefore, it is very unlikely that these bills were used for everyday transactions. In that case they would have amounted to more than 9 percent of the total of notes in circulation. As the cash holdings of the banks do not show any large increases during 1931, all the additional currency must have been absorbed by the public and then either been hoarded at home, or transferred abroad. Both of the components of the de-

[16] A very similar phenomenon occurred in Switzerland, where the expansion of the monetary base in 1931 was mainly due to large bills with the amount of 1,000 and 500 franc bills almost tripling (see Weber 1980, 112).

[17] There were seventy-two households in the sample, with eighteen spending less than 3,000 schillings per year, and seven more than 7,000 (see *Wirtschaftsstatistisches Jahrbuch* 1932, 348).

Table 6.7. *Note circulation in Austria, 1931–2 (number of 1,000-schilling bills circulating)*

Month	Bills
Jan. 1931	87,597
Feb.	86,924
March	88,647
April	87,121
May	190,845
June	168,610
July	218,085
Aug.	156,130
Sept.	187,157
Oct.	209,788
Nov.	219,813
Dec.	226,800
Jan. 1932	207,486
Feb.	174,992
March	105,589
April	83,910
May	66,535
June	49,449
July	41,686
Aug.	36,626
Sept.	33,137
Oct.	30,586
Nov.	28,614
Dec.	26,600

Sources: *Mitteilungen des Direktoriums der Oesterreichischen Nationalbank,* Nr.1/1932, 16, and Nr.1/1933, 14.

posit currency ratio worked then in the same direction, putting downward pressure on this ratio. Most of this decline occurred between May and July 1931.

For the reserve ratio, we do not have the same amount of indirect evidence. As far as deposits are concerned, everything that has been said for the D/C ratio applies also for the D/R ratio. The reserves of the banking sector consisted of three basic components: vault cash, deposits at other banks, and deposits at the central bank. Since the interbank deposits cancel out for the aggregated banking sector, only cash and deposits at the ANB are relevant. Monthly data on demand deposits at the ANB are available, and as Table 6.8 shows,

Table 6.8. *Deposits at the Austrian National Bank in 1931, monthly (in million schillings)*

Month	Deposits at ANB
December 1930	92.7
January 1931	111.1
February	82.7
March	66.4
April	64.1
May	142.2
June	180.4
July	94.4
August	121.1
September	74.5
October	90.8
November	140.1
December	128.1

Sources: *Mitteilungen des Direktoriums der Oesterreichischen Nationalbank*, various issues.

those assets of the commercial banks more than doubled during May 1931, increased further in June, and showed large fluctuations during the following months.[18] Finally, in December, they were 53 percent above their April and about 38 percent above their December 1930 level.

For vault cash, no monthly data are available. Our estimates for December 1930 and December 1931 suggest a drop of about 13 percent, or about 9.3 million schillings. This small decline was more than offset by the increase in the banks' balances at the ANB. The reserve ratio then declined for both definitions of money, at an annual rate of 60 percent for M1 and at a rate of 46 percent for M2.

The fluctuations in the banks' balances at the central bank suggest, however, that the reserve ratio did not show the same continuous decline as the currency ratio, reflecting the fact that it is more difficult for banks to strengthen their liquidity during a financial crisis than it is for the public. The banks were, nevertheless, most instrumental for the large declines in the money stock, since bank lending was one of the sources of potential increases in M1 and M2. The close relationship between loans and money, especially for M1, was

[18] They showed also a very strong weekly pattern, reaching their lowest levels at the last day of the month, when the demand for currency was at its peak.

owing to the fact that the Austrian banks' assets were largely "current account loans," a combination between a credit line and a demand deposit. These loans were typically given to businesses and served them as their sources of financing everyday business. Compensating balances were then held in the form of "current account" deposits. Any changes in the amount of loans extended to the businesses would then lead to changes in the volume of deposits and create a high correlation between loans and especially M1.[19] Historic accounts report that banks became very restrictive in their lending policy during 1931 (and afterward), so that even low-risk customers could hardly find banks willing to lend them money. The Viennese business newspaper, *Wiener Börsen-Kurier,* reports on August 17, 1931 (2), that the banks had embarked on a "safety first" policy, and that consequently, liquidity and mobility were increased far above the usual levels.

For 1931, we can then conclude that both ratios worked together to create this unprecedented decline in the money stock, and Friedman and Schwartz's conclusion for the United States that "bank failures deserve special attention . . . because they were the mechanism through which the dramatic decline in the stock of money was produced . . ." (1963, 352) finds strong confirmation in Austria during and after the Credit-Anstalt crisis of 1931.

International comparison of money stocks

The depression of the late 1920s and early 1930s, although worldwide in scope, affected different countries to different degrees. The depth as well as the length of the decline showed significant variations from country to country, suggesting that the policies pursued by the respective governments and/or monetary authorities might have affected the depression experiences of those countries.

As Jonung (1981, 287) points out, American economists have generally regarded the American record as the benchmark case. Moreover, the American experience is the one most intensively studied by economists. Comparing the Austrian record to the American one gives us very interesting insights into the common factors and the basic differences. Because of the very different roles these countries

---

[19] For a related discussion of the correlation between bank loans and the money supply in the United States, see Cacy (1976).

have played in the world economy of the 1930s, it will be of interest to find out if, nevertheless, similarities in economic developments can be found. Especially, since the depression in the United States is considered to have been generated domestically and been exported to the rest of the world, something that is not claimed for the Austrian depression, but is frequently claimed for the Austrian financial crisis.

A country much more similar to Austria in size and economic importance was Sweden. Both nations were small open economies and thus subject to foreign developments. Nevertheless, the character of the depression in these two countries was very different, so different indeed that Sweden never considered its business downturn of the early 1930s as the Great Depression (Jonung 1981). A comparison of these two economies could then reveal possible impacts of different policy approaches.[20] Germany seems to be interesting for a comparison with Austria for two very different reasons. First of all, there is wide-ranging evidence, anecdotal as well as empirical, that German economic developments had considerable effects on the Austrian economy (large country–small country case) and second, the banking systems of these two countries were very similar.

In this section we want to concentrate only on the similarities and differences in the monetary experiences of these countries. A comparison of the development of the money stocks (M2) in the four countries is shown in Table 6.9. It is immediately obvious that, while Austria, Germany, and the United States suffered very large reductions in their respective money stocks, Sweden did not have the same record (and even had some slight increases).

The American money stock declined from 1929 to 1933 by about 33 percent and then recovered until 1937 to about 97 percent of its 1929 level. The German monetary aggregate started its decline in 1930 and leveled out at about 32 percent below its 1929 level and started to recover from mid- to end 1933 on.[21] The available evidence suggests that it had recovered to its predepression level by 1937. The Austrian money stock shows a quite different picture. M2

---

[20] But differences in the institutional setting, in the historic background, etc., cannot be disregarded when we try to make any comparisons.

[21] As James (1984, 71) reports, the monetary contraction started in June 1930 led within twelve months to a decline by 17 percent.

Table 6.9. *International comparison of money stocks (1929=100)*

Year	Austria	U.S.	Germany	Sweden
1929	100	100	100	100
1930	103	98	93	104
1931	83	91	76	104
1932	76	76	70	103
1933	75	67	68	104
1934	73	72	73	106
1935	76	83	74	108
1936	75	92	78	112
1937	na	97	84	122

Sources: Austria: author's own estimates.
U.S.: Jonung 1981.
Germany: Saint-Etienne 1984.
Sweden: Jonung 1981.

increased slightly during 1930 and started its decline only in May 1931. Although its decline was not as deep as in the United States or Germany, it was more prolonged. Actually, no recovery could be detected through 1936, while the United States and Germany had regained 97 and 84 percent of their 1929 levels. In particular the strong expansion occurring in the United States in 1935 and 1936 was not present in Austria. In contrast, the money stock in Sweden had never really declined and showed in 1936 and 1937 very considerable growth (bringing it to 21 percent above the 1929 level).

While in the United States the money stock started to decline from February 1929 on, in Germany from June 1930 on and in Sweden from July 1930 on, in Austria we could not find any indication of a consistent fall before May 1931.[22]

More information about the underlying reasons for the different movements of the money stocks in these countries can be gained from an analysis of the two ratios: the currency ratio and the reserve ratio (Table 6.10).

The currency ratio exhibited a very different behavior in Sweden

[22] Except for a short decline in fall 1929 due to withdrawals caused either by the stock market boom in the United States, or the political riots in Austria, or the rumors about the illiquidity of the Boden-Credit-Anstalt (or any combination of the three). M1 had declined during 1930 by about 2.4 percent due to declines in current accounts, but those were more than offset by increases in savings deposits, leading to a rise in M2.

Table 6.10. *International comparison of currency–money and reserves–deposit ratios*

Year	Austria	U.S.	Germany	Sweden
Currency–money ratio (in percentages)				
1929	18.8	8.4	24.1	11.8
1930	18.6	8.2	23.9	11.9
1931	25.2	9.6	31.7	11.9
1932	21.6	14.0	29.7	11.8
1933	22.4	16.3	30.0	12.0
1934	22.6	13.8	29.0	12.8
1935	21.6	12.5	na	14.2
1936	21.9	12.1	na	15.7
Reserves–deposit ratio (in percentages)				
1929	4.2	7.7	1.5	1.8
1930	4.0	7.8	1.6	1.8
1931	6.4	8.5	2.0	1.8
1932	8.8	9.7	1.9	3.6
1933	7.3	12.2	2.1	6.7
1934	8.8	15.7	1.7	9.4
1935	11.6	5.6	na	8.4
1936	10.2	17.8	na	8.4

Sources: Austria: author's own estimates.
U.S.: Jonung 1981.
Germany: James 1984.
Sweden: Jonung 1981.

from that in the other countries in our sample.[23] Although none of the countries showed any significant changes in the currency ratio between 1929 and 1930, with Austria, Germany and the United States, each experiencing declines of 0.2 of a percentage point, and Sweden a rise by 0.1 of a percentage point, in 1931 the situation changed dramatically. The currency ratios of the three countries that suffered banking crises during that year, Austria, Germany, and the United States, increased between 1.4 and 7.8 percentage points or showed growth rates between 15.8 and 30.4 percent. The United States had the smallest growth rate, while the Austrian and the German currency ratios were almost equally affected (30.4 and 28.2

[23] In order to make an international comparison easier, we use here the ratio of currency to the money stock and not the ratio of currency to deposits.

percent). Sweden, on the other hand, without any runs on its banks, did not show any changes at all. It is then obvious that these jumps in the currency holdings of the public exerted downward pressure on the respective money stocks. For the United States, this run for high-powered money would have reduced the money stock between June 1930 and September 1931 by about 10.6 percent, for Austria during 1931 by more than 25 percent.

These developments provide strong support for Jonung's (1981, 297) claim that the constancy in the currency ratio in Sweden can be explained by a strong public confidence in the solvency of the Swedish commercial banking system, which prevented any runs on Swedish banks and resulted in the absence of any bank defaults or payment suspensions in Sweden during the 1930s. That the Austrian, the German, and the American public did not have the same amount of confidence is well known. All three countries fell victims to bank runs. In Germany and in Austria, these runs were basically limited to one single year, 1931, but the United States had a multitude of financial failures spread out between late 1930 and early 1933. This difference in the occurrence of the banking failures is reflected in the behavior of the respective currency ratios in 1932. Not only did the United States ratio keep on increasing, but its largest jump occurred in 1932, namely from 9.6 to 14 percent. Both of the other countries had significant reductions in the currency holdings of the public, reflecting increasing confidence on part of the depositors. The further occurrence of bank failures in early 1933 in the United States resulted in another year of increased relative currency holdings, with the C/M ratio reaching its highest level (16.3 percent) for the 1929 to 1937 period. Germany remained basically unchanged, since it had successfully finished its restructuring of the banking sector, while Austria showed some additional increases in currency holdings that might be related to the fact that two of the remaining large banks (Niederösterreichische Escompte-Gesellschaft and Wiener Bank-Verein) had to be reorganized with government help after suffering heavy losses during the Great Depression.

In 1934, the Swedish public started to increase its currency holdings, but these increases were unrelated to the monetary chaos of the 1930s (Jonung 1981, 297). The declines in the German and in the American ratios reflect the tendency toward more normal conditions, while in Austria it took another year until the currency ratio showed a considerable drop.[24]

The changes in the reserve holdings of the banks were not less dramatic, although they show a very different pattern, over time as well as from country to country. The Austrian, Swedish, and American banks' behavior shows considerable changes during the 1929 to 1936 period, and especially the latter two confirm Cagan's (1965, 30) view that the banks' reserve ratio adjustments tend to lag relative to the currency ratio, or as Schwartz (1981, 29) sums up historical evidence on banking crises as "a uniform story of a shift from deposits to currency by the public once the economy is engulfed in panic and of a belated attempt by banks to increase reserves relative to their deposits once the panic subsided."[25]

In the case of Germany it is remarkable that in spite of the German banking crisis, the reserve holdings were only increased from 1.6 to 2 percent of the deposits, an initial ratio already considerably lower than in the United States or Austria,[26] and stayed at this level through 1934, while Sweden, for instance, which used to have about the same low degree of reserve holdings, increased its ratio even without a banking crisis. Thus, while the banks in Austria, the United States, and Sweden became increasingly more cautious and built up their reserves, in order to be able to prevent further runs, German banks did not see any reason to do so.[27]

The behavior of the monetary base reflects very different developments in these four countries. While Sweden and the United States expanded their issues of high-powered money from 1930 to 1936, the Austrian as well as the German central banks exhibited very contrasting behavior. Austria, as we recall, expanded its mon-

[24] Only after the final stage of the reorganization of the Austrian banking sector, after the merger of the Credit-Anstalt with the Wiener Bank-Verein.

[25] This might not happen voluntarily but is owing to the fact that large conversions of deposits into cash will reduce the banks' reserves and deposits first quite equally, and only later will banks be able to call in some of their loans and thus to increase their reserve ratios.

[26] This is sometimes attributed to the banks' reliance on a very liberal discounting policy of the German Reichsbank (see, e.g., McGouldrick 1984).

[27] This might also be related to the fact that Germany – fast and efficient as its reputation claims – had finished the restructuring of its banks by spring 1932 (see Born 1977, 499), while Austria had not done so until mid-1934 and the United States until spring of 1933.

etary base in 1931 by 10.1 percent, as a reaction to the liquidity needs of the troubled financial intermediaries. In 1932, however, after a change in leadership at the National Bank, a change in policy followed, which resulted in the first and the largest drop in the monetary base during the interwar period: a reduction by 13.8 percent.[28] Another deflationary reduction in the volume of base money, this time by only 3 percent followed in 1933.

In Germany, high-powered money growth had virtually stagnated in 1930, basically because of large foreign withdrawals following the elections in September 1930, which brought large gains to the National Socialist Party and a defeat for the chancellor.[29] Similar to Austria, the banking crisis of spring 1931 resulted in increased amounts of base money, and similarities can be found again in 1932 and 1933, when both countries' monetary bases shrank (just as their money stocks did). Although both countries showed moderate increases in their endowments of base money during 1934, their money stocks developed differently, because of different behavior of their respective banking sectors.[30] Thus, one can expand Jonung's (1981, 297) conclusion that in both countries, Sweden and the United States, the expansion of the total amount of base money after 1933 was closely linked to the rise in the volume of base-money reserves held by the commercial banking system, to include Austria, as well.

The importance of bank failures on the behavior of the money stock was, therefore, an international phenomenon, as seen in a comparison of countries as diverse as the United States, Germany, Sweden, and Austria. With reference to countries without such banking failures, we have ascertained that the money stock in Austria (or in any of the countries with banking crises) would not have fallen by any comparable amount had it not been for difficulties of the banking system and the subsequent failure of the authorities to arrest them in time. The bank failures and panics were highly instrumental in bringing about the money supply shocks from which these countries suffered.

[28] We have to recall, however, the caveat about the ANB's power to influence the monetary base in interwar Austria.
[29] Considering the fact that, around the end of the year, high-powered money was usually higher because of seasonal factors, it had actually declined in 1930.
[30] See the above discussion on the reserve ratios.

The demand for money

The money market is a critical component of virtually all theories that explain the evolution of aggregate economic activity. Consequently, an analysis of the Great Depression has to pay due attention to this subject, since its accurate understanding is crucial for the evaluation of the monetary policies of that period. The previous section dealt with the supply side of the money market, while this section will focus on the issues on its demand side. A thorough insight into both of these aspects will then allow us to draw out how – through the interplay of money supply and money demand – economic activity in interwar Austria was influenced.

The focus of this section will then be on the choice of the variables that explain the movements in the estimated monetary aggregates and the empirical estimation of their respective importance in Austria during the interwar period. Since the alleged instability of the relationship between the quantity of money and its explanatory variables (mainly income) played what Klovland (1982) termed a "strategic role" in those views of the Great Depression that tended to stress the ineptitude of monetary policy, some consideration will be given to this subject, too.[31,32]

We estimated traditional simple money demand functions for both monetary aggregates, relating real demand to income and the interest rate. To allow for partial adjustment between the amounts desired and actually held, we added a lagged dependent variable. In order to capture the effects of the financial crisis on money demand, a dummy variable was added for the years 1931 and thereafter.

As the results in Table 6.11 show, all the coefficients estimated had the signs expected by theory, and the relevant ones were significant at the 10 percent level. The overall fit of the equations was equally satisfactory.

These results give us confidence in our money series. It is encouraging that for Austria during this time of economic upheaval, the standard formulation of money demand performs very well and

---

[31] Stability (and instability) are here used in a statistical sense, i.e., whether the estimated coefficients of the explanatory variables remain constant over time.

[32] The relatively small size of our data sample restricts, however, the extent of our analysis. Quarterly data would be necessary to conduct a more thorough investigation based on state-of-the-art statistical methods.

Table 6.11. *Money demand in Austria, 1923–1936, with adjustment for financial-crisis effects*[a]

Independent variables[b]	Dependent variable[b]			
	M1	M2	M1	M2
Constant	− .9697	.2930	−1.5765[c]	.4402
	(−1.7922)	(.4911)	(−2.7827)	(.4858)
Income	.3958[c]	.9026[c]	.2161	.9561[c]
	(1.8593)	(3.5670)	(1.0468)	(2.6840)
Interest Rate	− .0824[c]	− .1789[c]	− .0956[c]	− .1793[c]
	(−2.4623)	(−6.3269)	(−3.2339)	(−5.9910)
Lagged Money	.5360[c]	.3776[c]	.5732[c]	.3620[c]
	(6.2555)	(3.9575)	(7.5249)	(2.9841)
Dummy	− .2418[c]	− .0580	− .2493[c]	− .0520
	(−14.8438)	(−1.7046)	(−17.1419)	(−1.1903)
Inflation	—	—	−.3447[c]	.0555
	—	—	(−1.8692)	(.2319)
R-square	.994	.994	.997	.995
R-square (adjusted)	.991	.991	.994	.991
SER	.031	.028	.027	.030
RHO	− .664	− .623	− .667	− .666

[a] t-values in parentheses.
[b] In logarithmic form (except the inflation variable).
[c] Significant at the 10 percent level.

produces results comparable to other countries during more "normal" time periods.

Up to this point we can claim that our results throw light on three issues of crucial importance in assessing the role of money in the economy of interwar Austria. In particular:

1. The predictability of the demand-for-money function: Our previous discussion and in particular the goodness of fit of the functions that were estimated show that this function was predictable enough for the time period under consideration (at least for the broad total).[33]

2. The role of interest rates: The vast majority of our equations show that the rate of interest played a crucial role for money demand, leaving us with no doubt that the rate of interest influenced

[33] Since our sample was relatively small, we could not perform any out-of-sample predictions.

the demand for money in Austria, just as it did in most other countries.

3. The role of the banking crisis on aggregate money demand: The narrow total witnessed a considerable reduction in demand, as the deterioration of the quality of those deposits – that is, the increase in the perceived risk made them inferior assets to hold. This effect apparently overpowered any increases in desired money holdings caused by increased uncertainty. For the broader total, we could not detect any lasting effects emanating from the crisis.

The results are precise enough to bear the weight of preliminary but firm conclusions about money demand in the Austrian interwar economy. The standard errors of the parameter estimates (as well as of the equations) are reasonably small, allowing us to determine the parameter values quite precisely. The relatively simple textbook money demand function (with adjustment for the crisis) explains the behavior of the Austrian monetary sector very well.

The first two issues in the theory of the demand for money as identified by Johnson (1962) – the relevant definition of the money aggregate and the choice of variables explaining movements in this aggregate – have been resolved satisfactorily for the interwar period in Austria and the long disputed issue of the interest elasticity has been answered, too. So, we can now turn to the third problem, the stability of the functional relationship. Stability in this context requires, as Spinelli puts it, "that the values of the estimated parameters do not shift in any erratic fashion in the long run" (1980, 87).

The period of the Great Depression has been studied very carefully concerning the question of stability of the demand for money,[34] as the "alleged instability of the relationship between the quantity of money and income in these years played a strategic role in the view that tended to stress the ineptitude of monetary policy" (Klovland 1982, 252), while the

economists associated with the monetarists or "quantity theory school" have argued that the ineffectiveness of monetary policy during the Great Depression was in fact the result of the [United States] Federal Reserve's failure to use its powers to reverse or halt the contraction that was occurring in the supply of money rather than the consequence of any breakdown or instability in the functional relationship between money and income (Gandolfi 1974, 970).[35]

[34] Gandolfi (1974), Khan (1974), Klovland (1982).
[35] Khan, Gandolfi, as well as Klovland, the first two for the United States, and the

As for money demand in Austria during the interwar period, several causes might have resulted in an instability of the relationships estimated above. For one, the institutional changes following the unprecedented banking crisis might have led to changes in the role of the commercial banks, as well as in the roles of certain assets. Furthermore, the introduction of exchange controls, restricting the movements of financial assets between Austria and the other countries, could have altered the preferences of the Austrians between holding their assets in domestic or in foreign money balances. Finally, the omission of a variable measuring the quality of deposits, since the banking problems might have increased the risk of holding bank deposits, and therefore, since they were noninferior assets, reduced the demand for them. In regard to estimation, we introduced a dummy variable to detect any shifts in the relationship after the outbreak of the banking crisis of 1931. For the time period 1931 to 1936, we recall, the results for M1 did show a large decline in demand, by about 24 percent below the corresponding level before the crisis (holding all the other variables constant). For the broader total, however, we could not detect such persistent changes in behavior. The inclusion of this dummy variable captures the overall shift in the relationship – that is, a change in the intercept, but not changes in the parameters themselves, the slope coefficients.

Was money demand during the interwar period in Austria unstable and consequently unpredictable for policymakers? In order to answer this question we performed stability tests on both aggregates. We used the so-called "forward and backward cusum of squares test," as developed by Brown and Durbin (1968).[36] By using a significance level of 5 percent, the analysis of the results for M2 – the money stock we considered to be more relevant for the Austrian institutional framework – did not reveal indications for any long-run instabilities.[37] For M1, however, we found some indication

latter for Norway, concluded that there was no detectable significant instability in the respective money demand relationships during the 1930s, when all relevant variables had been included.

[36] This test is based on an examination of the residuals of the relationship. In essence it tests whether the squared one period prediction error from a set of recursive regressions cumulate at an approximately constant rate. We dropped the dummy variable for the after crisis period from the equation.

[37] As an alternative, we analyzed the data for any impact effects of the 1931 crisis, and found the dummy variable to be significant for M2, indicating a 10 percent

of a change in the fundamental relationship.[38] However, to conclude
from this evidence that the demand for M1 was unstable would be
premature. The specification used does not account for possible
changes in the quality of deposits, especially current account deposits, and could therefore be biased. The inventory models of
money demand "imply that the cost of converting interest-earning
assets into money is a significant determinant of the fraction of
income held as cash balances" (Higgins 1978, 25), and M1 and its
behavior conform to those inventory (and transactions) models. The
banking crisis of 1931 changed the cost of conversion of deposits
into high-powered money and rendered the assumption of constant
cost unrealistic, since the perceived risk of not being able to convert
increased, and therefore, the value of deposits declined. Lothian
(1976, 56) states in this context that "under some circumstances the
omission of these variables (e.g., quality of deposits) can have a
serious effect on the stability of conventional deposit-inclusive definitions of money. . . ." His solution to this problem would then be
to return to a definition of money that is of "constant quality over
time and space" (ibid.), namely high-powered money.[39] Our dummy
variable for the postcrisis period is only a very rough proxy for the
reduced quality of deposits, since it assumes a one period shift in
quality, instead of gradual changes that a more direct measure could
pick up.

We can conclude that our preliminary results do not indicate any
consistent instability in the demand for M2, while for M1 no firm
conclusions can be drawn without explicit adjustment for changes
in quality of deposits. The demand for the broad and more relevant
monetary aggregate did not show permanent changes in the coefficients reaching beyond the immediate crisis period, and therefore
instability in the demand for real balances cannot be taken as an
argument against the use of monetary policy in interwar Austria.[40]

impact decline in money demand caused by the banking problems, an effect
that dissipated after 1931.

[38] We have to keep in mind, however, that the small sample size does not allow
us to make any firm conclusions, and precludes the use of more rigorous methods.

[39] Klovland (1982), in his study of money demand in interwar Norway, used an
alternative approach to this problem and found that his measures of quality of
deposits were significant, and their inclusion resulted in stable money demand
functions for the interwar period.

[40] This conclusion does not imply, however, that expansionary monetary policy

Table 6.12. *Money demand in Austria, disaggregated, 1923-36*[a]

| Independent variables[b] | Dependent variable[b] | | | |
	Currency	Checking accounts	Current accounts	Savings accounts
Constant	−1.2099	.4151	−1.8775	1.0714
	(−1.6218)	(.2102)	(−1.5493)	(.8194)
Income	1.2284[c]	1.3931[c]	.1567	1.3073[c]
	(4.6955)	(2.1047)	(.3667)	(3.1514)
Interest rate	.0410	− .2100	− .0583	− .3701[c]
	(.7941)	(−1.6959)	(− .7075)	(−4.2485)
Lagged dependent	.0198	.2969	.5775[c]	.4005[c]
	(.1047)	(1.6498)	(3.9206)	(4.7778)
Dummy	.1793[c]	− .2405[c]	− .3677[c]	.1087
	(2.6799)	(−2.7179)	(−10.4088)	(1.1852)
R-square	.946	.940	.987	.992
R-square (adjusted)	.918	.910	.979	.988
SER	.046	.097	.072	.065
RHO	—	—	.641	—
DW	2.765	1.669	—	1.776

[a] t-values in parentheses.
[b] In logarithmic form.
[c] Significant at the 10 percent level.

Disaggregated demand functions

In order to get a clearer picture of the underlying relationships, we disaggregated the money stock into its components. While our monetary aggregates are simple summations of different types of assets with equal weights attached to all of them, implicitly assuming that they all had the same degree of "moneyness," some of our results in the previous section suggested the desirability of further disaggregation, and of separate estimation of demand functions for those components of the money definitions: currency, checking accounts, current accounts, and savings accounts.

Table 6.12 shows the results for the log linear demand functions for currency, checking accounts, current accounts, and savings accounts for the specification including lagged adjustment and a

with a simultaneous adherence to the gold exchange standard might have been a more successful policy alternative (see also chapters 4 and 7).

dummy for the after-crisis period.[41] The explanatory power of the disaggregated demand functions is comparable to that of the aggregates. Especially the functions for the larger components of money, namely current and savings accounts, show the same goodness of fit as the aggregated functions. The respective coefficients allow us to capture the different roles these monetary assets played in the portfolios of the Austrian public and we analyze the different reaction patterns to changes in underlying economic conditions.

We expected the banking crisis to exert a significant influence on the public's demand for currency. Our analysis of the overall money supply showed a very large drop in the deposit-currency ratio during 1931, reflecting the scramble for liquidity on the part of the public after the events of May 1931. Under normal economic conditions, at any moment in time the value of one schilling in deposits should be equal to the value of one schilling in cash. A banking crisis, with its concurrent deterioration in the level of confidence in the banking sector, however, can lead to a change in the exchange value of deposits for currency in favor of currency. Deposits are no longer perfect substitutes for cash,[42] and notes and coins are traded at a premium, as people place a higher value on them than on their – nominally – equivalent deposits. Under these circumstances we would expect the demand for currency to take a quantum leap upward (ceteris paribus).

The results indicate very clearly that this scramble for liquidity did take place. They suggest that the public increased its demand for currency over the years following the crisis, on average by about 18 to 20 percent, as compared to the precrisis period (ceteris paribus).[43]

The largest impact of the financial crisis was felt on the demand for current account deposits, the working balances of businesses. Their level after 1931 was about 37 percent below the precrisis level

---

[41] These disaggregated series are not corrected for interbank deposits, since no breakdown into these components was available.
[42] In "normal" times they must be superior to cash, otherwise they would not constitute such a large fraction of real cash balances held.
[43] The fact that – because of widespread fear of devaluation – many Austrians considered foreign currency an even better substitute for deposits than Austrian schillings might bias our results somewhat. Currency holdings increased by more than suggested here as people converted their deposits first into schillings and then those schilling holdings into dollar or pound notes.

for the same interest rate–income combinations. Historic accounts of the 1930s in Austria stress the fact that companies – even financially sound and well managed ones – were faced with a considerable credit shortage.[44] Since the holdings of current accounts were largely based on current account loans extended to private businesses, the large decline in these deposits also reflected the very restrictive and cautious business policy of the banking sector after the traumatic experiences of 1931. If, consequently, the amount of current account deposits was – indirectly – more supply determined than demand determined, this should be reflected in the other coefficients of the demand function. We would expect it to be unresponsive to the "normal" influences on money demand – that is, the amount of transactions or the level of interest rates – and moreover, the speed of adjustment from desired to actual holdings of deposits should be low, since these institutional constraints did not allow for speedy return to equilibrium.

The results show that neither the income nor the interest rate variables have coefficients significantly different from zero. Lagged adjustment of current account holdings turns out to be slower than for any one of the other components of money. Only about 42 percent of the gap between actual and desired holdings are closed within 12 months' time, as compared to full adjustment in currency and checking deposits and somewhat speedier adjustment for the volume of savings (60 percent). These results suggest that those economic observers of the 1930s who attached great importance to the role of restrictive business policies – on the part of the banking sector – in accounting for the delay in the recovery of the Austrian economy were right. It seems unreasonable to accept a view that utility (profit) maximizing businesses would not try to adjust their portfolios to changes in income (transactions), yields, and opportunity cost, if they were free to do so. During the 1930s in Austria, the banks' policies prevented them from doing so.

The most interesting feature of the demand function for savings is the insignificance of the postcrisis dummy. No shift in the inter-

[44] A report of the Austrian Institute for Business Cycle Research (OIfK) of July 1938 (140) points to the fact that in the aftermath of the banking crisis the money market was controlled by the private banks, and especially by the largest one of them, the Creditanstalt-Bankverein, and that loans to industries were either completely unavailable or only available at very high interest rates.

cept term could be detected after the 1931 crisis. This result gives strong support to the view that the crisis did not affect savings deposits in the same way as it affected current account deposits, checking deposits, or currency. Since the overwhelming majority of savings deposits were liabilities of the savings banks to the ultimate wealth holders, the ability of these financial institutions to survive the crisis without a single default might be reflected in this lack of a significant shift after 1931. This type of financial intermediary managed to keep the confidence of the public, and so to preserve its volume of savings liabilities.[45]

At the same time, the lack of alternative investment possibilities for the lower income people – the majority of the holders of savings deposits – might influence our results. Nevertheless, it is surprising that we could detect such an unusually strong negative interest elasticity. We have, however, some doubts about assigning any causality to this observed correlation. Investigation of the data reveals that it was the total disappearance of savings during the hyperinflation of the early 1920s[46] that caused the holdings of savings accounts to show a consistent upward trend, only interrupted in 1931. This development, then, was mainly owing to previous events and not necessarily related to changes in interest rates.

The analysis of the disaggregated functions revealed very clearly the underlying reasons for the differences in the two monetary aggregates. It showed further the different roles these components of the money stock played and the resulting differences in their reactions to changes in the main variables that influence the demand for money. The expected increase in the demand for the most liquid of all assets, namely currency, was fully confirmed by the data, as was the reduced attractiveness of certain deposits. The signs of all other coefficients were as the theory led us to expect, and they were overwhelmingly significant.

---

[45] In the very first weeks after the outbreak of the CA crisis, savings banks witnessed even increased inflows, i.e. money was diverted from commercial bank accounts toward savings banks.

[46] As Schmidt (1925, 28) reports, the real volume of savings deposits was in June 1922 – just before the climax of the hyperinflation – down to about 0.2 percent of its 1913 (prewar) level and estimates it for September 1922 at about 0.07 percent, i.e. 2 million gold crowns compared to 3 billion in December 1913. By the end of 1930, it had recovered to about 37.2 percent of the 1913 level (*Wiener Börsen-Kurier*, January 5, 1931, 4).

Table 6.13. *Gross National Product (in million schillings) and the income velocity of money*

Year	GNP	V1	V2
1924	9,257	3.954	3.638
1925	10,296	3.810	3.248
1926	10,283	3.287	2.640
1927	11,110	3.140	2.429
1928	11,678	3.088	2.292
1929	12,087	3.051	2.190
1930	11,560	2.938	2.018
1931	10,360	3.011	1.971
1932	9,550	3.499	2.124
1933	9,020	3.731	2.115
1934	8,980	3.940	2.149
1935	9,140	4.145	2.176
1936	9,319	4.274	2.187

Sources: GNP: Kausel et al. 1965.
Money: Author's own estimates.

The income-velocity of money

How then was velocity, money's "second dimension" (Higgins 1978), affected by these developments?

In Table 6.13 we report Gross National Product and the income velocities for both the narrow (V1) and the broad money stock (V2).[47]

Two years, 1931 and 1932, deserve special attention. Empirical evidence for other countries, like the United States, Canada, and Sweden,[48] showed that the income velocity of money during the depression moved as a rule in the same direction as the changes in the money stock – that is, movements in velocity did not offset the effects of the changes in the money stock. As this behavior was characteristic for most of the American business cycles of the last century, Friedman and Schwartz (1963, 302) concluded that "ve-

[47] Since GNP is a flow item, measured over the course of one calendar year, but the money stock constitutes a stock item, measured on the last day of the respective years, we adjusted the monetary data by taking averages between two adjacent time periods. Since most of our previous analysis suggested that M2 was the more appropriate measure of the money stock, we will concentrate here on the velocity of this aggregate.

[48] See Friedman and Schwartz (1963), and Jonung (1981).

locity tends to rise during the expansion phase of a cycle and to fall during the contraction phase." Although for 1930 the Austrian evidence supports this conclusion, it is not so for 1931 and 1932. In those years of declining business activity, velocity in Austria first stagnated (1931) and then made a considerable upward jump (by 7.5 percent in 1932).

In order to explain this apparently odd behavior, we have to identify the forces that affected velocity. For one, the banking crisis, with its effect on the attractiveness of deposits, reduced the demand for the sum of currency and deposits, for currency – although an alternative to deposits – was not a perfect one. Second, currency substitution reduced the demand for Austrian schillings, as people demanded and hoarded foreign currency notes.[49] And, third, uncertainty about the course of the economy increased the demand for money relative to income.

In 1931, then, the overall effect of the first two forces just about canceled out the forces emanating from increased uncertainty. In 1932 they were stronger than the third force, because uncertainty about the future course of the economy was reduced and expectations consolidated. But the effects of the banking and currency crisis persisted. The strongly deflationary business policies of the banks after the 1931 experience reduced the public's money holdings below what they desired, and the public reacted with an increased turnover of the existing money stock. The amount of money fell by more than income did, and velocity increased by 7.5 percent, bouncing back to its precrisis level.[50]

While the United States witnessed a 29 percent decline in velocity

---

[49] We recall, e.g., that the Bank of England had to send pound notes to Austria (in May 1931) in order to enable the Austrian National Bank to meet the increased demand for British currency (Kernbauer 1981b, 22). At the same time the Swiss National Bank had to send considerable quantities of Swiss francs to the ANB (Weber 1980, 111). Further, we know that foreign notes were sold at a premium compared to other forms of foreign assets and that the ANB allocated only certain percentages of the foreign notes demanded. Hurst (1932, 644–45) pointed out in this context that "much of the fleeing capital did not seek banks but was hoarded in whatever currency was thought to be safe." Gresham's Law suggests that foreign currency would not actually be used for transactions, since its real value exceeded its official exchange value.

[50] This is consistent with our finding that the speed of adjustment of current account deposits was very low, as the supply of current account deposits was controlled by the banks through their power to allocate current account loans.

between 1929 and 1933, and Canada even a 41 percent drop (Friedman and Schwartz 1963, 352), Austria's income velocity was about equal in both of these years, since an 8 percent decline in 1930, plus no change in 1931, was offset by an almost equal increase in 1932. This apparent discrepancy in the results for these three countries can, however, be resolved.

The difference between Canada's (much larger) decline in velocity and the one witnessed by the United States economy was due to the fact that Canada had not encountered any bank failures that would have reduced the demand for money and would have offset some of the harm they had done to the supply of money. In the United States, on the other hand, the diminished attractiveness of deposits caused by the collapse of banks had reduced the overall demand for currency and deposits. Therefore, the stock of money in Canada did not have to fall by more than 13 percent to create a decline in income by 49 percent (while the respective numbers for the United States were 33 and 53 percent). "The bank failures, by their effect on the demand for money, offset some of the harm they did by their effect on the supply of money" (ibid., 353). The same reasoning can therefore explain why in Austria velocity did not change at all in 1931 and increased in 1932. The banking crisis was of a much larger relative importance for the Austrian economy than it was for the American economy, as the Credit-Anstalt was the dominant bank of interwar Austria. As the banking crisis was of much larger weight in Austria, its effects must have been relatively stronger, reducing money demand more than in the United States, and thus resulting in a complete offset of the increased demand that might have resulted from the great increase in uncertainty, the reduced attractiveness of equity, etc., that occurred as a consequence of the large business downturn. In 1932, the same forces led to an increase in velocity.[51]

Interaction of money supply and money demand

As the preceding analysis showed, the banking and currency crisis of 1931 influenced money supply as well as money demand and, through these effects, economic activity. The results support the

[51] The fear of inflation and of currency depreciation might have added to these effects, increasing velocity above what it would have been otherwise.

conclusion that the money stock fell because of a supply shock (a shift in the supply curve), rather than only through reduced demand (a shift in the demand curve along the given supply curve). The reductions in the money stock were considerably larger than the impact effects of the crisis on the demand for money. The behavior of the interest rates should then reflect this fact quite clearly.[52]

If our analysis of the interplay of money supply and money demand is correct, we expect to observe an increase in the level of interest rates just after the occurrence of the unanticipated monetary contraction. As liquidity is suddenly reduced, interest rates will have to go up as the public tries to readjust its disturbed portfolio by attempting to replace all kinds of assets by cash.[53] The income effect and the price anticipation effect should, at some (not exactly specified) later point in time, reduce the level of interest rates from its new peak (back to or even below the initial rate). According to Temin's (1976, 103) review of the literature this "peak of the rise in interest rates following a fall in the supply of money (or the rate of change of this supply) should be reached in the first quarter following the change in the supply of money," and this effect on the interest rate "should be easily apparent if the reduction had any important macroeconomic impact" (ibid., 126). A strong effect is crucial since "we want to know not simply if the supply of money fell, but if it fell enough to explain a major movement of income" (ibid., 99).

The behavior of some of the key interest rates before, during, and just after the financial crisis of 1931 is shown in Figure 6.5. A strong upward trend is apparent in all the series.[54] This rise is especially

[52] The interest rates represent the price of credit and not of money per se, the price of money being the inverse of the price level. Nevertheless, the amount of money will affect the level of the interest rates.

[53] We assume implicitly that the first effect of the reduced money stock is not on prices.

[54] Ideally we would need the rates on very "moneylike" assets, i.e. with low risk, fixed yields, and short time to maturity. We cannot fulfill all of these requirements simultaneously. However, most of the rates available show a very similar pattern. A different behavior can be observed for the League of Nations bond due in 1943, as its yield actually declined in Vienna. This was due to the fact that it was dollar denominated and had an international guarantee, making it very attractive as a secondary liquidity reserve, as well as a hedge against the expected depreciation of the currency and the financial weakness of the Austrian state.

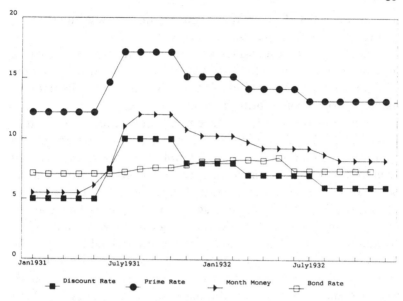

Figure 6.5. Interest rates in Austria, 1931–2 (monthly, in percent).

pronounced for the short rates, while the bond yields rise much more slowly (but more steadily). These figures represent nominal interest rates – that is, they include the anticipated rates of price change. This might explain some of the discrepancy between the short rates and the rates for the long-term bonds. As we have pointed out repeatedly, inflationary fears, based on the behavior of domestic credit and the monetary base, were very strong in mid-1931, and those fears might be reflected in short-run interest rates. The behavior of the interest rates provides us then with evidence for unexpected monetary stringency in 1931.[55] The downward trend in

[55] Schwartz (1981) uses the inverse of the United States wholesale price index as a measure of monetary stringency during the Great Depression in the United States, and finds that every relevant monetary event is reflected in this ratio. For Austria, however, there are problems in replicating those results. For one, it constituted a small open economy, so that the prices for all traded goods should have been determined exogenously. The vast amount of tariffs and import restrictions might have muted this link. But even the prices of nontraded goods were subject to regulations and rigidities that broke the link to money. Additionally, the reported price series do not reflect the de facto devaluation of the currency from September 1931 on, and would have to be adjusted for the gold value of the currency.

interest rates that had prevailed since mid-1929 was interrupted, and this interruption was quite marked.[56]

Temin (1976, 127) identifies another avenue through which "a decrease in the supply of money would have affected the economy without leaving traces behind of the sort we have been discussing," namely through some form of credit rationing.

Although we do not have direct empirical evidence on this matter – that is, knowledge of specific potential borrowers who were refused loans at any interest rate – there is ample reference in the different economic reports relevant to this fact.[57] The conservative lending policy of the banking sector resulted in sound debtors – as well as not-so-sound ones – being precluded from acquiring financial liabilities at any price. This credit rationing can, however, only affect economic activity if those potential borrowers could not get the required funds from alternative sources. The selling of stocks was only possible for very few and large companies,[58] industrial bonds were basically nonexistent, and foreign sources of money had dried up after 1931 (and were never open to anyone except a small privileged group of debtors). Credit rationing, therefore, seemed to have restricted the overall supplies of money available to corporations as well as individuals, independently of the prevailing market interest rates.

This leads us then to the third and final channel of transmission of financial crises to economic activity, namely the nonmonetary effects, as identified (among others) by Bernanke (1983).

The nonmonetary effects of the crisis

Bernanke (1983) showed for the United States that the reductions in the money supply during the Great Depression were not sufficient to explain all of the subsequent fall in output, and that the financial crisis of 1930 to 1933 also affected the macroeconomy directly by

---

[56] The expected subsequent decline in the interest rates, owing to the other two effects, can also be observed.

[57] We had already mentioned the report of the Austrian Institute for Business Cycle Research that had pointed to the unavailability of loans for all types of industries during the years following the financial crisis.

[58] The relative inactivity of the Viennese stock market rendered this possibility a very theoretic one.

reducing the quality of certain financial services, especially credit intermediation. In his model, the real service performed by the banking sector is the differentiation between good and bad borrowers, and the cost of credit intermediation constitutes the cost of channeling funds from the lenders (savers) to the good borrowers. Efficient and profit-maximizing banks will then try to minimize these cost by using their expertise, by establishing long-term relationships with customers and by offering loan conditions that encourage self-selection on the part of the potential borrowers. Hamilton (1987) argues along the same lines when he stresses the role of the disruption of the real services of intermediation on the part of the financial sector as a consequence of the American banking panic of 1930.

In Austria, the events of 1931 had a distinct impact on credit intermediation. First of all, we have to point out that, the more important the role of the banking sector is in providing businesses with the necessary capital, the larger this effect will be. As for Austria after 1931, there were hardly any alternative ways for firms to raise funds. Direct borrowing in capital markets by large private borrowers without the intermediation of banks was largely nonexistent.[59] This gave the domestic commercial banks an almost monopolistic role in providing business with capital, for long-term investment as well as for daily operations.

As the banks withdrew increasingly from the market for long-term business credits and placed their assets in more liquid forms, disintermediation took place. The *Wiener Börsen-Kurier* (November 16, 1931, 5) observed in this respect a complete change in the Austrian banking business. According to its analysis, following the crisis of 1931, liquidity has replaced rentability as the guiding principle of the banks. One aspect of this change was this fact:

The mortgage institutes are not disposed to grant fresh credits. The credits they are giving very seldom exceed 10,000 schillings, and the interest demanded on first mortgages is 12 percent. Private lenders are more accommodating, but when they lend rather large sums they demand both capital

---

[59] In Austria, the amount of securities held by the public was very small compared to Germany or to the amount of personal savings. Bank deposits were the preferred way to hold wealth, much more so than holding securities (see OIfK 1938, 150).

Table 6.14. *Loan portfolio of the most important Austrian banks (selected years)*

Year	Loans (in million schillings)	Loans/GNP (in percentages)
1924	1,394	15.1
1926	1,867	18.2
1928	2,265	19.4
1930	2,273	19.7
1932	1,149	12.0
1934	829	9.2
1936	682	7.3

Sources: Loans: OIfK 1938, 138; GNP: Kausel et al. 1965.

and interest service be in terms of gold schillings. It also appears that the Central Savings Bank of the Municipality of Vienna no longer accords credits so freely. (*The Economist,* November 14, 1931, 908)[60]

But the savings banks, the Postal Savings Bank, and the credit associations could not replace the commercial banks in this credit intermediation process, especially since they were relatively small and all served a very specific clientele. Table 6.14 shows the extent of disintermediation that took place after the crisis. In 1930, just before the outbreak of the CA crisis, the loan portfolio of the largest Austrian banks amounted to almost 20 percent of Austrian GNP, and then dropped continuously to only 7 percent in 1936. The relative size of bank financing for Austrian business declined in six years by almost two thirds. With it an important intermediate good in the production process became either rationed or more expensive. This decline in the supply of inside money had negative effects on economic activity. Part of the acquired expertise of these banks was lost for the Austrian economy, thus increasing the cost of intermediation and production.

Apart from these disintermediation effects, economic activity was

---

[60] This phenomenon was not limited to Austria, but prevailed in other parts of Europe as well, which is reflected in the following observation of the League of Nations (1931, 306):

There are signs that toward the end of the summer [1931] confidence in the financial stability of Europe had been so shaken that it became increasingly difficult even for first class financial houses and business firms to obtain renewal of short term credits granted by bankers in the financially strongest countries. This was one of the most serious aspects of the financial crisis in August.

Table 6.15. *Austrian foreign trade, 1929–37 (in million schillings)*

Year	Exports	Imports	Balance
1929	2,189	3,263	−1,074
1930	1,851	2,699	− 848
1931	1,291	2,161	− 870
1932	764	1,383	− 619
1933	773	1,149	− 376
1934	857	1,153	− 296
1935	895	1,206	− 311
1936	951	1,249	− 298
1937	1,217	1,454	− 237

Source: OIfK (1946, 19).

also negatively influenced by the combination of exchange controls and the overvalued schilling. "The restrictions on foreign exchange ... caused considerable limitation on trade" reported *The Economist* (October 31, 1931, 807), since "[t]he National Bank is still adhering to the practice of granting only 2 to 3 per cent of the applications for foreign currencies, even where important articles needed from abroad are concerned." At the same time, import tariffs were raised considerably (July 1931), and import quotas and prohibitions were introduced (April 1932). With several trading partners, so-called clearing arrangements were signed, basically requiring balanced trade between the partners. These arrangements restricted volumes of trade, as the exchange of goods was adjusted to the export volume of the less competitive country. The National Bank's adherence to the old exchange rate of the schilling, which no longer corresponded to the market's evaluation of the currency, imposed a tax on exports, and subsidized imports. Starting in mid-1932, private foreign exchange clearing at market prices was increasingly allowed and the official parity successively lost its importance. Table 6.15 shows the development of Austrian foreign trade between 1929 and 1937.

The crisis of the Credit-Anstalt put a heavy burden on the already strained finances of the Austrian state. Its participation in the reconstruction and its guarantees created large additional outlays, at a time of declining revenues due to the cyclical downturn. The government started very early into the crisis with its attempts to put its financial house back in order. In October 1931, parliament passed a law for expenditure control and revenue enhancement. Among other measures, a "crisis tax," a special tax on income and wealth, was introduced, and the gasoline tax was raised. Expenditures for state employees and retirees were drastically curtailed. In July 1932, the merchandise turnover tax was raised. These measures, as important as they might have been for the stability of the expectations concerning the future of the Austrian currency, exerted a rather contractionary effect on economic activity. The large cost of the CA crisis made fiscal policy more contractionary than otherwise necessary.[61]

Unfortunately, we cannot disentangle these nonmonetary effects of the crisis on economic activity from those of the monetary channel.[62] The persistence of the downturn, however, makes it very likely that the nonmonetary channel contributed its share to the conversion of the initial downturn into the protracted depression that kept Austrian economic activity at such consistently low levels through 1937.[63]

[61] Gratz (1949, 287) points out that the Austrian government changed its position concerning active stimulatory fiscal policy three times during the 1930s: in 1933, 1936, and 1937.

[62] Bernanke (1983) did this, by running output equations that included monetary surprises (or price surprises) and measures of disintermediation as independent variables. We attempted to perform a similar analysis for Austria, but the results were not satisfactory. This topic is open to further research once additional data become available.

[63] Real GNP in 1937 had not reached more than 86 percent of its 1929 level, while Germany was back to 117 percent, and the United States to 103 percent.

7. The financial crisis and the lender of last resort

When the market breaks down on occasion, we may need the medicine of a lender of last resort.

—C. P. Kindleberger, 1978

The lender of last resort is as common in European financial history as the deus ex machina in Greek tragedy.

—E. März, 1982

The domestic lender of last resort

One of the key elements of a financial crisis is that "the whole process [could be] arrested at the outset by a timely intervention of some authority [the lender of last resort] that lends freely at a penalty rate or engages in open market operations" (Bordo 1986a, 191).

The basic function of this lender of last resort is to "stand ready to halt a run out of real and financial assets into money, by making more money available" and thus to prevent a situation such that "each participant in the market, in trying to save himself, helps ruin all" (Kindleberger 1978, 161–2), or in other words, "the financial distress of the few must not be permitted to become a financial crisis for all" (Schwartz 1986, 22).

In Austria, in 1931, the crisis was not arrested at the outset, and a run on its banks and on its foreign reserves occurred, in spite of the quick intervention of the Austrian National Bank and the Austrian government. This suggests that the public had some doubts about the dependability of the arrangements and/or that the authorities were "unschooled" in their response to the bank failure.

The lender of last resort (LLR) can be defined very simply as an authority that can and does "expand its note issue and loans at a time when the prudent commercial banker is constraining his" (Humphrey and Keleher 1984, 284). This call for a domestic LLR "arises because of two institutional characteristics, namely fractional reserve banking and the government monopoly of legal tender issuance" (Barth and Keleher 1984, 62).[1] The fact that banks in the contemporary monetary system do not hold 100 percent of their deposits in reserves, but only a small fraction, makes them vulnerable to potential runs by frightened depositors. Since only the monetary authorities are allowed to issue legal tender, only they can meet these abnormal increases in the demand for currency. The role assigned to this LLR can be seen very generally as "a backstop or guarantor to prevent a panic-induced collapse of the fractional-reserve banking system" (Humphrey and Keleher 1984, 277) or, more specifically, as helping to prevent a credit crisis from becoming a monetary crisis – that is, "to prevent credit/debt contraction from producing monetary contraction" (ibid.). Besides stabilizing the money stock the LLR should also manage to prevent disruptions of the credit intermediation and disruptions of the payments system.

Most crucial, the task of the LLR is a macroeconomic one and not a microeconomic one. It does not have to secure the liquidity of an individual institution (especially if this one is insolvent), but the liquidity of the entire economy by "averting contagion, spillover, or domino effects which may adversely affect the stability of the entire monetary system" (ibid., 278). It should, therefore, focus on the rescue of the market but not on the rescue of unsound individual institutions. However, it is recognized that abrupt closure of a bank might have social costs and might lead to a contagious loss of confidence in other banks and that emergency assistance can mitigate or even prevent such effects. Even in the case of an insolvent bank, arguments can be found for last-resort lending if it might provide the supervisory authorities "with the time necessary to make an orderly and efficient disposition of the failed bank without interruption" (Guttentag and Herring 1987, 162). The basic responsibility of the lender of last resort is to ensure the stability of the financial system and the public's confidence in this stability. In order to do so, it should – ideally – fully acknowledge and widely announce its determination to preserve the stability of the system before any crisis occurs, so as to eliminate the incentive for the public to perpetrate a run on the banks if one or more fail because of unsound policies, or as Bagehot (1962, 85) put it, "the public have a right to know

[1]   There are, however, authors who argue against any lender-of-last-resort function (e.g., White 1984).

whether [the central bank] – the holders of ultimate bank reserve – acknowledge this duty, and are ready to perform it."

Nevertheless, should a crisis occur, then Bagehot's well-known principle prescribes "lending freely at a high [penalty] rate" as the feasible approach. Lending freely should ensure that credit is available and should therefore prevent any selling off of bank assets and the consequent fall in the prices of these assets, while the high rate serves the function of (1) rationing scarce reserves among eager borrowers, and (2) ensuring that central bank borrowing is really "last resort" – that is, that all market sources of liquidity have been used before turning to the LLR.

This free lending policy should, however, be restricted to "temporary periods of emergency that may last for only a few days" (Thornton 1939, 286), and should not constitute a continuous departure from restraint of and control over the rate of expansion of the note component of the monetary base.

Who then should perform this function of lender of last resort?

As we stated initially, the monopoly issuer of legal tender is ideally in a position to provide the necessary liquidity to the market in order to avoid crises. Therefore most of the writers argue for the central bank to serve as a LLR. But there are also alternative solutions, as März (1982, 187) points out so vividly:

The lender of last resort is a sort of protean being who appears in strikingly different guises – in the shape of the central bank of a country, or as a government agency like the treasury, sometimes as a consortium of banks, and not infrequently as an international body or group of bodies.

As mentioned in März's quote, the LLR is not necessarily a public authority, as the market could theoretically also take care of that role. As Claassen (1985) shows, however, imperfect information, the size of the troubled institution, and the potential free rider problem might prevent market solutions and therefore require, in his view, government intervention. Kindleberger (1978), pointing to the public good character of financial stability, claims that the private market is unable to provide this good, while Schwartz (1986) does not share his conclusions.

Before we turn to the Austrian situation in 1931, one specific point needs further consideration. We had pointed out that the LLR objectives should be widely announced to the public before a crisis occurs or that it should be well understood that the conversion of deposits into currency will be assured. Although this seems to be a necessary condition to prevent runs, it has to be recognized that a potential moral hazard might arise – that is, the danger that the insured institutions become less careful in preventing collapses, as the "insurance" might "encourage their improvidence" (Thornton 1939, 188), leading them to "laxity and recklessness" (Humphrey and Keleher 1984, 287) and induce increased risk taking. The subsidy implicit in the LLR action lowers the incentives for the banks to maintain prudent liquidity levels. "Even though the private cost of risk taking is reduced, the social cost in terms of damages will increase if more risk is taken" (Claassen 1985, 31). This can be avoided if the LLR does not assume responsibility for the rescue of the individual bank but only for the market – that is, if it does not prevent the triggering of events but only the secondary repercussions.[2] "Individual imprudence should (still) be punished by loss" (Humphrey and Keleher 1984, 287).

As far as Austria in 1931 is concerned, the LLR function was mainly in the hands of the Austrian National Bank. However, as we have shown above, the government also played a crucial role by influencing the policies of the central bank and by extending guarantees. We can, then, consider the LLR function as – de facto – a joint product of the government and the central bank. First, we will turn to the main actor, the Austrian National Bank.

The Austrian National Bank

We recall from chapter 2 that not only did the Austrian National Bank (ANB) participate in the initial rescue plan of the Credit-Anstalt, but – as an internal drain emerged, fueled by fears that means of payment would be unobtainable – the ANB also embarked on a very liberal rediscounting policy in order to support the banks that had suffered under the public's scramble for high-powered money.[3] The consequence of this policy of free lending was an external drain, as the domestic credit component of the money supply

---

[2] "To prevent excessive risk taking by banks confident of assistance, however, the lender of last resort must be certain to specify that in financial crises assistance will be available to the market, not to particular banks" (Barth and Keleher 1984, 63).

[3] Open market operations were not available to the ANB until 1955.

grew so fast as to create an efflux of international reserves through the balance of payments (capital account). The response to the initial internal drain had led to an external drain, and this then resulted in a feedback to the internal sector, since "unless you can stop the foreign exchange export you cannot allay the domestic alarm" (Bagehot 1962, 27).

The loss of reserves endangered the convertibility of the Austrian schilling. Since Austria constituted a small open economy under the gold exchange standard, the long-run objective of the central bank was "to maintain (fixed rate) convertibility of currency into international reserves (or gold)" (Humphrey and Keleher 1984, 279). This goal was stated quite clearly in Article 1 of the charter of the ANB; it identified the principal objective as "to prepare the introduction of cash payments (redemption of bank notes in specie) by forming a reserve of precious metal and deposits payable in stable currencies"; and, moreover, "the bank shall use all its means . . . to ensure that the value of its notes shall at least not depreciate."[4]

While the internal drain required an expansionary policy ("lending freely"), the external drain required a restrictive monetary policy ("at a penalty rate"). What then did the ANB do?

When the first signs of an internal drain occurred, it embarked on a policy of "lending freely," however not at a penalty rate but at the then going rate of 5 percent. As the Credit-Anstalt did not have enough rediscountable (commercial) bills,[5] the ANB – in violation of its charter[6] – rediscounted financial bills[7] issued by the CA.

The discount rate was not raised until four weeks after the out-

---

[4] In addition to that, the League of Nations had required from Austria in 1924 "to take steps to ensure that the National Bank shall so conduct its discount policy as to maintain the stability of the crown, not only in its relation to gold but also in its relation to goods" (LofN 1925, 3).

[5] Had to be short-term (up to ninety two days to maturity) commercial bills, since they were considered to be "self liquidating" (Reisch 1931, 216).

[6] But consistent with Kindleberger's (1985, 18) observation that "in crises, central banks have often found it necessary to cast aside their rules for the eligibility of assets discounted by banks in trouble." Even the governor of the Federal Reserve Bank of New York (Harrison) advised the Fed to advance money, "taking a margin of ineligible paper" during the crisis of the Bank of the United States in 1930 (see Lucia 1985, 412).

[7] These were neither short-term, nor self-liquidating, and could be subject to involuntary prolongation.

break of the crisis, at a point in time when the official foreign reserves had already declined from 855.5 million Austrian schillings (on May 7, 1931) to 677.1 million schillings.[8] This increase in the rate did not manage to stem the external drain. The focus of the attack had shifted from the CA to the National Bank, confirming Garber's (1981, 6) observation that "the attacked institution becomes an agent of the speculators and merely transmits the attack to the insurer. The insurer, not the insured institution, suffers the collapse in its assets." And the ANB's assets indeed collapsed.

Considering the size of these outflows of reserves – reserves that had been accumulated during only eight years, since the establishment of the ANB – it is amazing how unconcerned and optimistic the president of the ANB, Reisch, presented himself in 1931.[9] His point was that foreign exchange reserves are not self-serving but are means of defending the currency, and consequently they should be fully utilized in such times, even if this should lead to a temporary nonfulfillment of the minimum cover requirements (Reisch 1931, 219–20). He was also very optimistic about future inflows of foreign capital, since he considered it completely unlikely that a vacuum of capital would develop in a country without being replenished either through the return of domestic or through the inflow of foreign capital. This would then – automatically – lead to the restoration of the foreign currency reserves of the National Bank. He did not, however, rely completely on this automatic mechanism; he warned that the National Bank could not "remain passive" toward the panicky run on its foreign exchange reserves, and would have to take appropriate action. He mentioned most prominently a further rise in the discount rate[10] that should create enough incentives to keep the capital in the country. In case this penalty rate was insufficient

[8] The actual decline was considerably larger as some of the reserves used were originally included among "other assets," and moreover, the BIS loan had already been given to Austria.

[9] We are well aware of the fact that any crisis has a very strong psychological component, and that therefore optimistic speeches by policymakers cannot be taken necessarily at face value, as they serve as tools of policy-making. It is only in the context of observed actions that the speeches become real indicators of policy.

[10] Already at 7.5 percent at that time.

to stop the tide, he mentioned the possibility of introducing exchange controls or a moratorium.[11]

It took the ANB another two weeks[12] for the next raise in the discount rate (to 10 percent) and three months until the government could decide to introduce exchange controls. By that time most of the foreign exchange reserves had been lost.

What were then the main reasons for the apparent failure of the lender-of-last-resort intervention?

Before we deal with the policy mistakes, we have to point out, however, that some successes had also been attained. We recall that the general banking crisis, the run on all the Viennese banks, had only lasted for about four days. The public's fear for the convertibility of their deposits at those institutions was stopped by the apparently unrestricted availability of currency, made possible by the liberal rediscounting policy of the ANB. These institutions were fortunate in that at the time of their liquidity needs, the pursuit of (parts of) Bagehot's principle was not yet challenged. The ANB prevented a widespread run from forcing well-managed (or at least relatively "better-managed") banks into ruin.[13]

Uncertainty regarding the interventions arose in late May of 1931. Continuous discussions within the ANB emerged concerning the liberal lending policy pursued, with the president advocating such a policy and the vice president and the director general opposing it. If one studies the events, one recognizes that the public had every reason to doubt the dependability of the preventive arrangements. The ANB violated Bagehot's (1962, 85) advice that the public has a right to know whether the central bank acknowledges its duty and is "ready to perform it."[14] This would have been especially impor-

---

[11] Moreover, he was very optimistic about the possibilities for the defense of currencies, as created by the cooperation of central banks.

[12] Until ten days after the outbreak of the German banking crisis.

[13] As the events developed further, the ANB became more selective in its help, more geared toward "certain privileged groups or institutions of society" (März 1982, 187). When, in July 1931, the midsized Viennese Mercurbank became subject to a run, since it was owned by the then-failing German Danatbank, the ANB was only partially ready to come to its rescue, and the government refused to help at all, although it was a perfectly sound institution. This and other previous incidents led März (ibid., 191) to conclude that the "lender of last resort is an 'insurance scheme' of remarkable selectivity, accessible only to those whose interest are deemed more equal than others."

[14] This need to be explicit, however, is not unchallenged, especially because of

tant since the rediscounting of financial bills was in violation of the statutes of the ANB.[15]

After two weeks of lending freely, the ANB threatened to stop granting credits to the CA, but the government and the Bank of England advised them to keep on rediscounting. The director general of the ANB did not agree with this policy, but the president pursued it further, requiring a governmental guarantee for the credits to the ailing bank.[16] After the state assumed reponsibility (May 28), the National Bank decided to grant another 120 million schillings of credit, and the BIS advanced 100 million schillings to Austria. Only two weeks later, the vice president and the director general of the ANB demanded a liquidation of the Credit-Anstalt, but the central bank decided to grant further credits if they were "economically unavoidable" (Kernbauer 1981b, 53). The vice president resigned, and the bank set a rediscount ceiling of another 30 million schillings. Another five days later, the director general went on sick leave, since he could not agree with the policies pursued, and the ANB decided to extend further credits unconditionally, as it might have recognized that "in moments of stress, the existence of a limit increases the alarm," since "when the market feels that there may not be enough to go around, the rush to get there first is exacerbated" (Kindleberger 1978, 224).

It should be quite obvious that this type of policy is not likely to create (or preserve) confidence, as Bagehot's rule is intended to do. We can apply Schwartz's (1986, 20) conclusion that "a misinformed public can nullify the beneficial effects of actions designed to avert panic," and extend it to a confused public. The ANB had to recognize that "to make large advances in this faltering way is to incur the evil of making them without obtaining the advantage" (Bagehot 1962, 64), and that it might have been better to follow Bagehot's advice, and "either shut the bank at once, and say that it will not lend more than it commonly lends, or lend freely, boldly, and so that the public may feel you mean to go on lending," since, "to lend

---

fear that such an explicit commitment might erode market discipline and encourage excessive risk taking (see Guttentag and Herring 1987, 167–8).
[15] Nevertheless, they accounted for up to 83 percent of the bills portfolio of the bank.
[16] This was consistent with Bagehot's (1962, 97) words that "no advances indeed need be made" on assets "which the [central] Bank will ultimately lose."

a great deal, and yet not give the public confidence that you will lend sufficiently and effectually, is the worst of all policies" (ibid.).[17]

An additional problem was that the penalty rate, once it was used, did not stop the capital flight by domestic citizens, nor did it attract new foreign capital.[18] Bagehot's (ibid., 97) "heavy fine on unreasonable timidity" did not perform its job.[19] Interest rates were of no material importance at a time when people were primarily interested in staying liquid and/or in a safe currency, or as Hurst (1932, 660) put it (for England), "it was probably true that the panic ... was of a depth not to be checked by any manipulation of the bank rate." Moreover, it is more likely that, given the circumstances, foreigners as well as Austrians "took raising of the discount rate as a sign not of strength but weakness, and sold rather than bought the currency . . ." (Kindleberger 1978, 183), since, "when possibilities of capital loss or gain outweigh considerations of rate of interest earned, the ordinary instrument of discount policy is not merely ineffective but may well have the opposite result from that intended" (Hodson 1931, 213). Due to the uncertainty of the situation people were willing to pay this price, and money did not seek the highest nominal yield, but rather the safest yield. Under these conditions it seemed rational to convert deposits into Austrian schillings and those into foreign currency (and so into gold) as the expected yield was higher than in Austria.

In Bagehot's defense, we have to state that he advocated the use of the penalty rate "early in the panic, so that the fine may be paid early, that no one may borrow out of idle precaution without paying well for it" (Bagehot 1962, 97). Moreover, this penalty rate should force the banks to "exhaust all market sources of liquidity" (Humphrey and Keleher 1984, 301). But the Credit-Anstalt was too big relative to the Austrian market, so that none of the Viennese banks

---

[17] Foreign influences and pressures had played an important role in the pursuit of these misguided policies. Many promises for international aid and threats to withdraw credits had been made whenever the ANB had planned to implement a moratorium.

[18] It was raised from 5 to 6 percent on June 8, to 7.5 percent on June 16, and to 10 percent on July 23.

[19] Although even in September 1931, after most of the foreign reserves had been lost, the president of the ANB, Reisch, still insisted that the discount rate would fulfill at least some of its planned effects. He rejected all those statements that considered the bank rate as ineffective (*Wiener Börsen-Kurier*, September 14, 1931, 1).

could have provided it the necessary liquidity, especially since they had to deal with their own liquidity problems and since money and capital markets were very underdeveloped at that time.

Bagehot has to be defended even further, as he would never have assisted the CA at all, since his rule did not apply to insolvent banks but only to illiquid ones; unsound banks should be allowed to fail, but failure should not be allowed to spread to sound institutions. To the Austrian National Bank's defense we have to reiterate that – on the basis of the initially reported losses and considering the first rescue plan – the CA would have been a solvent bank. Moreover, as Humphrey (1975, 9) points out correctly, the determination of a bank's condition is time-consuming and therefore "it may be necessary to extend last-resort loans to distressed banks simply to purchase the time required for the authorities to make an informed judgment of the conditions of the banks." But solvency of a bank is often rather difficult to determine on such short notice and "the LLR may be forced to act before it is possible to verify the soundness of the bank seeking assistance" (Guttentag and Herring 1987, 164–5). This was especially so in the case of the Credit-Anstalt with its incomplete and incorrect record keeping. The president of the ANB, Reisch, had pointed out – as early as 1925 – that if having the choice between supporting an unworthy bank (and thus securing the existence of thousands of its victims) and letting this unworthy bank and its victims go under, one would have to choose the first alternative (Kernbauer 1981b, 130). Reisch's main goal was to prevent the potentially heavy costs of an abrupt closure of the largest bank, on which a large part of Austrian industry was financially dependent. And in 1931, he acted accordingly.

As the true extent of the problems started to emerge, the point of no return might already have been crossed.[20] The ANB had already become the principal creditor of the failing bank.

But the Austrian National Bank was not only the principal creditor of the CA and its lender of last resort, it was also its "investor of last resort." It was very actively involved in the recapitalization of the ailing bank. As we recall from chapter 2, it participated with 30 million schillings in the initial reconstruction plan, in exchange

---

[20] Kernbauer (1981b, 130) states that by May 25, 1931, the government must have had knowledge of the fact that the losses were much larger than 140 million schillings.

for 17.6 million schillings worth of new CA shares, which subsequently lost their value. All in all, it accepted about 44 million schillings of the losses of the CA.[21]

Uncertainty and lack of information are the "ideal" conditions for rumors and panics. Therefore, in a situation of crisis, full and timely information of the market is of utmost importance. Unfortunately, this rule was not respected by the Austrian National Bank during the CA crisis. As the problems developed, the public eagerly awaited the periodic information, especially so the weekly statements of the National Bank and the monthly figures on bank deposits. The former was regularily available and reflected the mounting troubles, but the latter was suppressed. At the height of the crisis, it was not published "due to belated arrival of the data," as the official justification said. This fact did not help to calm the fears of the public, quite the contrary. The *Wiener Börsen-Kurier* (August 27, 1931, 2) put it very aptly, when it criticized the Austrian authorities for their belief that "the fire could be fought by breaking the thermometer."[22]

As the preceding discussion points out, the handling of the crisis by the Austrian National Bank was by no means optimal. Its failure to arrest the process at the outset was – partly at least – the result of policy mistakes. Still one has to be careful not to make the mistake of evaluating the behavior of the authorities in 1931 by the standards of the late 1980s. Most importantly, one has to recognize the almost complete lack of information available to the policymakers. The crucial decisions had to be taken by the authorities under conditions of extreme uncertainty. The true state of affairs at the ailing bank was not known to the decision makers in May 1931.[23] The ANB had no power (or possibility) to supervise and regulate the bank adequately. Only through the granting of discount credits could the central bank gain some insight into the nature of the business deals on which the commercial bills were based. The only systematic forms of information were the annual balance sheets and profit-and-loss accounts of the banks. And they were – unfortunately – not

---

[21] See Rutkowski (1934, 105). Notel (1984, 171) estimates that between 1923 and 1938 the Austrian National Bank spent almost 170 million schillings on bank rescues.

[22] Translation of the author.

[23] It took British chartered accountants (C.P.A.s) several months to sort out the true situation of the bank's assets.

always correct. How dependent the ANB was on the willingness of the banks to provide information is expressed very drastically in a quote from the annual report of the Austrian National Bank for 1927:

During the past year the Austrian banks have for the first time decided to publish half yearly balance sheets on June 30, 1927, in accordance with the wish expressed by the Austrian National Bank, hereby taking the first decisive step toward the publication of the interim balance sheets. We [i.e., the ANB] can not but express the hope that the first step will be followed by other improvements in the same direction, such as earlier publication of the yearly balance sheets, their greater uniformity and the more frequent publication of interim balance sheets.[24]

What a sign of regulatory impotence! Moreover, the hopes of the ANB were not fulfilled and even the half yearly balance sheets lasted only three years.

It was in this informational vacuum that the Austrian National Bank and all the other parties involved had to make all their decisions concerning the solvency and liquidity support of the Credit-Anstalt – a position rather different from that of today's central banks and bank supervisors.

The Austrian State

The psychological factor dominates the economic crisis affecting most nations to-day, and it is for politicians, above all, to influence men's minds by spreading through the world by their actions, a general feeling of confidence.
—League of Nations, General Report of the
Co-ordination Subcommittee on Economic Questions,
cited in *The Economist*, September 19, 1931

As we mentioned above, the state played a crucial role in functioning as the lender of last resort. One can argue that the observed behavior of the LLR was the outcome of a joint production between government and the National Bank.[25]

The government's interest in a financial crisis can be explained by the fact that "certain negative externalities are commonly as-

[24] English translation, quoted from *Federal Reserve Bulletin*, June 1928, 402.
[25] Unfortunately, these principal players did not coordinate their actions to a degree that would have been necessary for a more successful intervention.

sociated with monetary instability" (Humphrey and Keleher 1984, 277). A government that wants to reduce these unfavorable externalities might find it worthwhile to intervene in the workings of the market, despite a laissez-faire philosophy – as in the case of the Austrian government.

In the Credit-Anstalt crisis, the Austrian state had another strong reason to get involved, namely, the way the Boden-Credit-Anstalt (BCA) crisis in October 1929 had been solved. We recall that the government had put considerable pressure on the CA to take over and rescue the ailing BCA.[26] The CA's willingness to help the government and the Austrian economy in such a case of distress made it – implicitly – eligible for government support in the case of any difficulties, especially if they should – partly at least – arise from this forced merger. In May 1931 then, the CA announced that the relatively largest share of its losses (60 million out of 140 million schillings) was owing to the depreciation of former BCA assets (over and above the adjustments that were already made at the time of the merger in 1929). This put moral pressure on the government to get involved, and linked it to the CA rescue attempt, independently of any negative externalities.[27] Moreover, one could argue that by merging with the BCA in 1929, the CA had contributed to the financial stability in Austria, and since a considerable part of its losses resulted from this merger, the state (taxpayers) had to "pay" for this service of prolonging financial stability by one and a half years.

Initially, by subscribing 100 million schillings of the losses and reconstruction advances the government had thought to have paid its dues vis-à-vis the CA.[28] But this assumption proved to be incorrect, for repercussions from the financial distress of this large institution could not be prevented by the initial rescue plan. The subsequent events required further action (or reaction).

[26] Chancellor Schober is quoted saying that Rothschild had to be convinced "not with a pistol, but a machine gun at his chest" (see Ausch 1968, 308).

[27] Unfortunately, we cannot assess whether the large relative weight given to depreciated former BCA assets was not done deliberately in order to make it impossible for the government not to come to the rescue of the Credit-Anstalt. In any case, "it raced to the financial rescue like a knight in shining armour" (Minister Weidenhoffer, as quoted in Stiefel 1983a, 418).

[28] "As far as the Austrian government was concerned the Credit-Anstalt crisis ended with their brave reconstruction measures. They had helped to cover the losses and also to restore the capital of the Credit-Anstalt. All further details were left to the bank itself" (Stiefel 1983a, 421).

The Austrian National Bank assumed the LLR role, but since it recognized that the attacked institution (CA) became an "agent of the speculators" in Garber's (1981, 6) sense, transmitting the panic to the insurer (ANB) and so to the Austrian currency, it required the government to give a guarantee for the CA's financial bills,[29] which were "only accepted by the National Bank with the permission of the Austrian government" (Stiefel 1983a, 421). Around May 26 the ANB had wanted – for the first time – to stop granting credit, but the government (and the Bank of England) had persuaded it to go on lending freely. After initial hesitation, the government provided that guarantee and became the ANB's partner in the provision of the LLR function. The forced guarantee for all the external liabilities of the CA in exchange for a two-year standstill agreement with the international creditors resulted in the state's deepest involvement in the CA crisis. It even led to the collapse of the government.

The rationale for giving away such an extended guarantee without receiving a substantial long-term loan (i.e. new money) in exchange was criticized immediately, not only by the minister of interior, who resigned, but also by others in Austria (e.g., see *Daily Telegraph,* June 17, 1931, 13). But it has to be recognized that the government had to deal with two very shrewd representatives of the foreign creditors, Sir Robert Kindersley and Mr. Gaunon. Their threat to withdraw 500 million schillings worth of foreign short-term credits, should the state not sign the guarantee, came very close to blackmail.

Theoretically, the government could have "substituted its own credit abroad for that of the banks that have come under pressure" (Freedman 1987, 193) by issuing foreign-currency loans to provide the foreign currency to the banks – via the ANB – and enable them to repay foreign depositors and to offset the capital flight of the Austrians. But in accordance with the Geneva Protocols of 1922, Austria needed the approval of the committee of control of the Guarantor States of the League of Nations loan for any foreign issues. The complicated formalities made any quick action impossible.[30] Capital imports by the government, to offset the effects of

[29] By June 11, 40 percent of the note circulation was already covered by financial bills of the Credit-Anstalt.

[30] It had taken Austria from October 1926 to July 1930 to receive all the necessary

the capital exports of the private sector on the foreign reserves of the central bank, did not represent a realistic option.

The transformation of the CA bills in the ANB's portfolio into a government debt in 1932 made the state – ex post – the true lender of last resort for the financial crisis of 1931, just as the gold schilling had become the true victim of the crisis. But in the final analysis, the Austrian taxpayers were the true lenders of last resort and especially the true victims of this crisis.

The delayed introduction of exchange controls (October 1931) can also be traced to the behavior of the government. Although the ANB had requested this rather drastic policy as early as June 1931, in order to be able to check the capital flight, the government refused to pass such a bill until October. This was definitely too late, especially since most of the countries around Austria (e.g., Germany, Hungary) had introduced similar restrictions much earlier, and most of the foreign exchange reserves had been lost by that time.[31]

As the state, just like the ANB, had only been confronted with the problems of the CA at the eleventh hour, it had only three days at its disposal to determine the future course of action, and, moreover, it had only very limited information on the true state of affairs. With hindsight, we know that it was a mistake to believe uncritically the reports of the leaders of the CA. More healthy skepticism on part of the government and central bank officials could have prevented some of the damage that occurred. As Chancellor Ender pointed out in June 1931 (only about a month after the initial announcement of the crisis), with the knowledge available at that time, the Credit-Anstalt laws would – most probably – not have been passed.[32] He claimed that the government would have let the CA settle its own debts and claims, and would have restricted itself to providing for the needs of the industries belonging to the CA. He

approvals and finally to raise a portion of the so-called Austrian Government International Loan of 1930.

[31] Austria was not only one of the last in Central Europe to impose restrictions making for fictitious exchange rates, it was also "the first to take a definite step towards the restoration of more normal conditions" in the autumn of 1933 (*Bankers' Magazine*, October 1933, 549).

[32] After the initial Credit-Anstalt law of mid-May 1931, the Austrian parliament had to pass nine additional ones until the end of the reconstruction of the bank in 1934.

stated further – with the tone of one about to resign – that with the amounts of money used for the CA rescue, a lot could have been accomplished (cited in Ausch 1968, 373).

Whether this approach could really have been followed is questionable, since, from the very beginning, the foreign creditors linked the problems of this bank to the Austrian state. For them it was not a problem of a private joint stock bank but a state affair.[33] The government, however, did not want to assume responsibility and did not provide leadership in the crisis. It restricted itself to reacting to the demands of the foreigners (and the ANB), but it did not act according to a consistent plan. Initially, it tried not to become principal shareholder of the CA. This approach had resulted in the first rescue plan, which was very favorable and generous to the original shareholders. Eventually, it had to accept the majority of the share capital of the reconstructed Credit-Anstalt.[34]

At no point, however, did the public have any reason to assume that the government was in command of the situation and that it was able to restore confidence. The state guarantees were outgrowths of hesitant policies, pursued in such a faltering way that the Austrian state had to "incur the evil of making them without obtaining the advantages" (Bagehot 1962, 641). The first guarantee was formulated in such a way that most of its intended effect (to create confidence) was lost, since the public was confused about its true contents, and the second guarantee led to the immediate resignation of the government that had signed it.

It has to be recognized, however, that the Austrian government had no adequate means of banking regulation available. All that was at its disposal was discretionary "protective" regulation – that is, it could offer guarantees to the depositors, but without any means of "prudential" or "preventive" regulation aimed at controlling the level of risk assumed by the banks.[35] It could only reduce the cost of failure without reducing the probability of such a failure occur-

---

[33] One result of this approach was the fact that four foreign banks, among them the Rothschild bank in London, refused the ANB access to its foreign exchange deposits, as these banks were also creditors of the ailing CA (see Kernbauer 1981b).

[34] The rest went to the foreign creditors as part of the debt repayment plan (see chapter 2).

[35] For a detailed description of these forms of regulation, see Baltensperger and Dermine 1987.

ring. The fact that the approach to protecting the safety of the banking system was "discretionary" – that is, it was not granted for sure, so that private risk remained – did not help to bring about stability. Both the LLR and the guarantees lost a lot of their potential power in the largely unregulated banking business of Vienna in the early 1930s.

Apart from lack of information, the basic noninterventionist philosophy, and the domestic political problems and quarrels, the main contributor to these unfortunate policies was excessive reliance on a foreign deus ex machina. The hope for timely and adequate foreign help was, however, unfounded, just an illusion and another relic from the hyperinflation period.[36] The chances for international help were very slim, especially since the question of a customs union with Germany overshadowed everything. Toynbee (1932, 63) used a very drastic but accurate description of Austria's position in mid-1931, when he wrote that it was "like a victim on the international altar, tied and bound, and with a knife at her throat." There were several knives, however, not only that of French politicians but also those of international bankers. The victim was rather helpless and only became more determined when most of the damage was already done.

For too long, the authorities – especially the government – were overly sensitive to the cost imposed on foreigners, stockholders as well as creditors, by a failure of the CA. They considered themselves very dependent on them (the foreign investors) and therefore they did not want to offend them. Too late, the Austrian authorities recognized that the only interest of the foreign creditors was self-interest. They wanted to get as much as possible out of the CA or out of Austria. They did not care who would pay, as long as they were paid. Excessive concern for the foreign creditors and stockholders cost Austria very dearly.

The international lender of last resort

It follows from the international propagation of financial crises, and from the efficacy under certain circumstances of lending in

---

[36] One of the side effects of the way the hyperinflation was overcome – namely with the help of a foreign loan (coordinated by the LofN) combined with foreign control over all aspects of economic policy (until 1926) – was the belief that the solutions to problems have to be sought abroad.

> the last resort, that there is room for an international lender of
> last resort.
>
> —C. F. Kindleberger, 1978

The well-established case for a lender of last resort has been predominantly made in a domestic context. Kindleberger (1973, 1978)
has to be credited with reigniting interest in an international equivalent to the domestic LLR function.[37] Since the initial appearance
of his contributions, a number of authors have touched upon this
problem.[38]

The domestic LLR is relatively clearly defined and well understood, and there exists widespread agreement in the literature, but
the international LLR, in contrast, appears "in strikingly different
guises."[39]

In most general terms, the idea behind this concept is an agency
or institution that lends to central banks (or governments) in need
of international liquidity. It performs therefore the functions of an
LLR for central banks.[40] The domestic LLR, the central bank, creates domestic bank reserves. Therefore, it has the resources to meet
any potential demand for domestic liquidity. But if a large part of
the bank's liabilities is denominated by foreign currency, the domestic LLR "may lack adequate resources to provide emergency
liquidity assistance without compromising its exchange rate objective or undermining its own international liquidity position" (Guttentag and Herring 1987, 173–4). And that is exactly what happened
in Austria in the summer of 1931.

As for the 1931 episode, the role of the international LLR could
be considered as an agency that could (should) have stopped the
"ball from rolling," that is, halted the international disintermedia-

---

[37] Humphrey and Keleher (1984, 310) show that as early as the pre-1914 gold
standard international LLRs have existed and that the economic literature had
taken notice of them (e.g., Withers 1909, or Hawtrey 1932).

[38] E.g., Moggridge (1982), Griffiths (1983), Barth and Keleher (1984), Claassen
(1985), Eichengreen (1987), Guttentag and Herring (1987).

[39] Applying März's (1982, 187) observation to the international LLR.

[40] Claassen (1985), however, seems to understand the international LLR as a lender
to international banks in need of liquidity, rather than to central banks. Humphrey and Keleher (1984, 310) define its role as "to provide a backstop or a
mechanism to prevent sharp contractions of the world money supply, preventing
world shocks (such as credit crises) from developing into world monetary
crises."

tion, and, as Kindleberger (1978, 197) points out, "the first opportunity to halt the international disintermediation came in May 1931 with the collapse of the Credit-Anstalt in Vienna."

The foreign creditors of the CA could not liquidate their assets at the ailing bank; they were frozen for two years. In this situation there would have been a need for an international lender of last resort, which would have helped to avoid the foreign repercussions of the bank's illiquidity. Great Britain especially was affected, as the largest part (about $27 million) of the foreign debt of the CA was owed to British creditors.

Even before the problem of the Credit-Anstalt had been announced to the public, the Austrian government and the National Bank had contacted the Bank of England (BofE), the Bank for International Settlements (BIS), and the League of Nations (LofN) for help. What Austria initially asked for was not the help of an international lender of last resort but rather a loan for the Austrian government. As we recall, Austria had wanted a credit amounting to 150 million schillings in order to cover its share in the reconstruction plan for the CA and to raise additional liquidity for strengthening its position for possible further emergencies.

The initial reaction of the three institutions was very different. The BIS sent a director to Vienna, Mr. Rodd, who recognized immediately the danger of the situation and reported to London concerning this request for a loan that "if this permission is given at once the situation will be remedied promptly, but if it is not given very grave difficulties will arise."[41] The BofE and the LofN, however, "passed the buck" to the BIS, the BofE stating:

You may be sure that we should wish to co-operate in any helpful way, but the position has been essentially changed . . . by the foundation of the BIS. Individual action by Central Banks, for reason of sympathy or even material interest, in such circumstances, has been superseded by corporate action through Basle. . . .[42]

The potential role of the BIS as a form of international LLR was widely recognized very early in the crisis, as indicated by the following report in the *Financial News* of May 13, 1931 (6):

At the present stage, such support is not required, for the National Bank is in a very liquid position. . . . If, however, conditions become worse

[41] As quoted in Kernbauer 1982, 13.
[42] Ibid., 13.

through any withdrawals of foreign credits or deposits, it is reassuring to know that there is a "second line of defense." It would be, indeed, a typical case in which the Bank for International Settlements could and should take action in the interest of international stability.

The BIS, in recognition of the potential for international repercussions, began "as soon as the crisis broke . . . to sound out the major central banks about aid to Austria" (Clarke 1967, 187). The resources at the direct disposal of the BIS were rather limited: paidup capital of about $4 million, permanent deposits of about 12 million, and liquid funds placed with it by central banks amounting to about 35 million (Quesnay 1931, 116). By May 14 the German Reichsbank, the National Bank of Belgium and the Bank of England had agreed to participate, and the Federal Reserve Bank of New York joined them the following day. The latter participated in the form of "an agreement to purchase prime Austrian commercial bills . . . as it [was] not empowered to make direct loans" (*Wall Street Journal*, June 2, 1931, 1). It was, however, only more than two weeks later that the rediscount credit was really advanced to Austria, but then amounting to not more than 100 million schillings,[43] instead of the requested 150 million schillings and only for three months. By that time, May 31, the sum was much too small to have any impact on the course of events. What produced a large impact on the future course of events, however, was the fact that this shortterm emergency loan was tied to a governmental guarantee for the credits extended to the Credit-Anstalt. Establishing a link between this loan and the guarantee had also been the cause of the delay in its allocation. Overnight, the financially ailing Austrian state stood guarantor for an unspecified and uncertain amount of liabilities of the CA. The effect on the public's confidence in the state of Austrian public finance was disastrous. The BIS was convinced that, with its reserves and this loan, the ANB would be able to secure the stability of the Austrian schilling, but quite opposite to its expectations, this loan with the parallel guarantee became the fundamental reason for the run on Austria's foreign reserves.[44] The purpose of the loan had also shifted from strengthening the Austrian treasury toward sup-

---

[43] Consisting of a 40 million schilling credit by the BIS and of 60 million schillings of rediscounting quotas at eleven central banks, namely those of England, France, Italy, Germany, Belgium, the Netherlands, Czechoslovakia, Poland, Greece, Switzerland, and the Federal Reserve Bank of New York.

[44] See the discussion of the causes of the currency crisis in chapter 4.

porting the currency. But during the period May 7 to May 31, the volume of reserves lost amounted to more than the overall volume of the BIS loan.

By June 5, this credit had been depleted and the ANB had to request another one. Although it was arranged within a week (for 100 million schillings), it was again subject to special conditions, namely to a successful placement of a foreign treasury bond loan of 150 million schillings. Political blackmail by France prevented the issue and therefore also the second BIS loan. It was only at this point that the BofE showed initiative and assumed the role of an international LLR by advancing 150 million schillings on the planned issue of treasury bonds.[45]

Although this action was perceived as a very positive signal in the Austrian and the international press,[46] it produced no lasting effect on the course of events, especially so since it coincided with the extension of the governmental guarantee to all foreign liabilities of the CA (amounting to another 500 million schillings), and the consequent resignation of the Austrian government.[47] These events were rather unfit for rebuilding confidence in Austria or its currency.

Hawtrey's (1932, 229) theoretical insights can be applied most appropriately:

As a general rule, if credits are to be granted to a central bank in difficulties at all, they should be granted up to the full amount needed. There should be no limit. If the amount is inadequate, and the exchange gives away after all, the sums lent are completely wasted. . . .[48]

The BofE's reasons for giving this loan had not been to solve any of the underlying problems, however, but rather to prevent a closing of the Austrian banks. It feared that such a moratorium could spread to adjoining countries, and especially to Germany,[49] freezing much larger foreign credits there than in Austria. According to Clarke

---

[45] For seven days, but renewable on a week-to-week basis.

[46] "International diplomacy was strangling Austria, international finance was rescuing her" (*Contemporary Review*, July 1931, 113).

[47] After "stiff opposition within the Austrian cabinet to the guarantee of the Credit-Anstalt's foreign liabilities" (Clarke 1967, 188).

[48] For Austria they were wasted, but not so for the BofE, since, as Kernbauer (1981b) shows, it made a considerable profit on this loan.

[49] In both countries, Austria and Germany, the United States and England were the largest creditors. However, the amounts advanced to Austria were relatively small, whereas the German indebtedness to those countries was very considerable.

(1967, 188–9), the motive of the BofE for this credit was to "avoid a crisis in Central Europe" and "afford the Austrian government some time to turn around and to negotiate for the sale of the bonds." This clearly constituted an extension of Thornton's and Bagehot's ideas to an international context, as the rationale for the lending was to avoid a moratorium's potential secondary repercussions, its spillover or contagion effects. But the amounts lent were inappropriate. "The last occasion . . . on which the Bank of England was able to play its traditional role of helping to keep the world-wide machinery of international finance in working order" (Toynbee 1932, 72) had passed unsuccessfully.

The second BIS credit, although promised and arranged in early June, was never granted, and placing a large bond issue in international financial markets was basically impossible. Foreign creditors were reluctant to lend to a country that had issued an unlimited guarantee for the liabilities of its largest commercial bank. Despite repeated reports in Austrian newspapers about favorable conditions for large foreign credits, and despite the Austrian government's efforts to please potential foreign creditors,[50] initially no long-term help was made available. The Austrian government had turned to the League of Nations in early August 1931 with a request for an inquiry into the financial situation of Austria. In September 1931, after an investigation, the LofN recommended a foreign bond issue for Austria in order to secure Austria's financial reconstruction. As the financial experts of the main countries did not act accordingly, nothing happened. In early May 1932 the Austrian government issued a desperate plea to the LofN describing the hopeless foreign exchange situation. Finally, in July 1932, the so-called Lausanne Protocols were signed by Austria on the one hand, and England, France, Italy, and Belgium on the other. These countries – similar to the Geneva Protocols of 1922 – agreed to guarantee an international loan for Austria. The signing of this treaty halted the instability of the value of the Austrian currency (as reflected in the agio on the gold price),[51] although the actual inflow of the funds was delayed for another year. The loan amounted to 308.6 million schil-

---

[50] We recall in this context, among others, the generous treatment of the shareholders of the CA (about 50 percent foreigners), the governmental guarantee for the CA liabilities, and a discount rate policy geared toward foreign demands.

[51] See Table 5.15.

lings and had to be used in its entirety to repay debts to the BofE, the Austrian National Bank, and to Austrian commercial banks. Apart from stabilizing the currency by removing the fundamental cause of the currency crisis (namely the uncertainty about the future of public finance), it had no positive effect on the Austrian economy since it was too small to allow for any investment expenditures or other fiscal policy measures.

Summarizing the impact of these international agencies on the Austrian financial crisis, we have to conclude that the "story of the international lender of last resort is ultimately one of failure."[52] The domestic lender of last resort had initially functioned relatively well, but it could only provide the banking system with domestic liquidity. This action, however, in a system of fixed exchange rates created a need for foreign liquidity (i.e., foreign exchange). The ANB had relied on the BIS's promise to help, but the BIS did not keep its promise. An alternative would have been to have the government import the necessary foreign exchange, but that avenue was not open without the consent of the League of Nations. Therefore, the LofN had a key function in stopping the currency crisis by helping to provide Austria with foreign exchange credits. But it took until 1933 to raise such a loan.

From the very beginning of the CA crisis, foreign central banks were involved in the process, either directly, like the BofE, or indirectly, through the BIS. As we learn from the minutes of the ANB,[53] the BIS and the BofE had advised the Austrian National Bank to finance the Credit-Anstalt's liquidity needs by use of the printing press, with the government assuming the credit risk through a guarantee and the BIS promising to help the ANB to support the currency, should the need arise. While the ANB followed this – illfated – advice and lent freely to an insolvent institution, the BIS did not satisfactorily assume its promised responsibility as an international lender of last resort for the stability of the currency.[54] The *Wall Street Journal* was overly optimistic when it announced:

[52] Adapted from Eichengreen (1984, 66).
[53] Geschäftsbericht der Generalratssitzung, 29/5/1931; cited in Kernbauer 1981b, 27.
[54] But we have to recognize, just as in the case of the ANB, that this initial plan had been based on the assumption, and Austria's specific reassurance, that the CA was a solvent bank and that its losses amounted to "only" 140 million schillings.

Thanks to the prompt measures taken by central and private banks to defend the Austrian exchange and to extend credits to the Austrian Credit-Anstalt, there is every chance now that Europe will weather successfully the storm which was produced by what has been described in responsible banking quarters as the biggest bank failure in history. There was serious danger at one time of financial panic throughout central Europe. (June 5, 1931, 7)

This credit did not produce the intended positive effects. Although Fraser's (1936, 460) positive assessment that "solidarity between central banks" had never been "more clearly demonstrated" was basically correct, the credit actually increased the plight of Austria and its currency by being tied to the ill-fated governmental guarantee for the credits granted to the CA. Thus the fundamental causes of the currency crisis, namely the sad state of Austrian public finance, were reinforced.

One of the two vice presidents of the ANB, Mr. Thaa, was among those who recognized some aspects of this problem. He objected to this credit, since, in his opinion, it could only be used to show a higher note cover than was justified, and it could not be used in any productive manner because it had to be repaid within three months, and no inflow of foreign exchange could have been realistically expected during this time period (Kernbauer 1981b, 55). The credit did not calm anxieties in Austria, and it did not prevent the spreading of financial panic throughout Europe.[55]

As we recall, the second BIS credit, although arranged by June 8, was never made available to Austria. But it would not have had any positive impact on the events, either. Small, short-term credits were not what Austria needed, and they were inappropriate for stopping the international repercussions of the Austrian crisis. If their only purpose was to buy time, the time was not properly used, and therefore the credits were wasted and counterproductive, because they made possible a postponement of the necessary adjustments. Once the government had accepted the leading role in the initial rescue attempt, without knowing the true situation of the bank and without having the necessary funds at its disposal, the CA crisis became a state affair. The BIS and the BofE were ill advised to

[55] Large-scale foreign exchange swap operations were not possible, at least not in the necessary amounts. Moreover, they would only have increased the potential gains to the speculators if they were not accompanied by the necessary changes in the underlying policies.

recommend liberal lending to a bank whose status was rather unclear and that turned out to be insolvent. The public's experience
with the hyperinflation and its resultant "paranoia about inflation"[56]
were not taken into account by the policy makers. Given its limited
information level, the public had every reason to assume a return
to inflationary times and started a run on the currency. The promised help from the BIS did not materialize, at least not in an amount
and with such promptness as to restore confidence.

What then went wrong with the international lender of last resort
in Austria?

First of all, we have to emphasize that neither the BIS nor the
LofN were what Humphrey and Keleher (1984, 311) termed "genuine
full-fleged" lenders of last resort, since they did not have the ability
to create money. They could only redistribute existing credit. Only
the foreign central banks that participated in the BIS loans could
create international reserves by extending rediscounting facilities to
the ANB. Both the BIS and the LofN could only negotiate and
coordinate the cooperation.[57]

In the cases of both organizations, the Public Choice School's
objections against an international LLR were confirmed, as they
contend "that the bureaucrats who would manage such an institution would (like anyone else) pursue their own interest and service
the needs of their constituents, rather than the public interest"
(Humphrey and Keleher 1984, 313). The bureaucrats did not recognize the potential repercussions of the unchecked Austrian crisis,
and were overwhelmingly concerned with the – mainly political –
interests of their constituents, most prominently with the opposition
to the proposed Austro-German customs union. The very fierce
reactions to and discussions about that proposal coincided with and
overshadowed the Credit-Anstalt crisis.

But as Stiefel (1983a, 425) reports, the LofN also supported very
actively the interest of the foreign creditors of the CA; Sir Otto
Niemeyer is quoted as saying that the creditors (i.e. foreign creditors

---

[56] Kindleberger (1978) uses this expression in the context of the German public,
but it was just as valid for Austria.

[57] However, both institutions had strong influence on economic policy-making.
One example is a small note in *The Economist* (November 21, 1931, 958) concerning the Austrian discount rate stating that "the high bank rate was maintained at the explicit wish of the Bank for International Settlements even though
the Austrian economy suffered seriously under the burden."

committee) "must be sure that they have the support of the League" and "we must use the influence of the financial committee [of the LofN] conjointly with that of the creditors."

These conflicts of interest did not advance the purpose of the international LLR, and were counterproductive in the effort to stop international disintermediation and to rebuild confidence.

The failures, however, cannot be blamed exclusively on these myopic policies of pursuing the short-term interest of the constituents. There were also valid arguments against foreign loans, namely "that the [currency] crisis was believed to have been caused by a flight of domestic rather than foreign withdrawals."[58] Mr. Bruins, the LofN's adviser to the ANB, had stated in June 1931 that foreign countries could not be asked to help the Austrian currency, if the Austrians transfer their schillings abroad (Kernbauer 1981b, 53).

All the problems mentioned above were reinforced by the considerable lack of reliable information. We recall that the Austrian National Bank and the government had no clear picture of the state of affairs, and neither had the international organizations. They had to rely mainly on the information they received from the domestic authorities. The BIS, for instance, was misinformed about the true extent of foreign short-term indebtedness of Austria, and was therefore in the belief that the Austrian foreign exchange reserves were considerably larger than its foreign debts. This was not only a wrong assumption, it also disregarded the possibility of domestic citizens trying to convert their schilling holdings into foreign exchange – a very crucial ommission.

Clarke (1967, 185) attempts to rationalize these shortcomings of the potential international LLR by stressing the fact that "no comparable international financial difficulties had occurred before" so that the "authorities had no previous experience by which to guide themselves," or in Schwartz's (1986, 12) words, the authorities were "unschooled in the practices that preclude such a development." *The Economist* (June 20, 1931, 1311) was not only premature but also too optimistic when it pronounced that "when the history of this difficult period comes to be written, it may well emerge that

---

[58] This argument was used by Kindleberger (1978, 198) for Germany, but it was equally valid for Austria, as the majority of capital flows were initiated by frightened Austrians, while the foreign creditors had agreed to a two-year standstill in exchange for a governmental guarantee and very generous interest rates.

the newly-founded B.I.S. will have played a great role in staving off financial disaster."

"The Bank of England," on the other hand, "from which leadership might ordinarily have been expected, was in no position to organize an adequate cooperative effort" (Clarke 1967, 186), and had to fight with its own liquidity problems.[59]

Summing up, we have to observe that the run on the schilling did not reflect a temporary loss of confidence in the stability of the fixed parity, but it was based on economic fundamentals. Therefore, we have to agree with Eichengreen's (1987, 47) point that "no amount of short-term lending would have done more than delay the crisis in the absence of measures to eliminate the underlying imbalance. The existence of an international lender of last resort could have affected the timing but not the fact of collapse."

Austria was ill-advised to rely on the intervention of an international deus ex machina and, therefore, to weaken its self-reliance – another ill-fated consequence of 1922.

[59] On September 16, 1931, at the height of the problems in England, Austria had to repay 50 million schillings of the BofE loan, while the remaining 100 million schillings as well as the BIS credit were due on October 16, but were then extended several times.

8. Alternative policies and policy implications

History may not repeat itself, but some of its lessons are inescapable. One is that in the world of high and confident finance little is ever really new.

—J. K. Galbraith, 1987

Alternative policies

Policy errors helped to shape the rather unfortunate developments. Therefore the question arises, whether any alternative policies could have been more successful in containing the crisis and in preventing or alleviating the negative effects on economic activity.

Economists are in the unfortunate position of having no laboratory experiments at their disposal, so that their conclusions about policies that have not actually been used can only be circumstantial. Always keeping in mind the idiosyncrasies of any observed case, one can compare the fate of the Credit-Anstalt to that of other banks, and the fate of Austria to that of countries that followed different policies.

In addition to the Credit-Anstalt, there were three large banks in Vienna. Among those the Niederösterreichische Escompte-Gesellschaft and the Wiener Bank-Verein had to be reorganized with government assistance in 1934. Their losses were considerably smaller than those of the Credit-Anstalt (in absolute as well as relative terms). The third one, the Länderbank, did not suffer any losses at all. This suggests that other, more cautious and sounder policies could have been followed. Managerial ineptitude played an important role. Therefore, alternative business policies could have limited or prevented some of the losses.

As far as the policies of the authorities are concerned, the Austrian record can be contrasted with that of other countries. Germany experienced a banking crisis similar to that of Austria, but it reacted quite differently. It immediately implemented banking holidays, exchange controls, and bank mergers, and required a purge of the inept bank managers.[1] Consequently, it had solved its banking problems long before Austria, and confidence returned sooner. Its economic upswing occurred long before the one in Austria.[2]

In 1931, Austria adhered to the international gold exchange standard and pegged its currency directly to the value of the dollar, thus linking itself to United States monetary policy. Both countries witnessed strong declines in their respective money supplies. Therefore the question arises whether Austria could have fared better by breaking this link to the dollar and by switching to flexible exchange rates. Choudhri and Kochin (1980) present evidence that those countries that did choose flexible exchange rates, in particular Spain and to a lesser degree the Scandinavian countries, Finland, Denmark, and Norway, isolated themselves rather successfully from the deflationary spiral of the gold standard and enjoyed stability of output and prices. Eichengreen and Sachs (1986) show that in ten European countries during the 1930s there was statistically significant negative correlation between the extent of depreciation of a country's currency and its level of industrial production. Further evidence results from the case of Great Britain, which devalued in September 1931, thus "fostering a remarkable recovery of output" (Saint-Etienne 1984, 57), and from Sweden, which left the gold standard and made price stability the official goal of the central bank, thus counteracting any contractionary impulses and keeping income and employment high (Jonung 1979, 1981). Gordon and Wilcox (1981, 83) conclude then that "devaluations in Britain, Scandinavia, and other countries in September 1931 stimulated early recoveries there while deepening the slide in the United States and Germany," and, we have to add, Austria. "Germany, Austria, and Hungary did not devalue their currencies like most of the other countries and thus followed the United States monetary lead to the bitter end" (Vaubel, 1984, 264).

Why then did Austria refuse to devalue and why did it follow the United States further into deflation and depression? One reason that influenced the policymakers' decisions might have been the rela-

---

[1] In Austria, by contrast, it took months for the leading managers to be replaced by new ones.

[2] Speedy banking reconstruction was not the only reason for Germany's earlier and stronger revival, but it was a precondition.

tively large foreign debt.[3] A devaluation would have increased the real burden of debt over and above the real increases suffered because of the ongoing deflation.[4] Moreover, according to the reconstruction plan of 1922, the League of Nations required the Austrian National Bank to maintain the stability of the exchange rate. More important than both of these reasons seems to be the factor that we had already encountered so often as decisive for the public's and the authorities' reactions, namely the painful experience with hyperinflation. It influenced the decision to remain on a fixed exchange rate in two ways: First, the trauma of hyperinflation had created a widespread association of devaluation with inflation, and second, there was a fear that devaluation would send unfavorable signals to potential foreign creditors. Austria adhered to the old gold parity of its schilling and preferred to accept an outflow of its reserves, the establishment of parallel markets for schillings at large discounts, and the introduction of exchange controls.

During the course of the financial crisis, many other decisions had to be made, and alternative approaches could have changed the flow of events. The question arises, then, why certain (potentially better) policies had not been used.[5] But we are not in a position to judge how the outcome would have differed. It seems then more relevant to discuss some of the policy implications for today and tomorrow that result from the events in Austria in 1931.

Policy implications

At the outset we have to reiterate that we have dealt with a single country's plight at a certain period in history, so that all our observations and conclusions might be subject to those "eccentricities

---

[3] Total public debt in foreign currencies at the end of 1930 amounted to about 2,173 million schillings (Institute of International Finance 1936, 23).

[4] The League of Nations loan of 1923 had as security, in addition to the guarantees of some European governments, the gross receipts from the customs and tobacco monopoly. The pledged revenues had to be turned over to the trustee, who retained the sum necessary for the service of the loan and returned the balance to the government. Higher debt service in domestic currency – due to a devaluation – would have reduced the amounts returned to the government and increased the budget deficit. That was undesirable, especially at a time when the public paid so much attention and reacted so strongly to budget deficits.

[5] For instance, what would have happened had the government supported the dependent industries instead of the Credit-Anstalt?

of specific cases," and that general policy conclusions have to be drawn in a very careful way. We have to keep in mind that behind the economic events observed and analyzed, there was a plethora of psychological, sociological, and especially political influences that helped to shape them. Such factors exist in any such crisis and can, therefore, lead to very different outcomes, even if the economic variables are the same.

The institutional arrangements at the beginning of the 1990s differ in a number of important ways from those of the 1930s. Markets are more efficient, communications, information, and technology have been improved, prudential supervision has been exter.ied and strengthened, management techniques have improved, and deposit insurance is institutionalized. In most countries regulatory changes have contributed to more stable banking systems.[6] Minimum reserve requirements, capital adequacy requirements, limits on debt exposure, increased information requirements, deposit insurance, supervision, and many other new tools have been crucial in creating a financial environment that is, on balance, less likely to experience runs than the unstable and unregulated banking sector of the 1920s and 1930s. But banking is still – and even more than ever – a highly leveraged business, bank debtors still go bankrupt, and dishonest or corrupt bankers still exist. Errors in judgment are still being made, partly out of information asymmetries. And bad government policies are still common.

Banks and their business dealings are no longer such terrae incognitae as they were sixty years ago. Nevertheless, banks still collapse,[7] and, therefore, historic experiences can give us valuable guidelines concerning the proper precautionary actions and correct reactions.

If one very general conclusion can be drawn from the Austrian financial crisis of 1931, it is that "a misinformed public can nullify the beneficial effects of actions designed to avert panic" (Schwartz 1986, 20). Unfortunately, this was not recognized by the authorities at that time. Lack of information, misinformation, and contradictory information are all ideal breeding grounds for rumors and pan-

---

[6] Regulations have not only stabilized the banking systems but also contributed to banking problems, especially so in the United States.
[7] In the United States, for instance, at the end of the 1980s the number of bank failures reached the highest rate since the Great Depression.

ics, and they all contributed very decisively to the Austrian crisis. Financial crises usually spread most quickly when information is least complete, and Bagehot's conclusion that the public have a right to know whether the central bank will intervene as a lender of last resort is still as valid as during the nineteenth century. Not only did the public lack reliable information but the government and the central bank made most of their decisions on the basis of a very limited or even distorted knowledge of the facts. Although in this kind of situation, when the speed of intervention is such an important factor, decisions under uncertainty are unavoidable, the Austrian authorities were ill-advised to take those crucial steps without sufficient information, or without investigating more thoroughly the information provided.

Several policy recommendations can be drawn from this case study of a financial crisis. Very generally, we can divide them into three categories, one dealing with avoiding the recurrence of the collapse of such a bank, one concerning the proper reaction of the authorities should such a financial crisis occur, and one consisting of recommendations with respect to a more stable economic environment.

Innovation, globalization, securitization, and many other factors have changed the business of banking in the decades since the Great Depression. But, as the popular saying goes, "the more things change, the more they stay the same." Many of the banking issues of the early 1930s are still relevant sixty years later. It is somewhat surprising to see that, in spite of the traumatic events of the 1930s, a lot of the issues that played an important role in the problems of the banks are still contributing to bank failures.

The fact that the Credit-Anstalt collapsed, and that for months the true state of affairs was not known, was to a considerable extent owing to the lack of adequate supervision. The government and the central bank participated in the rescue and guaranteed the deposits without knowing the true extent of the problems – a very costly mistake. Astonishing parallels exist to the crisis of the United States thrift industry at the end of the 1980s. Inadequate supervision in a time of large (regulatory) changes prevented the timely recognition and solution of the problems. The combination of (implicit) deposit insurance and lack of adequate supervision in a largely deregulated world was a crucial contributing factor to the Credit-Anstalt crisis, and it played an important role in the American thrift crisis. In the interwar period, protective regulation without adequate preventive regulation cost the taxpayers of Austria considerable amounts of money, and it will do the same to the American taxpayers during the 1990s.[8] The ideal mix of these two forms of regulation has still not been found by the regulators.

The Credit-Anstalt crisis should also teach present and future bank managers and regulators about the dangers inherent in an extremely close link between banks and other industries. The peculiar Austrian banking structure, which was also common in Germany, was a crucial factor in the bank's plight. As we recall, this bank was shareholder and creditor of a considerable part of Austrian industry, and its directors sat on many company boards. Large parts of its assets were locked up in industrial undertakings. The extensive equity holdings of the CA and of other Austrian banks had resulted from unsold share issues and from later share purchases in order to support the share prices of client firms. The difficulties of these industries – caused by the business depression – had multiple repercussions on the bank. Its loans became immobilized, and its securities portfolio became frozen and suffered in value. The bank had no choice but to extend further credits to these sick industries in order to protect the value of its own portfolio.

Tendencies to erode the separation between banking and commerce are today an issue in the financial systems of the United States and Japan. Leveraged buyouts and similar transactions as well as regulatory changes lead to financial institutions acquiring equity stakes in commercial firms. Some regulators view with concern and alarm the consequences of such a "commingling of commercial and banking institutions," and are concerned about "the growing tendency of investment banks to be sizeable equity holders in firms for which they render a wide variety of investment banking services" (Corrigan 1989, 5).

In consideration of banking history, these concerns are well-founded and should not be disregarded when the United States goes about breaking down the Glass-Steagall regulations. This intermingling of commercial and banking institutions poses not only a problem to the banks, but also to the bank regulators and the lender of

[8] For a detailed description of preventive and protective regulation, see Baltensperger and Dermine, 1987.

last resort. Such arrangements can easily lead to an extension of the safety net to include the commercial activities and institutions of the banks – something that would not necessarily be in the best interest of the central banks or the deposit insurance systems. Although a complete separation of banking and commerce might be neither desirable nor necessary, excessive cross ownership should be avoided, as the Credit-Anstalt example showed so drastically.[9]

The Credit-Anstalt was by far the largest bank in Austria, accounting for more than half of the business of all commercial banks. It had reached this position by a sequence of (more or less) forced mergers with failing Viennese institutions. Consequently, when the crisis broke, it was too large to be assisted by the other Austrian banks, and it even turned out to be too large for the rescue attempts of the Austrian state. One has to agree with *The Banker* (July 1931, 14) that "it is decidedly a sounder situation if there are several banks of approximately equal importance, for if any one of them gets into trouble, the others are in a position to help." Whether they actually do help is then a different issue.

Today, in most industrialized countries, the banking situation is very different from that of Austria in the 1930s. None of the countries has such a dominant financial institution as the CA was for Austria. But nevertheless, as Europe gets ready to create the Single Market and banks start looking for other banks to merge with, this lesson from the 1930s might become more relevant again. Despite the possible economies of scale and scope, banking concentration to the extent it happened in interwar Austria has to be prevented, not only to avoid monopolistic price setting but also to avoid an unsound banking situation. A single institution must not become "the market."[10]

Another issue raised by the Credit-Anstalt crisis, which has survived the six decades since the traumatic events of the interwar

[9] Concern about the potential problems with a very close association between banks and nonbanking institutions has led the European Community to put limits on banks' holdings of equity in other industries.

[10] The creation of a single European financial area with banks operating in all EC countries with one single license extends each bank's market beyond the national borders. Therefore, each bank becomes smaller relative to its market. But as long as there is no common European central bank, the lender-of-last-resort function remains a national function, and the banks become larger relative to their respective lenders of last resort.

years, is the issue of banks buying their own shares or having friends or clients buy them to support their value. As we recall, the Credit-Anstalt had bought a large part of its own shares in order to support the price, without reducing the published equity accordingly. Similar transactions occurred at the Danatbank in Germany. One of the results of these buy-backs was manipulation of the share prices, so that they no longer reflected the market's evaluation of the value of the particular company. At the same time, the equity bases of the institutions were reduced, making them less resilient to eventual shocks.

A similar but somewhat more sophisticated technique was used by the Bank of the United States, which failed in 1930 and evoked much controversy at that time. It gave loans to affiliates for the purpose of supporting the bank's stock and encouraged depositors into purchasing it (Lucia 1985). The bank even offered them a commitment to repurchase the stocks at a fixed price.

Despite the disastrous effects these attempts had, similar techniques are still around. A very drastic example occurred in Israel in the early 1980s. Banks offered their shares to their clients as liquid investment opportunities and secured an attractive return on them by supporting the prices. With the collapse of the bull market in the spring of 1983, the banks could no longer afford to support their shares, and a run on the banks seemed to be imminent. The state intervened, guaranteed the prices, and suspended the trading of the bank stocks, and finally nationalized the banks. A less dramatic but still potentially dangerous practice was discovered in Spain in 1989. Spanish retail banks were caught by their supervisors selling shares to friendly clients and employees at heavy discounts, mainly using soft loans in order to encourage the buyers (*Financial Times*, March 17, 1989).

It is then a challenge to the lawmakers and the bank supervisors around the world to ensure that these lessons of the 1930s are understood and not allowed to be repeated.

The Credit-Anstalt and all the other Austrian and German banks of the interwar period were known for their large hidden reserves, resulting from an undervaluation of assets. There was the implicit assumption that losses could be easily absorbed by those institutions, simply by realizing parts of their enormous hidden assets. As a consequence the public remained unconcerned in view of the recurrent news of losses and collapses of many industrial enterprises, which were closely linked to these banks. On May 11, 1931, there was a rude awakening in Austria and two months later in Germany. The cushions of reserves were more imaginary than real, and the large banks – thought to be unsinkable – had to reveal the losses of most of their equity. The misguided trust in the hidden assets had reduced the necessary precaution. Instead of contributing to the stability of the system by allowing the banks to smooth out variations in performance, the hidden reserves had actually reduced stability by concealing important information.

Sixty years later hidden reserves still exist in some banking systems, especially in continental Europe, and they still create problems for bank regulators interested in the truthfulness of the published accounts. Swiss law, for instance, continued to allow banks to build up and dissolve hidden reserves with no obligation to reflect changes in the reserves in their annual reports by the end of the 1980s. As a result, more than half of the banks in Switzerland dipped into their hidden assets to improve their reported performance after the 1987 stock market correction (*International Herald Tribune,* February 25–6, 1989, 11). This led then to a reevaluation of the guidelines about drawing up published accounts.

Large hidden reserves enable banks – at least for a while – to cushion losses, to manipulate earnings, and to hide underlying problems, thereby protecting confidence. If a problem is solved immediately, then using such reserves might contribute to stability, but if they serve to avoid corrective action, then they are more likely to worsen the results. Without adequate information on the status of the banks, depositors cannot choose correctly. It is a challenge for the bank supervisors to find the right balance between the advantages and drawbacks of hidden reserves.

Securities constituted a large part of the portfolio of the Credit-Anstalt,[11] and they form an even larger part of the portfolios of many contemporary commercial banks. Holding securities creates for a bank the impression of potential liquidity, allowing it to dispose of them in well-functioning capital markets whenever needed. The international trend toward securitization has reinforced this feeling of liquidity. But as the crisis of 1931 and the events around

[11] Based on the published accounts of June 1930, almost 20 percent of the assets were in the form of securities.

the stock market correction of October 1987 showed so vividly, in times of crisis, liquidity might be an illusion. An individual bank or financial institution cannot face a liquidity problem, since it can increase its liquidity by selling assets in the market at their going market price. However, when most of the market participants attempt to sell or when the one trying to dispose of its assets is very large relative to the market and the mood of the market is very bearish, liquidity can only be bought at a very high price – by selling assets at very unfavorable prices. At the present time, characterized by large-scale securitization, bankers as well as their supervisors are challenged to make a realistic assessment of the liquidity of the individual institutions under possible crisis scenarios. Forced selling can quickly turn illiquidity into insolvency.

We recall that the CA had lost more than 60 percent of its loans to foreign debtors, highlighting very clearly the dangers of foreign lending. The present-day problems of many banks in the industrialized countries originated from just the same source. Foreign lending involves more aspects of risk, since exchange rate risk and political risk have to be added to the risk of default. It is also accompanied by a much larger informational asymmetry between the borrower and the lender than domestic lending. Disregard of these principles contributed very prominently to the painful experience of the CA, just as it did to many of the internationally engaged commercial banks in the 1980s. The international trend toward liberalization of capital flows and banking services will further increase the share of foreign business in bank balance sheets and with that the risks mentioned will pose a tremendous challenge to bankers as well as their supervisors.

Maturity mismatch was one of the fundamental problems of the Austrian banks, and its dangers are valid at any time and anywhere. It is part of the banks' services, and the banks are paid for bearing this risk. Increased mobility of funds, large interest-rate volatility, a growing number of financial investment alternatives add potentially to this problem. On the other hand, real investment projects become larger and require longer payback periods, increasing the difficulties of financial intermediaries to match the maturities of their assets and liabilities. The experience of the savings and loan industry in the United States during the 1980s is but one example of the potential dangers involved in refinancing long-term assets with short-term liabilities, especially if the first carry fixed and the latter variable interest rates.

As far as the handling of incipient crises is concerned, the events of 1931 provide valuable policy implications. While the initial run on the other Viennese banks was successfully stopped by the liquidity injections of the Austrian National Bank, the case of the attempted CA bailout highlights some of the potential mistakes. In this episode, the ANB had violated some of the key points of Bagehot's rule by assisting an insolvent bank, by following a stop-go approach, and by accepting "bad bills or bad securities."

Can Bagehot's rule, then, be used as an unambiguous policy recommendation for such crises? His general advice is that it is sufficient to provide liquidity to the "solvent merchants and bankers" who comprise the "great majority" of the market (Bagehot 1962, 97). In the case of the failure of one or more small banks, this rule seems to be rather straightforward, but in the case of a large bank failure, it becomes more ambiguous. Should large banks be allowed to fail? "Bagehot did not think it appropriate for the central bank to extend aid to poorly managed key banks" (Humphrey and Keleher 1984, 303), as long as the sound majority is protected. In a situation like the CA crisis, however, the correct policy approach becomes more complicated, since the insolvent bank constituted "the unsound majority." Its balance sheet total was in excess of 50 percent of the total of all commercial banks in Austria, and as we mentioned above, a very considerable part of Austrian industry was heavily dependent on this bank. From the perspective of optimal resource allocation, it would still seem correct to let this bank fail, but the overwhelming relative size of the bank might be considered a characteristic special enough to "invalidate the traditional argument for permitting failure" (Mayer 1975, 603).[12,13] The money supply should, in any case, not be allowed to fall – that is, the secondary repercussions of the crisis have to be avoided.

In general terms, the lender-of-last-resort function is much better understood today than it was sixty years ago – in a national as well

---

[12] "Failure" includes also the possibility of a merger with another institution. For arguments for and against letting large banks fail, see Mayer (1975).

[13] Since the rescue of the Continental Illinois Bank in 1984, it is clear that the U.S. government is not prepared to let any of the large commercial banks fail.

as in an international context. The failures of the 1930s taught the policymakers the lesson that a credit squeeze and a drop in the money supply had to be avoided. The most vivid and most publicized example was the famous one-sentence statement issued by the chairman of the U.S. Federal Reserve Board the day after the 22.6 percent drop in the New York Stock Exchange in October 1987: "The Federal Reserve, consistent with its responsibilities as the nation's central bank, affirmed today its readiness to serve as a source of liquidity to support the economic and financial system" (Wall Street Journal, November 25, 1987, 7). This statement, very short but very clear, calmed the fears of the market that a credit crisis might follow the stock market crisis. The explicit and publicized commitment by the Fed immediately restored confidence in the system, and no other crisis followed.[14]

Less than two years later, in spring 1989, the Federal Reserve saw another need to intervene as lender of last resort by offering liquidity to the savings and loan industry in order to help it cope with the potential threat of withdrawals by depositors. This time, however, considerable criticism was voiced, since many of the thrift institutions were considered insolvent, not merely illiquid, and their collateral was judged to be rather dubious.[15] Once again, the old conflict over the traditional role of the lender of last resort re-emerged.

As Eichengreen and Portes (1987, 33) point out, "there are also stronger domestic lenders of last resort ... with more extensive supervisory and regulatory roles now than fifty years ago." But continuous developments toward deregulation, liberalization, and innovation require that supervision be constantly improved and in-

[14] It is worth mentioning that one of the first actions of Chairman Greenspan, following his appointment to the helm of the Fed, was to have his staff work out adequate action programs for various potential crises, one of them being a stock market crash. Since in times of crises the period to react is usually very short and the actions have to be clear and consistent, it is very crucial to be prepared. Unfortunately the Austrian authorities were not prepared to deal with the Credit-Anstalt crisis in 1931.

[15] The Fed announced that it was prepared to accept as collateral from thrifts with liquidity problems notes issued by the Federal Savings and Loan Insurance Corporation (FSLIC). The FSLIC, however, was already insolvent at that time, and the U.S. Congress never put its faith and credit behind these notes (see The Economist, March 11, 1989, 90).

ternationally coordinated. Banking supervision in interwar Austria was completely inadequate and could not perform its functions.[16] But that was largely a domestic problem. At the beginning of the 1990s, banking supervision is an international problem that requires international solutions. Deregulation has led to a free flow of capital and services, and made regulatory arbitrage possible. In order to avoid this form of competition in laxity, to create a "level playing field" for all internationally active banks, and to secure the soundness of the international financial system, the Basel Committee on Banking Regulations and Supervisory Practices of the Group of Ten countries meeting at the BIS adopted internationally agreed standards for minimum solvency ratios for internationally engaged banks. This move should inspire more confidence in the international banking system, contribute to financial stability, and help to reduce the probability of internationally transmitted banking problems, like those of the 1930s. "In banking and finance, public confidence is the bottom line and systemic risk is the ultimate threat" (Corrigan 1989, 6), and it is the goal of such international agreements to reduce this threat.

The question of permitting or preventing the failure of a large bank is intimately connected to the question of deposit insurance. The Austrian experience of 1931 suggests a very clear policy conclusion. The existence of deposit insurance is not enough to prevent or stop panicky withdrawals by frightened depositors. The crucial point in such a case is the perceived standing of the insurer. In Austria, the government became the insurer, and the withdrawals did not stop: Its financial situation was not sound enough to create confidence. Developments in the United States (in Ohio and Maryland) in 1985 led to similar conclusions. Private insurance funds were perceived as being insufficiently endowed, and runs developed, triggered by losses at the largest S&Ls. At the same time, no such runs occurred on federally insured banks or S&Ls.[17] This episode showed that formal insurance alone does not suffice. The security of the private sector's deposits must be assured beyond any rea-

[16] Inadequate supervision was also one of the factors contributing to the 1984 collapse of Johnson Matthey Bankers (JMB) in England. As the *Financial Times* (December 18, 1985, 12) remarked, supervision was "altogether too gentlemanly." Similarly the crisis of the American thrift industry could never have reached such a dimension had supervision been adequate.

[17] For a more detailed account see Gilbert and Wood, 1986.

sonable doubt, backed up by the monetary authority issuing high-powered money.[18]

The interdependence of international financial markets has grown tremendously since the 1930s, especially so during the 1980s, linking the markets more closely together than ever before. The probability of a run of depositors has been reduced in most industrialized countries by deposit insurance; nevertheless the tremendous growth in international interbank connections has increased the risk of a run by other banks. The refusal to provide short-term financing – like interbank loans on the Eurocurrency market – can easily bring a bank down. Because of the close links and the modern means of electronic transmission, an international chain reaction of collapses can occur within hours. Unfavorable rumors are all that is needed.[19] Accordingly, the need for international cooperation has increased. Although the fixed exchange rate system of the 1930s is no longer in existence, and therefore the probability of international propagation of a financial crisis via the monetary standard reduced, the multitude of international links and the existence of large unregulated international financial markets (such as the Eurodollar market) require widespread international cooperation, independently of political considerations.

The story of the international lender of last resort during the crisis of the 1930s was one of failure. None of the institutions that could have played this role in May/June 1931 performed it in a satisfactory way: not the Bank of England, not the Bank for International Settlements, not the Federal Reserve Bank of New York, and not the Banque de France. If there was a chance to stop the problem from spreading, it was not grabbed in time. All the actions were rather hesitant and therefore unsuccessful. In this matter, there is a clear case for speedy international cooperation and for clear rules concerning the respective responsibilities in times of crises.

In today's world the problem of an international lender of last resort appears to be much better understood, and there are international committees or organizations to deal with such problems

---

[18] The question is not whether insurance is provided by public or private institutions but rather whether it is considered to be sufficient.

[19] The collapse of the Continental Illinois Bank in 1984 gave an indication of how quickly such unfavorable news can travel around the globe.

To some extent the International Monetary Fund acts as an international lender of last resort, while also serving the capital market in a signalling capacity, providing information on domestic adjustment programs and helping to differentiate among borrowers. (Eichengreen and Portes 1987, 33)

By performing this function it is "reducing the risk that the difficulties of one [debtor country] will be transmitted infectiously to others who are creditworthy" (ibid., 49). But its procedures are rather slow in order to intervene as a LLR in a sudden crisis. A more functional international LLR is available to the members of the European Monetary System. Short-term foreign exchange credits are available to each of the participating countries should strong capital outflows endanger the exchange rate or the reserves. The purpose of this procedure is to calm fears and to provide time to remedy the underlying problems that have caused the outflow. But no comparable international arrangements exist in the case of bank collapses spreading around the world. The international lender of last resort for the Euromarkets does not yet exist.

On a more general level, the events of the 1930s showed very clearly the importance of an open world trading system for economic prosperity. This conclusion has not lost its relevance over the last sixty years. Debtor countries cannot service their foreign debts unless they are able to export. The easiest way to induce defaults is to make it difficult for borrowing countries to service their debts by inhibiting their exports. As *The Economist* (September 26, 1931, 553) pointed out, citing a report of the subcommittee of the British National Committee of the International Chamber of Commerce:

[I]nternational debts must be discharged by the transfer of goods, or services, or gold, or by balancing international investments either on long term or on short term. High customs tariffs have interposed a most serious obstacle to the discharge of these debts through the transfer of goods. . . . The creditor countries are failing to recognise the duty which lies upon the creditor of not preventing the debtor from paying. Great exporting and creditor nations are not realising the truth that they cannot sell unless they support the world market, either as buyers or as permanent investors.

This was true in the 1920s and 1930s and is still true as we approach the end of the twentieth century. Protectionism in all parts of the world, especially so in the Successor States of the Austro-Hungarian Empire[20] and in the United States (Smoot-Hawley Tariff Law of

[20] According to estimates of the Austrian Branch of the International Chamber of

June 1930), was an important contributing factor to the large drop in Austrian exports.[21] Between 1929 and 1932 exports fell in nominal terms by 65 percent, cutting Austria's capacity to service its debt by two thirds.[22]

Today the same problem is at the heart of the international debt crisis. Sixty years after the passage of the Smoot-Hawley Act, outright protectionism still remains a threat, and politicians are eager to use it for political purposes.[23] Unfortunately, protectionism is infectious. Within the General Agreement on Tariffs and Trade (GATT), there are formal mechanisms to deal with the problems of protectionism that were not available during the 1930s. But even such a formal mechanism can only be successful, if there is a large country (or a group of countries) that commits itself to keeping its market open and puts pressure on others to do the same. This kind of leadership is lacking since the lessons of the 1930s have still not been fully understood.

As Hertz (1933, 329) pointed out, "inflation poisoned the entire economic organisation of Austria and fostered a spirit of gambling which also greatly contributed to the ruin of the banks." Sixty years later this poison is still with the world economy, although the doses have varied throughout the decades and from country to country. Inflation with its destructive effects on the economy had been one of the starting points of the Austrian as well as the German banking problems of the 1930s. Similarly, the inflationary period of the 1970s planted the seeds for the crisis of the American thrift industry in

Commerce in 1927, tariffs in Austria amounted on average to about 19.2 percent of the value of the goods imported. Austrian goods, on the other hand, were subject to much higher tariffs in the countries of its trading partners: in Hungary 31.1 percent, in Czechoslovakia 36.4 percent, in Italy 38.6 percent, and in France even 58.1 percent (Hertz 1933, 328).

[21] It has to be recalled that foreign trade played a vital role in interwar Austria, more so than in most other countries. In 1929, per capita foreign trade of Austria amounted to $120, compared to only $81 for the United States, $82 for Czechoslovakia, and $107 for Germany (OIfK 1933, 27).

[22] The largest reductions in trade occurred in exports to the United States (−80 percent) and Czechoslovakia (−73 percent). Exports to all Successor States together dropped by 69 percent. Since Austria's export prices fell during this period by only about 20 percent, most of the reduction was in real terms.

[23] The passage of the U.S. Trade Bill in 1988 is a case in point, as are the multitude of bilateral voluntary export restraint agreements that the United States has forced on its trading partners during the 1980s.

the late 1980s.[24] In all three cases the destruction of the currency played a crucial part in the later banking problems. In the events of the 1930s, it destroyed the capital base of the banks, in the 1970s, the deposit base of the thrift institutions. In the end, in both cases, the taxpayers had to pay for the cleanup.

It has been shown that fiscal problems were fundamental to the currency crisis, as a result of fiscal excesses associated with inflationary finance. When the public perceived a breakdown of budgetary discipline, it questioned the value of the currency and fled into foreign assets in order to protect its wealth. Sixty years later the financing of large fiscal imbalances by money creation is still the driving force behind inflation and even hyperinflation in parts of the (developing) world. Investors shift away from domestic into foreign assets in order to avoid having to pay the inflation tax brought about by large fiscal imbalances. Therefore, all adjustment programs, like those of the International Monetary Fund, attach primary importance to fiscal correction as a precondition for general adjustment, just like the League of Nations' stabilization programs of the 1920s.

The economic disasters of the interwar period were not unavoidable; they did not have to happen. After six decades we have come to understand many of the causes, but many problems are yet unresolved. The purpose of this study is to add a few pieces to this puzzle, to add to our understanding of the economic dimensions of those events, and to add to our understanding of the policy mistakes, since "the policy mistakes that made it inevitable must not be repeated" (Saint-Etienne 1984, 104), and therefore they have to be properly understood.

[24] H. Robert Heller, a former member of the board of governors of the Federal Reserve Board, made this point very clearly, when he stated in a speech at the World Economic Forum in Davos, Switzerland, on February 1, 1989, that "the roots of the savings and loan problems lie in the inflationary excesses of the 1970s, that were followed by the high interest rates and the recession of the early 1980s."

9. Conclusions

History can repeat itself – with a vengeance.

—Henry Kaufman

The crisis of the Austrian Credit-Anstalt in 1931 is an interesting case study of a financial crisis with repercussions going far beyond the Austrian borders. The collapse of this bank opened the acute phase of the crisis, which shook the world economy to its foundations during the second half of 1931. The key areas covered by this study were (1) the analysis of the crisis in the context of leading theories of financial crises, (2) the identification of the causes of each stage of the crisis, (3) the examination of the market's efficiency in predicting the crisis, (4) the analysis of how the crisis was transmitted to the Austrian macroeconomy, (5) the study of the behavior of the authorities as lenders of last resort during the crisis and how their behavior shaped events, and, finally, (6) the identification of policy recommendations resulting from the events of 1931, which are still valid sixty years after the crisis. The comparison of the events in Austria with the three leading theoretic approaches to financial crises revealed that, for all the theories, the episode constituted a true financial crisis and not a pseudocrisis.

The financial distress of the Credit-Anstalt started this financial crisis with a short-lived run on the banking sector and a subsequent attack on the Austrian currency. The problems of the largest Austrian bank were caused by a plethora of reasons, and the banking panic by perceived similarities among the Viennese banks, but the currency crisis was a reaction to the way the initial episodes were handled. As far as the timing of the outbreak of the crisis is concerned, limited information prevents us from pointing to a certain date because the day of the announcement of the Credit-Anstalt's problems had no special connection with the occurrence of the financial distress. In considering the causes of the financial distress

185

of this prestigious banking institution, we have to distinguish between the causes of its insolvency and those of its illiquidity. The initial problem of the bank was the question of solvency, and that led to a problem with liquidity, as the public revised its expectations concerning the bank and became increasingly unwilling to hold its liabilities.

A further distinction seemed important, namely between those causes that were directly responsible for the problems (proximate causes), and those that had set the stage long before the events actually occurred (fundamental causes). The main proximate causes – the effects of the business depression and management errors – resulted in a crisis, because they affected a bank (or a banking system) that was fundamentally unstable. The main origins of this instability were the effects of the breakup of the monarchy, and the subsequent hyperinflation and its consequences, the ill-fated speculation of 1923–4, and the maturity mismatch between the bank's assets and liabilities. The collapse of the Credit-Anstalt was merely the climax of a difficult adjustment in the Austrian banking sector that began with the events of 1918–24 and ended in 1934.[1]

The perceived similarities among the Viennese banks and the fact that the largest and most prestigious among them experienced financial distress caused the public's short-lived run on the other financial institutions. The depositors as well as the creditors of the bank faced the question whether the Credit-Anstalt failure was due to bank-specific causes or whether it represented a shift in the risk of the whole banking system. After four days, the majority knew that the causes were largely bank-specific.

The attack on the currency was not an irrational and unexplainable panic by a confused public but rather a rational response to perceived inconsistencies in policy. Domestic credit growth to alleviate the liquidity problems of the ailing bank was seen to be inconsistent with the adherence to the gold exchange standard, and the public attacked the foreign exchange reserves of the Austrian National Bank. It recognized the potential for capital gains in hoarding foreign exchange instead of holding Austrian schillings, which

---

[1] The final chapter occurred in 1934, when the Niederösterreichische Escompte-Gesellschaft was incorporated by the Credit-Anstalt, and the Wiener Bank-Verein merged with this "new" Credit-Anstalt, becoming today's Creditanstalt-Bankverein.

were expected to be devalued. The refusal by the Austrian authorities to stop these inconsistencies led to a chronic shortage of foreign exchange and reduced allocations of foreign exchange, to the emergence of black (coffeehouse) markets in foreign currencies, and finally to exchange controls. Fundamental to this attack was the public's fear that the enormous potential increases in government debt – owing to its guarantees for all CA liabilities – would eventually be monetized because the prospect for alternative methods of financing appeared dim (until the signing of the Lausanne Protocols in July 1932).

The investigations of the efficiency of the market in predicting the crisis of the Credit-Anstalt and of the Austrian currency were mixed. Since the bank had intervened very heavily in the market for its stocks, no prior discounting of the bank's collapse could be detected. On the other hand, evidence was found in the bond market that beginning with the announcement of the Credit-Anstalt crisis the market's evaluation of the Austrian currency deteriorated.

The occurrence of the crisis and the way it was handled had disastrous effects on the real economy in Austria, deepening and extending the downturn, and postponing the nadir by more than a year and a half, and pushing unemployment above 25 percent. The money supply shock that followed the events of May 1931 exerted a strong downward pressure on the real sector. Rates of decline in excess of 20 percent occurred in 1931 followed by further reductions in the following three years.[2]

Just as in other countries that experienced banking crises, the deposit-currency ratio was the main determinant of this monetary shock. The public's scramble for high-powered money, following the announcement of the bank's collapse, more than offset the considerable increase in the monetary base. This – together with increased reserve holdings by the frightened banks – reduced the money supply.

Money demand and velocity were affected by these unprecedented events, with the different components of money being subject to very different changes, as the public switched into more liquid assets.

---

[2] Since those estimates were only based on Austrian schillings held by the public, substitution into foreign currencies might have biased our estimates of the true money stock in Austria downward and thus exaggerated the rate of destruction of money.

In spite of the turbulence, however, the standard money demand specification generated results very much in line with those for other countries and other periods. The preliminary test for the stability of the demand relationship did not reveal any indications of instabilities. The overall behavior of the money market in Austria during the financial crisis of 1931 was very similar to the behavior observed for other countries that had experienced bank collapses – for instance, the United States and Germany – thus, strengthening those earlier results by adding another conforming case study.

Historical accounts as well as economic theory suggest that the behavior of the monetary authorities is crucial during a potential financial crisis. Real financial crises only occur when relevant institutions are absent or authorities unschooled in their response to an arising crisis (Schwartz 1986, 12). The analysis of the behavior of the authorities in Austria during the crisis of 1931 is that they did not succeed in reducing the severity of the crisis. A misunderstanding of Bagehot's principle, excessive reliance on a deus ex machina from abroad, and the incorrect assessment of the adverse political reality in Europe all contributed to the unfortunate outcome. There was no shortage of lenders of last resort, domestic as well as international, but their respective commitments were rather partial, and therefore they could not restore confidence and stop the secondary repercussions of the failure of the Credit-Anstalt. The cost of those lender-of-last-resort actions had to be incurred without achieving any of the potential benefits. This episode was one additional confirmation for what Eichengreen and Portes (1987, 12) identified as "the critical role played by institutional arrangements in financial markets as a determinant of the system's vulnerability to destabilizing shocks." And the Austrian system was extremely vulnerable.

The crisis in Vienna had repercussions on the rest of Europe, especially on Germany, Hungary, and the other neighboring states. The shock waves were also felt in Paris, London, and even New York. Very soon after the outbreak of the crisis in Austria, the problems of Germany entered center stage, and the Austrian calamities became of only secondary importance. The traumatic events in Germany and England would, however, have occurred irrespective of the collapse of the Credit-Anstalt.

Interesting policy conclusions can be drawn from the events in

Vienna, which are still valid sixty years later. They comprise such issues as banking supervision, capital adequacy, maturity mismatch, hidden bank reserves, the role of the domestic and international lender of last resort, protectionism, inflation, fiscal imbalances, and international financial cooperation. Remarkable parallels to contemporary events can be detected, giving new life to Santayana's words: "Those who cannot remember the past are condemned to repeat it."

Bibliography

Akerlof, G. A. 1970. "The Market for 'Lemons': Qualitative Uncertainty and the Market Mechanism." *Quarterly Journal of Economics* 89 (3):488–500.

Andersen, L. C., and J. L. Jordan. 1968. "The Monetary Base – Explanation and Analytical Use." *Federal Reserve Bank of St. Louis Review,* August, 7–11.

Armstrong, H. F. 1932. "Danubia: Relief or Ruin." *Foreign Affairs* 10 (4):600–16 (July).

Ausch, K. 1968. *Als die Banken fielen.* Wien: Europa Verlag.

Bachinger, K., and H. Matis. 1974. *Der Oesterreichische Schilling.* Graz, Wien, Köln: Verlag Styria.

Bachmayer, O. 1960. *Die Geschichte der österreichischen Währungspolitik.* Heft XII, Wien: Schriftenreihe der Oesterreichischen Bankwissenschaftlichen Gesellschaft.

Bagehot, W. 1873. *Lombard Street.* Reprint 1962. Homewood, Ill.: Richard D. Irwin.

Balbach, A. B., and A. E. Burger. 1976. "Derivation of the Monetary Base." *Federal Reserve Bank of St. Louis Review,* November, 2–8. Reprinted in *Current Issues in Monetary Theory and Policy,* 2d ed., edited by Th. M. Havrilesky and T. J. Boorman, 256–78. Arlington Heights, Ill.: AHM Publishing Corp., 1980.

Ball, R., and P. Brown. 1968. "An Empirical Evaluation of Accounting Income Numbers." *Journal of Accounting Research* 6:159–78.

Baltensperger, E., and J. Dermine. 1987. "The Role of Public Policy in Ensuring Financial Stability: A Cross-country Comparative Perspective." In *Threats to International Financial Stability,* edited by R. Portes and A. K. Swoboda, 67–90. Cambridge: Cambridge University Press.

Barry, L. M. 1988. "FDIC Responds to Increasing Bank Failures." *Banking & Finance,* Federal Reserve Bank of St. Louis, Spring, 1–2.

Barth, J. R., and R. E. Keleher. 1984. " 'Financial Crises' and the Role of the Lender of Last Resort." *Federal Reserve Bank of Atlanta Economic Review,* January, 58–67.

Batchelor, R. A. 1986. "The Avoidance of Catastrophe: Two Nineteenth-Century Banking Crises." In *Financial Crises and the World Banking System,* edited by F. Capie and G. E. Wood, 41–73. New York: St. Martin's Press.

Batra, R. 1987. *The Great Depression of 1990.* New York: Simon & Schuster.

Bernanke, B. S. 1981. "Bankruptcy, Liquidity, and Recession." *American Economic Review* 71 (2):155–9 (May).

—— 1983. "Nonmonetary Effects of the Financial Crisis in the Propagation of the Great Depression." *American Economic Review* 73 (3):257–76 (June).

Beyen, J. W. 1949. *Money in a Maelstrom*. London: Macmillan.

Blejer, M. I. 1978. "Exchange Restrictions and the Monetary Approach to the Exchange Rate." In *The Economics of Exchange Rates: Selected Studies,* edited by J. A. Frenkel and H. G. Johnson. Reading, Mass.: Addison-Wesley Publishing Company, Inc.

—— 1979. "On Causality and the Monetary Approach to the Balance of Payments." *European Economic Review* 12:289–96 (July).

Boorman, J. T. 1980. "The Evidence on the Demand for Money: Theoretical Formulations and Empirical Results." In *Current Issues in Monetary Theory and Policy,* 2d. ed., edited by Th. M. Havrilesky and J. T. Boorman, 315–60. Arlington Heights, Ill.: AHM Publishing Corp.

Bordo, M. D. 1984. "The Gold Standard: The Traditional Approach." In *A Retrospective on the Classical Gold Standard, 1821–1931,* edited by M. D. Bordo and A. J. Schwartz. Chicago: University of Chicago Press.

—— 1986a. "Financial Crises, Banking Crises, Stock Market Crashes and the Money Supply: Some International Evidence 1870–1933." In *Financial Crises and the World Banking System,* edited by F. Capie and G. E. Wood, 190–248. New York: St. Martin's Press.

—— 1986b. "Explorations in Monetary History: A Survey of the Literature." *Explorations in Economic History* 23 (4):339–415 (October).

Born, K. E. 1967. *Die deutsche Bankenkrise 1931.* München: P. Piper & Co. Verlag.

—— 1977. *Geld und Banken im 19. und 20. Jahrhundert.* Stuttgart: Alfred Kröner Verlag.

Boughton, J. M. 1981. "Recent Instability of the Demand for Money: An International Perspective." *Southern Economic Journal,* January, 579–97.

Boughton, J. M., and E. R. Wicker. 1979. "The Behavior of the Currency-Deposit Ratio During the Great Depression." *Journal of Money, Credit and Banking,* November, 405–18.

Braun, M. S. 1932. "Gegenwartsprobleme der österreichischen Wirtschaftspolitik." *Archiv für Sozialwissenschaften und Sozialpolitik* 67:561–78.

Brown, R. L., and J. Durbin. 1968. *Methods of Investigating Whether a Regression Relationship Is Constant over Time.* Selected Mathematical Papers, European Meeting, 26. Amsterdam: Mathematical Center Tracts.

Brown, R. L., J. Durbin, and J. M. Evans. 1975. "Techniques for Testing the Constancy of Regression Relationships over Time." *Journal of the Royal Statistical Society,* Series B, 149–63.

Bryant, R. C. 1980. *Money and Monetary Policy in Interdependent Nations.* Washington, D.C.: The Brookings Institution.

Burnham, J. B. 1984. "World Debt and Monetary Order: Learning from the Past." *The Cato Journal* 4 (1):71–80 (Spring/Summer).

Butschek, F. 1983. "Vom Zusammenbruch zur 'Genfer Sanierung': Oesterreichische Wirtschaftsentwicklung 1918-1923." *Wirtschaft und Gesellschaft* 3:421-40.

Cacy, J. A. 1976. "Commercial Bank Loans and the Money Supply." *Federal Reserve Bank of Kansas City Monthly Review*, November, 3-10.

Cagan, P. 1965. *Determinants and Effects of Changes in the Stock of Money, 1875-1960.* New York: Columbia University Press.

Chandler, L. V. 1970. *America's Greatest Depression, 1929-1941.* New York: Harper & Row.

————— 1971. *American Monetary Policy, 1928-1941.* New York: Harper & Row.

Choudhri, E. U., and L. A. Kochin. 1980. "The Exchange Rate and the International Transmission of Business Cycle Disturbances: Some Evidence from the Great Depression." *Journal of Money, Credit, and Banking* 12 (4): 565-74 (November).

Claassen, E.-M. 1985. "The Latin American Debt Problem and the Lender-of-Last Resort Function." In *The Economics of the Caribbean Basin*, edited by M. B. Connolly and J. McDermott, 27-67. New York: Praeger.

Clarke, S. V. O. 1967. *Central Bank Cooperation: 1924-31.* New York: Federal Reserve Bank of New York.

Connolly, M. B., and D. Taylor. 1984. "The Exact Timing of the Collapse of an Exchange Regime and Its Impact on the Relative Price of Traded Goods." *Journal of Money, Credit, and Banking* 16 (2): 194-207 (May).

Cooley, T. F., and E. C. Prescott. 1973. "Varying Parameter Regression: A Theory and Some Applications." *Annals of Economic and Social Measurement* 2: 462-73 (October).

Corrigan, E. G. 1989. Remarks made before the 61st Annual Mid-Winter Meeting of the New York State Bankers Association on January 26, 1989. Reprinted in *Bank for International Settlements Review*, February 15, 1-6.

Coulbois, P. 1982. "Central Banks and Foreign-Exchange Crises Today." In *Financial Crises*, edited by C. P. Kindleberger and J.-P. Laffargue. New York: Cambridge University Press.

Credit-Anstalt 1928. *Geschäftsbericht 1927.* Wien.

————— 1931. *Geschäftsbericht 1930.* Wien.

Creditanstalt-Bankverein (1957). *Ein Jahrhundert Creditanstalt-Bankverein.* Wien.

Eichengreen, B. J. 1981. "Bank Failures, Balance of Payments and the 1931 Sterling Crisis." Harvard University, Discussion Paper No. 869, Cambridge, Mass.

————— 1983. "The Causes of British Business Cycles 1833-1913." *Journal of European Economic History* 12 (1):145-61 (Spring).

————— 1984. "Central Bank Cooperation under the Interwar Gold Standard." *Explorations in Economic History* 21.64-87.

————— 1987. "Hegemonic Stability Theories of the International Monetary System." The Brookings Institution, Discussion Paper No. 54, Washington, D.C.

Eichengreen, B. J., and R. Portes. 1987. "The Anatomy of Financial Crises." In *Threats to International Financial Stability*, edited by R. Portes and A. K. Swoboda 10–58. Cambridge: Cambridge University Press.

Eichengreen, B. J., and J. Sachs. 1986. "Exchange Rates and Economic Recovery in the 1930's." *Journal of Economic History* 45: 925–46.

Einzig, P. 1961. *A Dynamic Theory of Forward Exchange.* London: Macmillan.

Ellis, H. S. 1941. *Exchange Control in Central Europe.* Cambridge, Mass.: Harvard University Press.

Fama, E. F. 1970. "Efficient Capital Markets: A Review of the Theory and Empirical Work." *Journal of Finance* 25 (2):385–417 (May). Reprinted in *Modern Developments in Investment Management,* edited by J. Lorie and R. Brealey. New York: The Dryden Press, 1978.

Fama, E. F., L. Fisher, M. C. Jensen, and R. Roll. 1969. "The Adjustment of Stock Prices to New Information." *International Economic Review* 10 (1):1–21. Reprinted in *Modern Developments in Investment Management,* edited by J. Lorie and R. Brealey. New York: The Dryden Press, 1978.

Federn, W. 1925. "Die Kreditpolitik der Wiener Banken." In *Geldentwertung und Stabilisierung in ihren Einflüssen auf die soziale Entwicklung in Oesterreich,* edited by J. Bunzel. München, Leipzig.

—— 1932. "Der Zusammenbruch der Oesterreichischen Kreditanstalt." *Archiv für Sozialwissenschaft und Sozialpolitik* 67:403–35 (June). Translated by H. Jarecki in *Euromoney,* October 1976, 140–9, November 1976, 68–80.

Fisher, I. 1932. *Booms and Depressions.* New York: Adelphi.

—— 1935. "Are Booms and Depressions Transmitted Internationally Through Monetary Standards?" *Bulletin of the International Statistical Institute* 28 (1):1–29.

Flood, R. P., and P. M. Garber. 1980. "An Economic Theory of Monetary Reform." *Journal of Political Economy,* February, 24–56.

—— 1981. "A Systematic Banking Collapse in a Perfect Foresight World." National Bureau of Economic Research, Working Paper No. 691, Cambridge, Mass.

—— 1984. "Collapsing Exchange-Rate Regimes, Some Linear Examples." *Journal of International Economics* 17:1–13.

Francis, J. C. 1980. *Investments: Analysis and Management,* 3d ed. New York: McGraw-Hill.

Frankel, J. A. 1980. "Tests of Rational Expectations in the Forward Exchange Market." *Southern Economic Journal* 46 (4):1083–1101 (April).

Fraser, L. 1936. "The International Bank and its Future." *Foreign Affairs* 14 (3):453–64 (April).

Freedman, Ch. 1987. "Discussion." In *Threats to International Financial Stability,* edited by R. Portes and A. K. Swoboda. Cambridge: Cambridge University Press.

Frenkel, J. A. 1977. "The Forward Exchange Rate, Expectations and the Demand for Money: The German Hyperinflation." *American Economic Review,* September, 653–70.

—— 1980. "Exchange Rates, Prices, and Money: Lessons from the 1920's." *American Economic Review*, May, 235–42.

Friedman, M. 1968. "Factors Affecting the Level of Interest Rates." Reprinted in *Current Issues in Monetary Theory and Policy*, 2d ed., edited by T. M. Havrilesky and J. T. Boorman, 378–94. Arlington Heights, Ill.: AHM Publishing Corp., 1980.

Friedman, M., and A. J. Schwartz. 1963. *A Monetary History of the United States 1867–1960.* Princeton, N.J.: Princeton University Press.

—— 1970. *Monetary Statistics of the United States.* New York: National Bureau of Economic Research.

—— 1982. *Monetary Trends in the United States and the United Kingdom: Their Relation to Income, Prices, and Interest Rates, 1867–1975.* Chicago: University of Chicago Press.

Frowen, S. F., and P. Arestis. 1977. "The Demand for and Supply of Money in the Federal Republic of Germany: 1965–1974." In *Monetary Policy and Economic Activity in West Germany*, edited by S. F. Frowen, A. S. Courakis, and M. H. Miller. New York.

Galbraith, J. K. 1987. "The 1929 Parallel." *The Atlantic*, January, 62–6.

Gambs, C. M. 1977. "Bank Failures – An Historic Perspective." *Federal Reserve Bank of Kansas City Monthly Review*, June, 10–20.

Gandolfi, A. E. 1974. "Stability of the Demand for Money During the Great Depression – 1929–1933." *Journal of Political Economy* 82 (5):969–83 (September/October).

Gandolfi, A. E., and J. R. Lothian, 1976. "The Demand for Money from the Great Depression to the Present." *American Economic Review*, May, 46–51.

Garber, P. M. 1981. "The Lender of Last Resort and the Run on the Savings and Loans." National Bureau of Economic Research, Working Paper No. 823, Cambridge, Mass.

—— 1985. "The Collapse of Asset-Price-Fixing Regimes." In *The Economics of the Caribbean Basin*, edited by M. B. Connolly and J. McDermott, 287–301. New York: Praeger.

Genberg, A. H. 1976. "Aspects of the Monetary Approach to Balance-of-Payments Theory, An Empirical Study of Sweden." In *The Monetary Approach to the Balance of Payments*, edited by J. A. Frenkel and H. G. Johnson. London: Allen Unwin; and Toronto: University of Toronto Press.

Gilbert, R. A., and G. E. Wood. 1986. "Coping with Bank Failures: Some Lessons from the United States and the United Kingdom." *Federal Reserve Bank of St. Louis Review*, December, 5–14.

Glasgow, G. 1931. "Geneva, Chequers and Economics." *The Contemporary Review* 140 (787):101–16 (July).

Godfrey, M. D., C. W. J. Granger, and O. Morgenstern. 1964. "The Random-Walk Hypothesis of Stock Market Behavior." *Kyklos* 17:1–30.

Goldfeld, S. M. 1973. "The Demand for Money Revisited." *Brookings Papers on Economic Activity* 3(2):577–646.

Goldfeld, S. M., and R. E. Quandt. 1972. *Nonlinear Methods in Econometrics.* Amsterdam: North-Holland.

Goldsmith, R. W. 1982. "Comment." In *Financial Crises*, edited by C. P.

Kindleberger and J.-P. Laffargue. Cambridge: Cambridge University Press.

Gordon, R. J., and J. A. Wilcox. 1981. "Monetarist Interpretations of the Great Depression: An Evaluation and Critique." In *The Great Depression Revisited,* edited by K. Brunner. Boston: Martinus Nijhoff Publishing.

Gorton, G. 1983. "Banking Panics in Business Cycles." Federal Reserve Bank of Philadelphia. Mimeo.

Granger, C. W. J. 1969. "Investigating Causal Relations by Econometric Models and Cross Spectral Methods." *Econometrica* 37:428–38 (July).

Granger, C. W. J., and O. Morgenstern. 1963. "Spectral Analysis of New York Stock Prices." *Kyklos* 16:1–27.

Gratz, A. 1949. "Die österreichische Finanzpolitik von 1848 bis 1948." In *Hundert Jahre Oesterreichische Wirtschaftsentwicklung, 1848–1948,* edited by H. Mayer. Wien: Springer Verlag.

Griffiths, B. 1983. "Banking on Crisis." *Policy Review* 25:28–35 (Summer).

Gruber, F. 1930. "Der österreichische Bundeshaushalt in den Jahren 1923 bis 1930." *Oesterreichisches Jahrbuch 1929,* Wien: Bundespressedienst

Guttentag, J., and R. Herring. 1987. "Emergency Liquidity Assistance for International Banks." In *Threats to International Financial Stability,* edited by R. Portes and A. K. Swoboda. Cambridge: Cambridge University Press.

Haber, F. 1928. *Oesterreichs Wirtschaftsbilanz.* München und Leipzig: Dunker & Humbolt.

Haberler, G. 1976. *The World Economy, Money and the Great Depression 1919–1939.* Washington, D.C.: American Enterprise Institute.

Hamilton, J. D. 1987. "Monetary Factors in the Great Depression." *Journal of Monetary Economics* 19:145–169.

Hardach, G. 1984. "Banking and Industry in Germany in the Interwar Period 1919–1939." *The Journal of European Economic History* 13 (2), special issue (Fall).

Hawtrey, R. G. 1932. *The Art of Central Banking.* London: Longmans, Green.

Hertz, F. 1929. "Kapitalbedarf, Kapitalbildung und Volkseinkommen in Oesterreich." In *Kapitalbildung und Besteuerung,* edited by W. Lotz. Schriften des Vereins für Sozialpolitik, Band 174. München and Leipzig.

——— 1933. "The Economic Chaos in Central Europe." *The Contemporary Review* 143 (807):326–34 (March).

Higgins, B. 1978. "Velocity: Money's Second Dimension." *Federal Reserve Bank of Kansas City Economic Review,* June, 15–31.

Hirsch, F. 1977. "The Bagehot Problem." *The Manchester School of Economic and Social Studies* 46 (3):241–57 (September).

Hodson, H. V. 1932. "Nemesis: The Financial Outcome of the Post-War Years." In *Survey of International Affairs 1931,* edited by A. J. Toynbee. London: Oxford University Press.

Humphrey, T. M. 1975. "The Classical Concept of the Lender of Last Resort." *Federal Reserve Bank of Richmond Economic Review* 61(1): 2–9 (January/February).

Humphrey, T. M., and R. E. Keleher. 1984. "The Lender of Last Resort: A Historical Perspective." *The Cato Journal* 4. (1):275–318 (Spring/ Summer).

Hurst, W. 1932. "Holland, Switzerland, and Belgium and the English Gold Crisis of 1931." *Journal of Political Economy*, October, 638–60.

Husted, S., and M. Rush. 1984. "On Measuring the Nearness of Near Moneys, Revisited." *Journal of Monetary Economics* 14:171–81.

Institute of International Finance. 1936. "Credit Position of Austria." *Bulletin No. 83*, January, 1–30.

James, H. 1984. "The Causes of the German Banking Crisis of 1931." *Economic History Review*, February, 68–87.

Joham, J. 1935. "Die Gründung der Oesterreichischen Credit-Anstalt für Handel und Gewerbe am 31. Oktober 1855." *Mitteilungen des Verbandes Oesterreichischer Banken und Bankiers*, November, 261–76.

Johnson, H. G. 1962. "Monetary Theory and Policy." *American Economic Review*, June, 335–84.

Johnston, J. 1972. *Econometric Methods*, 2d ed. Tokyo: McGraw-Hill Kogakusha, Ltd.

Jonung, L. 1975. "Studies in the Monetary History of Sweden." Unpublished dissertation, University of California at Los Angeles.

——— 1981. "The Depression in Sweden and the United States: A Comparison of Causes and Policies." In *The Great Depression Revisited*, edited by K. Brunner. Boston: Martinus Nijhoff Publishing.

Judd, J. P., and J. L. Scadding. 1982. "The Search for a Stable Money Demand Function: A Survey of the Post-1973 Literature." *Journal of Economic Literature*, September, 993–1023.

Kaldor, N. 1932. "The Economic Situation of Austria." *Harvard Business Review*, October, 23–34.

Kamitz, R. 1949. "Die österreichische Geld- und Währungspolitik von 1848 bis 1948." *Hundert Jahre Oesterreichische Wirtschaftsentwicklung, 1848–1948*, edited by H. Mayer. Wien: Springer Verlag.

Kausel, A., N. Nemeth, and H. Seidel. 1965. "Oesterreichs Volkseinkommen 1913 bis 1963." *Monatsberichte des Oesterreichischen Instituts für Wirtschaftsforschung*, Sonderheft 14. Wien.

Kernbauer, H. 1981a. "Die Oesterreichische Nationalbank I." Mimeo.

——— 1981b. "Die Oesterreichische Nationalbank II." Mimeo.

——— 1982. "The Policy of the Austrian National Bank Before and During the 1931 Crisis." Paper presented at the Conference "The 1931 Crisis and Its Aftermath," Claire College, Cambridge, April 1982.

Kernbauer, H., E. März, and F. Weber. 1983. "Die wirtschaftliche Entwicklung." In *Oesterreich 1918–1938: Geschichte der 1. Republik*, edited by E. Weinzierl und K. Skalnik. Graz, Wien, Köln: Verlag Styria.

Keynes, J. M. 1924. *Monetary Reform*. New York: Harcourt, Brace & Co.

——— 1925. "The United States and Gold." In *European Currency and Finance*, Vol. I, edited by J. P. Young. Washington D.C: Government Printing Office.

Khan, M. S. 1974. "The Stability of the Demand-for-Money Function in the United States 1901–1965." *Journal of Political Economy* 82 (6):1205–19 (November/December).

Kindleberger, C. P. 1973. *The World in Depression, 1929–1939.* Berkeley: University of California Press.

——— 1978. *Manias, Panics and Crashes: A History of Financial Crises.* New York: Basic Books.

——— 1985. "Bank Failures: the 1930s and the 1980s." Paper prepared for the Federal Reserve Bank of San Francisco Conference "The Search for Financial Stability: The Last Fifty Years," Monterey, California, June 1985.

Kindleberger, C. P., and J.-P. Laffargue. 1982. "Introduction." In *Financial Crises,* edited by C. P. Kindleberger and J.-P. Laffargue. Cambridge: Cambridge University Press.

Klovland, J. T. 1982. "The Stability of the Demand for Money in the Interwar Years, The Case of Norway, 1925–39." *Journal of Money, Credit, and Banking* 14 (2):252–64 (May).

Laidler, D. 1985. *The Demand for Money: Theories and Evidence,* 3d ed. New York: T. Y. Crowell.

Laidler, D., and J. M. Parkin. 1970. "The Demand for Money in the United Kingdom 1956–1967: Preliminary Estimates." *The Manchester School of Economic and Social Studies* 38:187–208 (September).

Layton, W. F., and C. Rist. 1925. *The Economic Situation of Austria.* Geneva: League of Nations.

League of Nations 1931. *The Course and Phases of the World Economic Depression.* Geneva.

——— 1932. *World Economic Survey 1931–1932.* Geneva.

Leuthold, R. M. 1972. "Random Walk and Price Trends: The Live Cattle Futures Market." *Journal of Finance* 27:879–89 (September).

Lothian, J. R. 1976. The Demand for High-Powered Money." *American Economic Review,* March, 56–68.

Lucia, J. L. 1985. "The Failure of the Bank of United States: A Reappraisal." *Explorations in Economic History* 22:402–16.

McGouldrick, P. 1984. "Operations of the German Central Bank and the Rules of the Game, 1879–1913." In *A Retrospective on the Classical Gold Standard, 1821–1931,* edited by M. D. Bordo and A. J. Schwartz. Chicago: University of Chicago Press.

März, E. 1981. *Oesterreichische Bankpolitik in der Zeit der grossen Wende.* Wien: Verlag für Geschichte und Politik.

——— 1982. "Comments." In *Financial Crises,* edited by C. P. Kindleberger and J.-P. Laffargue. Cambridge: Cambridge University Press.

März, E., and F. Weber. 1983a. "Commentary." In *International Business and Central Europe, 1918–1939,* edited by A. Teichova and P. C. Cottrell. Leicester: Leicester University Press.

——— 1983b. "The Antecedents of the Austrian Financial Crash of 1931." *Zeitschrift für Wirtschafts- und Sozialwissenschaften,* Heft 5:497–519.

Mayer, T. 1975. "Should Large Banks Be Allowed to Fail?" *Journal of Financial and Quantitative Analysis,* November, 603–10.

Meltzer, A. H. 1976. "Monetary and Other Explanations of the Start of the Great Depression." *Journal of Monetary Economics* 2:455–71.

Minsky, H. P. 1977. "A Theory of Systematic Fragility." In *Financial Crises: Institutions and Markets in a Fragile Environment*, edited by E. I. Altman and A. W. Sametz, 138–52. New York: John Wiley & Sons, Inc.

——— 1982. *Can "It" Happen Again?* New York: M. E. Sharpe, Inc.

Moggridge, D. E. 1982. "Policy in the Crises of 1920 and 1929." In *Financial Crises*, edited by C. P. Kindleberger and J.-P. Laffargue. Cambridge: Cambridge University Press.

Morgenstern, O. 1931. "Kapital- und Kurswertänderungen der an der Wiener Börse notierten österreichischen Aktiengesellschaften 1913 bis 1930." *Zeitschrift für Nationalökonomie*, 251–5.

Nötel, R. 1984. "Money, Banking and Industry in Interwar Austria and Hungary." *Journal of European Economic History* 13 (2):137–202, special issue (Fall).

Nurkse, R. 1944. *International Currency Experience.* Geneva: League of Nations.

Oesterreichisches Institut für Konjunkturforschung. 1933. *Die Entwicklung der österreichischen Wirtschaft 1923–1932.* Wien.

——— 1946. *Der österreichische Außenhandel in den Grundzügen seiner Entwicklung.* Wien.

Pressburger, F. G. 1969. "Die Krise der Oesterreichischen Creditanstalt." *Revue Internationale d'Histoire de la Banque*, 2, Geneva, 83–118.

Pressburger, S. 1966. *Oesterreichische Notenbank 1816–1966,* Wien: Oesterreichische Nationalbank.

Quesnay, P. 1931. "Scope and Activities of the Bank for International Settlements." *The Banker* 18 (64):110–21 (May).

Reik, W. 1931. *Die Beziehungen der österreichischen Großbanken zur Industrie.* Wien, Berlin.

Reisch, R. 1923. *Stellung und Aufgaben der Oesterreichischen Nationalbank innerhalb des Wiederaufbauprogrammes.* Wien: Verband Oesterreichischer Banken und Bankiers.

——— 1931. "Schillingwährung und Oesterreichische Nationalbank." *Mitteilungen des Verbandes Oesterreichischer Banken und Bankiers*, July, 213–20.

Rothschild, K. W. 1947. *Austria's Economic Development Between the Two Wars.* London: Frederick Mullen Ltd.

Ruback, R. S. 1983. "The Cities Service Takeover: A Case Study." *Journal of Finance* 38 (2):319–30 (May).

Rutkowski, H. 1934. *Der Zusammenbruch der Oesterreichischen Credit-Anstalt für Handel und Gewerbe und ihre Rekonstruktion.* Bottrop in Westfalen: Buch-und Kunstdruckerei Wilhelm Postberg.

Saint-Etienne, C. 1984. *The Great Depression, 1929–1938: Lessons for the 1980s.* Stanford: Hoover Institution Press.

Santayana, G. 1905. *The Life of Reason.* Vol. I: *Reason in Common Sense,* New York: Scribners.

Sargent, T. J. 1982. "The Ends of Four Big Inflations." In *Inflation: Causes and Effects*, edited by R. E. Hall. Chicago: University of Chicago Press.

Schmidt, W. 1925. "Die Sparkassen." In *Geldentwertung und Stabilisierung*

200   **Bibliography**

in ihren Einflüssen auf die soziale Entwicklung in Oesterreich, edited by J. Bunzel. München, Leipzig.

Schwartz, A. J. 1981. "Understanding 1929–1933." In *The Great Depression Revisited,* edited by K. Brunner. Boston: Martinus Nijhoff Publishing.

—— 1986. "Real and Pseudo Financial Crises." In *Financial Crises and the World Banking System,* edited by F. Capie and G. E. Wood, 11–31. New York: St. Martin's Press.

Sokal, M. 1925. "Die Banken." In *Geldentwertung und Stabilisierung in ihren Einflüssen auf die soziale Entwicklung in Österreich,* edited by J. Bunzel. München, Leipzig.

—— 1935. "Neugestaltung und Zusammenfassung im österreichischen Bankwesen." *Mitteilungen des Verbandes Oesterreichischer Banken und Bankiers,* February, 1–40.

Sokal, M., and O. Rosenberg, 1929. "The Banking System of Austria." In *Foreign Banking Systems,* edited by P. H. Willis and B. H. Beckhart. New York: Henry Holt & Company.

Spinelli, F. 1980. "The Demand for Money in the Italian Economy: 1867–1965." *Journal of Monetary Economics* 6:83–104.

Stiefel, D. 1978. "Konjunkturelle Entwicklung und struktureller Wandel der österreichischen Wirtschaft in der Zwischenkriegszeit." Forschungsbericht Nr. 135. Institut für Höhere Studien, Wien.

—— 1983a. "The Reconstruction of the Credit-Anstalt." In *International Business and Central Europe, 1918–1939,* edited by A. Teichova and P. C. Cottrell. Leicester: Leicester University Press.

—— 1983b. "Managementprobleme und die österreichische Bankenkrise des Jahres 1931." In *Management und Organisation,* Veröffentlichungen des Vereines der wissenschaftlichen Forschung auf dem Gebiete der Unternehmensbiographie und Firmengeschichte, Heft 10, Wien.

—— 1989. *Finanzdiplomatie und Weltwirtschaftskrise.* Frankfurt am Main: Fritz Knapp Verlag.

Stolper, G. 1967. *The German Economy, 1870 to the Present.* New York.

Summers, L. 1989. "Planning for the Next Financial Crisis." Paper presented at the NBER Conference on Financial Crises, October 17, 1989.

Temin, P. 1976. *Did Monetary Forces Cause the Great Depression?* New York: W. W. Norton.

Thorton, H. 1802. *An Inquiry into the Nature and Effects of the Paper Credit of Great Britian.* Edited with an Introduction by F. A. von Hayek (1939). New York: Rinehart & Co.

Toynbee, A. J. 1932. *Survey of International Affairs 1931.* London: Oxford University Press.

Vaubel, R. 1984. "International Debt, Bank Failures and the Money Supply: The Thirties and The Eighties." *The Cato Journal* 4 (1):249–67 (Spring/Summer).

Wagner, M., and P. Tomanek. 1983. *Bankiers und Beamte, Hundert Jahre Oesterreichische Postsparkasse.* Wien: Oesterreichische Postsparkasse.

Walré de Bordes, J. van 1924. *The Austrian Crown, Its Depreciation and Stabilization.* London: P. S. King & Son Ltd.

Wärmer, G. 1931. "Der Bargeldumlauf in Oesterreich." *Mitteilungen des Verbandes Oesterreichischer Banken und Bankiers* 1/2, February, 35–9.

Webb, St. B. 1986. "Fiscal News and Inflationary Expectations in Germany After World War I." *Journal of Economic History,* 46 (3):769–94 (September).

Weber, E. J. 1980. "The Great Depression in Switzerland: A Monetary Analysis." Unpublished dissertation, University of Rochester, Rochester, New York.

White, L. H. 1984. "Bank Failures and Monetary Policy." *The Cato Journal* 4 (1):269–74 (Spring/Summer).

Wicker, E. 1980. "A Reconsideration of the Causes of the Banking Panic of 1930." *Journal of Economic History,* September, 571–83.

Withers, H. 1909. *The Meaning of Money.* London: Smith, Elder & Co.

World Bank 1989. *World Development Report 1989.* New York: Oxford University Press.

Wright, K. M. 1977. "A Projected Resilient Financial Environment." In *Financial Crises, Institutions and Markets in a Fragile Environment,* edited by E. I. Altman and A. W. Sametz. New York: John Wiley & Sons, Inc.

Yeager, L. B. 1976. *International Monetary Relations: Theory, History and Policy,* 2d ed. New York: Harper & Row.

—— 1981. *Experiences with Stopping Inflation.* Washington, D.C.: American Enterprise Institute.

Periodicals

Die Aktiengesellschaft.
Austrian Yearbook.
The Banker.
The Bankers' Magazine.
Barron's.
Business Week.
Commerce Yearbook.
Compass.
The Contemporary Review.
Daily Telegraph.
The Economist.
Euromoney.
Federal Reserve Bulletin.
Financial News.
Financial Times.
Foreign Affairs.

International Herald Tribune.

Mitteilungen des Direktoriums der Oesterreichischen Nationalbank.

Monatsberichte des Oesterreichischen Institutes für Konjunkturforschung (OIfK).

Moody's Manual of Investments.

Neue Freie Presse.

Neues Wiener Journal.

The New York Times.

Reichspost.

Statistisches Handbuch der Weltwirtschaft, Berlin.

Statistisches Handbuch für die Republik Oesterreich, Wien.

Statistische Nachrichten, Wien.

The Times.

Wall Street Journal.

Wiener Börsen-Kurier.

Wirtschaftsstatistisches Jahrbuch, Wien.

Index